Best of Friends 7

The yearbook of Creative Monochrome

Editor
Roger Maile

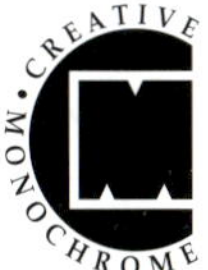

BEST OF FRIENDS 7
The yearbook of Creative Monochrome
Editor: ROGER MAILE
Editorial assistant: Alex Dilley
Image scanning: Nicholas Charlton

Published in the UK by Creative Monochrome Ltd
Courtney House, 62 Jarvis Road, South Croydon, CR2 6HU

British Library Cataloguing-in-Publication Data:
A catalogue record for this book is available from the British Library.

ISBN 1 873319 36 3
First edition, 2000

ISSN 1359-446X

Printed in England by The Burlington Press Ltd
1 Station Road, Foxton, Cambridgeshire, CB2 6SW.

Introduction

Photographs are made to be seen. That is the essential philosophy behind Creative Monochrome. We do, of course, have related objectives – such as providing information and education about the art and craft of monochrome photography – but bringing quality monochrome photography to the attention of the widest possible audience is the guiding light.

Why? The prime reason is the motivational effect of seeing what other artists are achieving through the same medium. I hope that photographers of all abilities will look at the images in this book and will be enthused and inspired by seeing what others are achieving. It is that spark which is essential to maintaining the development of the art – the 'how to' hurdles can always be overcome if the motivation is sufficiently strong. And having the potential reward of publication is in itself an incentive to keep talented photographers striving for new levels of achievement.

Some will misconstrue this as an apology for photography as a competitive activity. Of course, the primary aim of any artistic activity is self-fulfilment: the desire to express one's feelings in a visible form. But the artist remains human and most of us seek some sign of acceptance or approval for the products of our labours. A minority will even gain their satisfaction from rejection and disapproval. The key is to achieve some form of reaction; the most damning response for any artist is indifference, because that implies that one's feelings are of no consequence.

Writing about photography as a means of expressing feelings can also lead to misunderstanding. Of course, it can mean that images make a statement about the photographer's perception of the 'big issues' – the meaning of life, the human condition, environmental concerns and so forth. But much more commonly, the feelings can be as simple as exploring wonder, beauty, love or intrigue. The acts of pointing the camera and pressing the shutter in themselves express the photographer's feeling that this subject at this moment in time are worth preserving. Indeed, one of the key charateristics of photography as an artistic medium is this ability to preserve the moment.

We will not all be on the same wavelength as the photographer. In the course of selecting the images for this book, I have sifted through around 4,000 images submitted by almost 300 photographers. It is inevitable that in some cases, I will not be able to fathom why a photographer felt that this particular subject or particular moment was worth preserving. If we all had the same feelings, life would be a lot less interesting.

My personal challenge in selecting the images for this book is not to find the 'best' images – there is no such absolute standard in aesthetic terms. But it is to try to make the 'best' selection from the images submitted in terms of representing the range of subjects and styles, so that the book achieves its objective of stimulating and enthusing photographers. And part of that mission is to include some images which I know will challenge the sensitivities of some readers.

Any such process of selection will inevitably be subjective. I try to keep my own sensitivities open to a wide range of styles and subject matter. But I would not be human if I did not have my own likes and dislikes. One foible I am conscious of is a preference for technical quality, whatever the subject or style. I am occasionally berated for this by certain individuals who regard it as a form of artistic fascism on my part. I cannot apologise for it because it is fundamental to my beliefs about communication of feelings through photography. To my mind, sloppy technique detracts from the image and distracts from its message: it is as fundamental to me as my dislike of boiled cabbage – it is not something I can change.

Contrary to some people's expectations, choosing the images for Best of Friends is a hugely enjoyable task. I love looking at photographs. And rather like a gold prospector, there is the constant possibility of finding a nugget hiding in the next envelope. There is, of course, a strong sense of responsibility and an empathy for those whose images narrowly fail to secure a place in the book.

One moving moment this year was the realisation that an image by Clive Harrison, retained from the selection for *Best of Friends 6*, was included in the final selection. Clive, a Friend of Creative Monochrome from the earliest days, died at the beginning of this year. Clive's commitment to the art of photography was total. He lived and breathed photography. Like so many talented photographers, he was modest in his own achievements and fulsome in his praise and encouragement of others.

I want therefore to dedicate this year's edition of Best of Friends to Clive's memory and have structured the book to start with a selection of images of Clive's favourite subject, child photography. His pleasure in the innocence and spontaneity of childhood, celebrated in so many of his images, was coupled with technical skill and artistic integrity. But he was not just a great photographer, he was the best of friends.

The Friends group

Creative Monochrome exists to promote the art of monochrome photography. It is deliberately a broad church, encouraging all styles of work and diverse subject matter. We act as a forum for the exchange of information and as a medium for sharing images and thoughts on image-making. These objectives are achieved through the Friends of Creative Monochrome – a group of over 5,000 people with a shared passion for black and white photography.

There are two forms of subscription to the Friends of Creative Monochrome. The Mono subscription brings Friends our bi-monthly magazine, significant savings and special offers on a wide range of products, and entitlement to participate in the Best of Friends 'competition'. The subscription is £8.50 per year in Europe or £12.50 outside Europe. The Best of Friends subscription offers the same benefits and, additionally, a copy of the Best of Friends yearbook and calendar and a saving of £6 on each entry for Best of Friends. This subscription costs £30 in Europe and £40 elsewhere.

To subscribe, or to receive information about our other magazines, books and mail order catalogue, contact Creative Monochrome Ltd, Courtney House, 62 Jarvis Road, South Croydon, Surrey CR2 6HU (tel: 020 8686 3282; fax: 020 8681 0662; e-mail: roger@cremono.demon.co.uk).

Best of Friends Awards

Each year we ask Friends and their partners to vote for their favourite images in the book. These votes decide who wins the BoF Awards medals and which images will appear in the Best of Friends calendar for the following year. There are 12 medals: two gold, four silver and six bronze.

Anyone who has had the chance to view the images in the book is entitled to vote. You may vote for up to 10 different images. Photographers may not vote for their own photographs.

To vote, for each image selected, write down the plate number (not the page number) and the name of the photographer. As a small incentive to participate, we will pick six entries out of the hat in a prize draw for books from the Creative Monochrome Contemporary Portfolio series, so you also need to include your name and address on the voting sheet.

Please do not be tempted to debase the Awards: votes should be awarded on a sincere assessment of photographic merit. We reserve the right to disqualify votes which appear to have been awarded for other reasons.

Send your votes to Creative Monochrome Ltd, Courtney House, 62 Jarvis Road, South Croydon, Surrey, CR2 6HU to arrive no later than 31 March 2001. Alternatively, you can vote by fax (020 8681 0662) or by e-mail: roger @cremono.demon.co.uk.

The prints on this page are previous medal winners and are not eligible for these Awards.

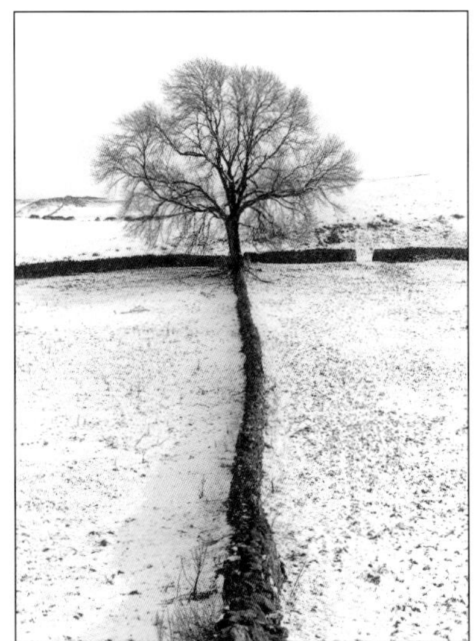

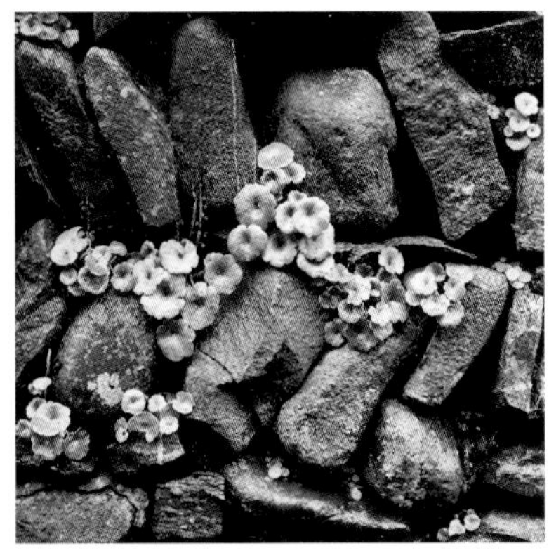

Award winners from Best of Friends 6:
(from the top)
Iceland poppy buds, *John Reed (gold)*
Tree of life, *Richard Ross (silver)*
Pennywort Wall, *Anne Newell (silver)*

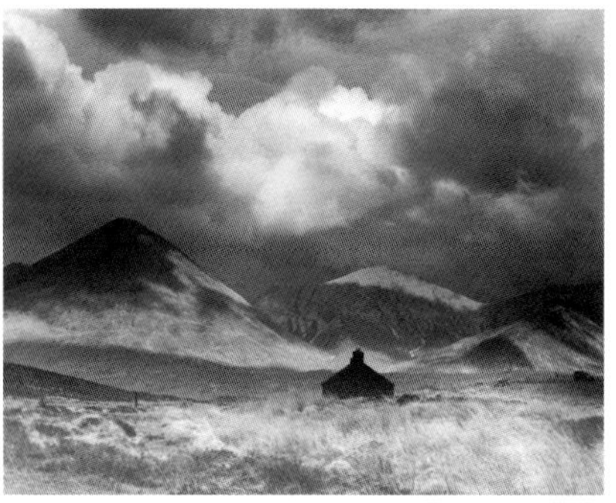

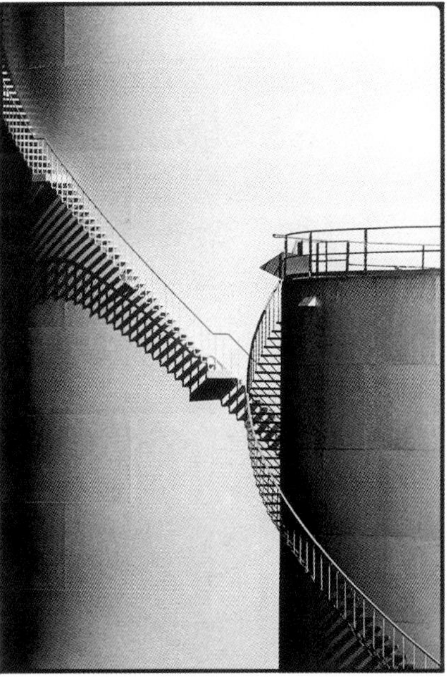

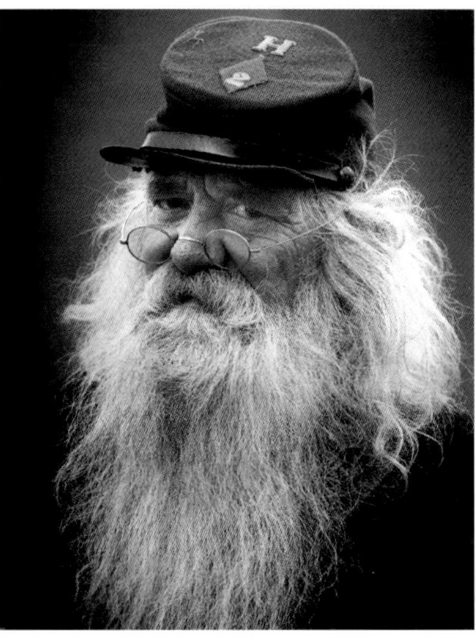

Award winners from Best of Friends 6:
(from the top)
Deserted croft, Skye, *Derek Singleton (gold)*
Untitled, *Peter Motton (silver)*
Soldier boy, *Garry Corbett (silver)*

Index of contributors

(The numbers shown are the plate numbers rather than the page numbers.)

Portfolio

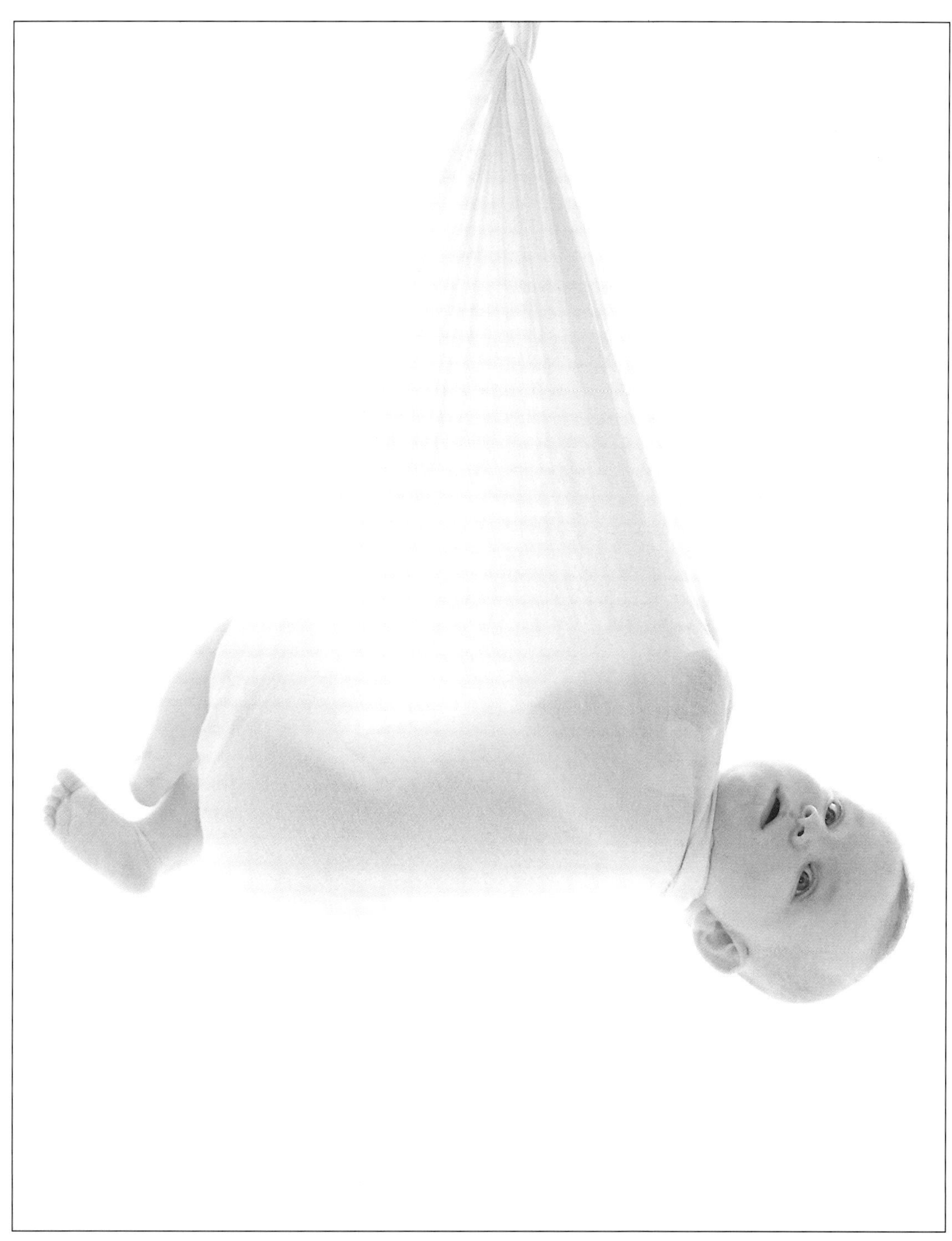

1
Ellie #3
Maggie McCall

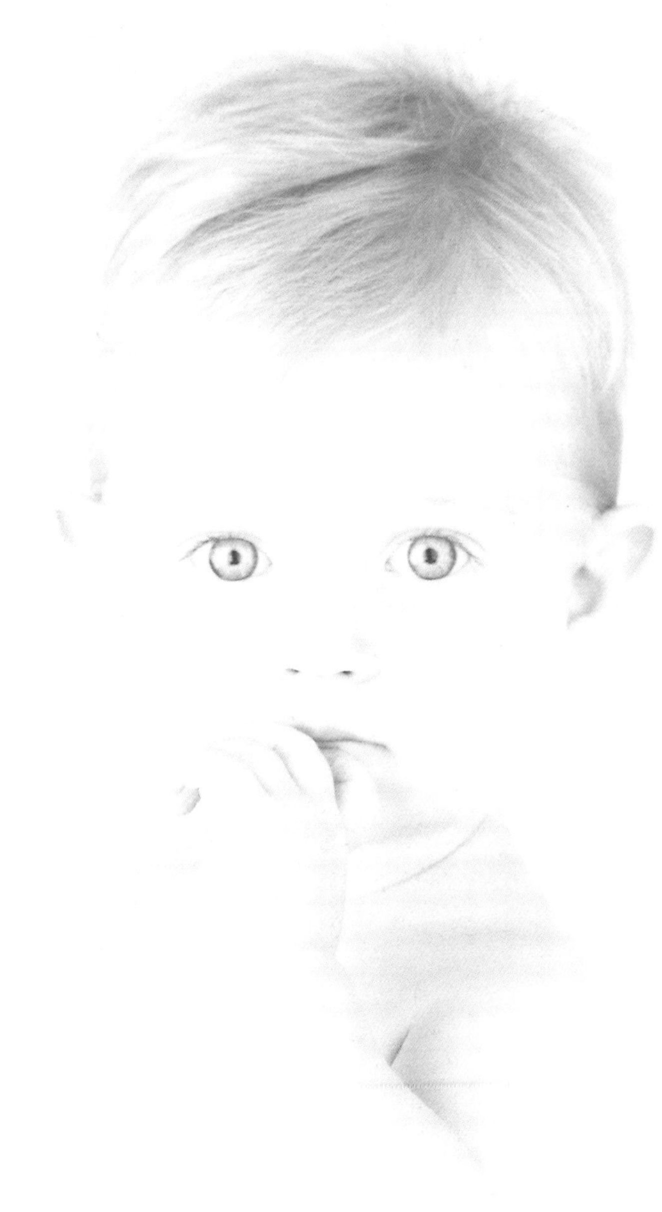

2
Joel
Gerry Coe

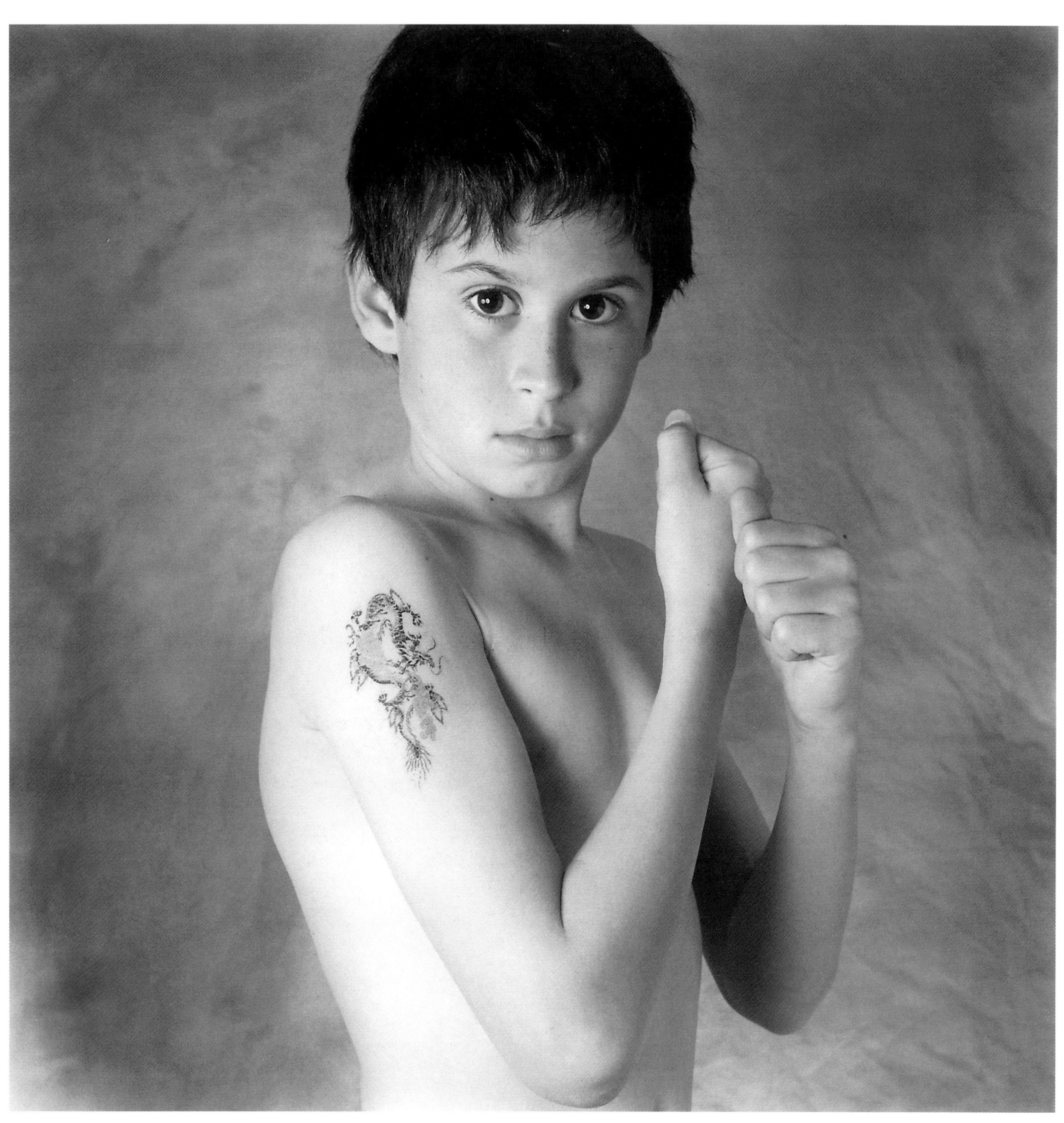

3
Reza #1
Mark Snowdon

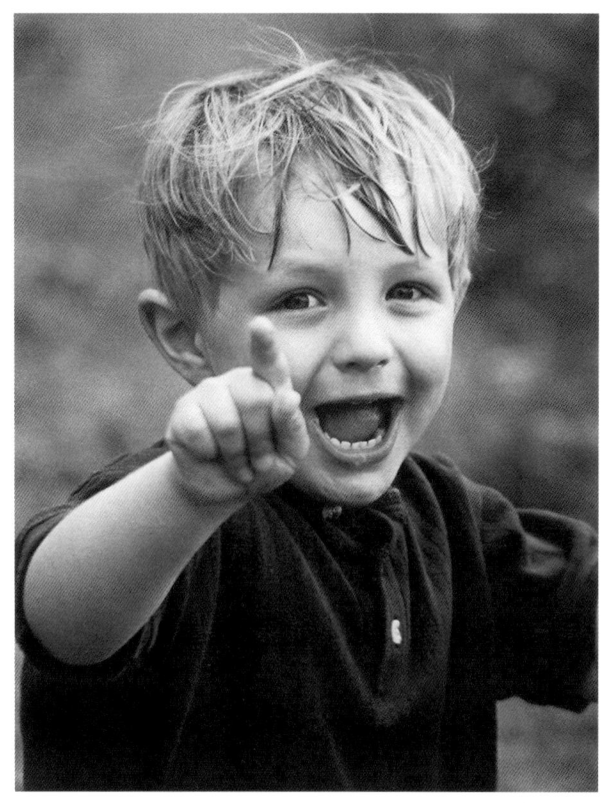

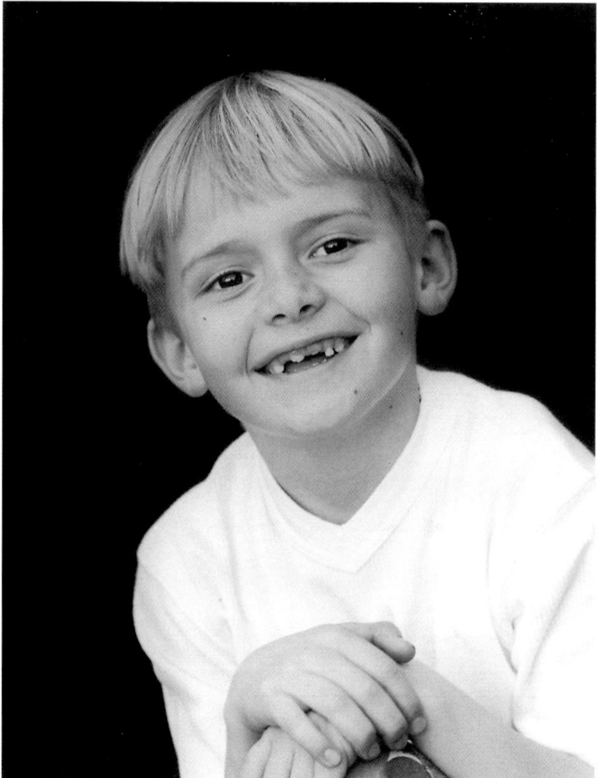

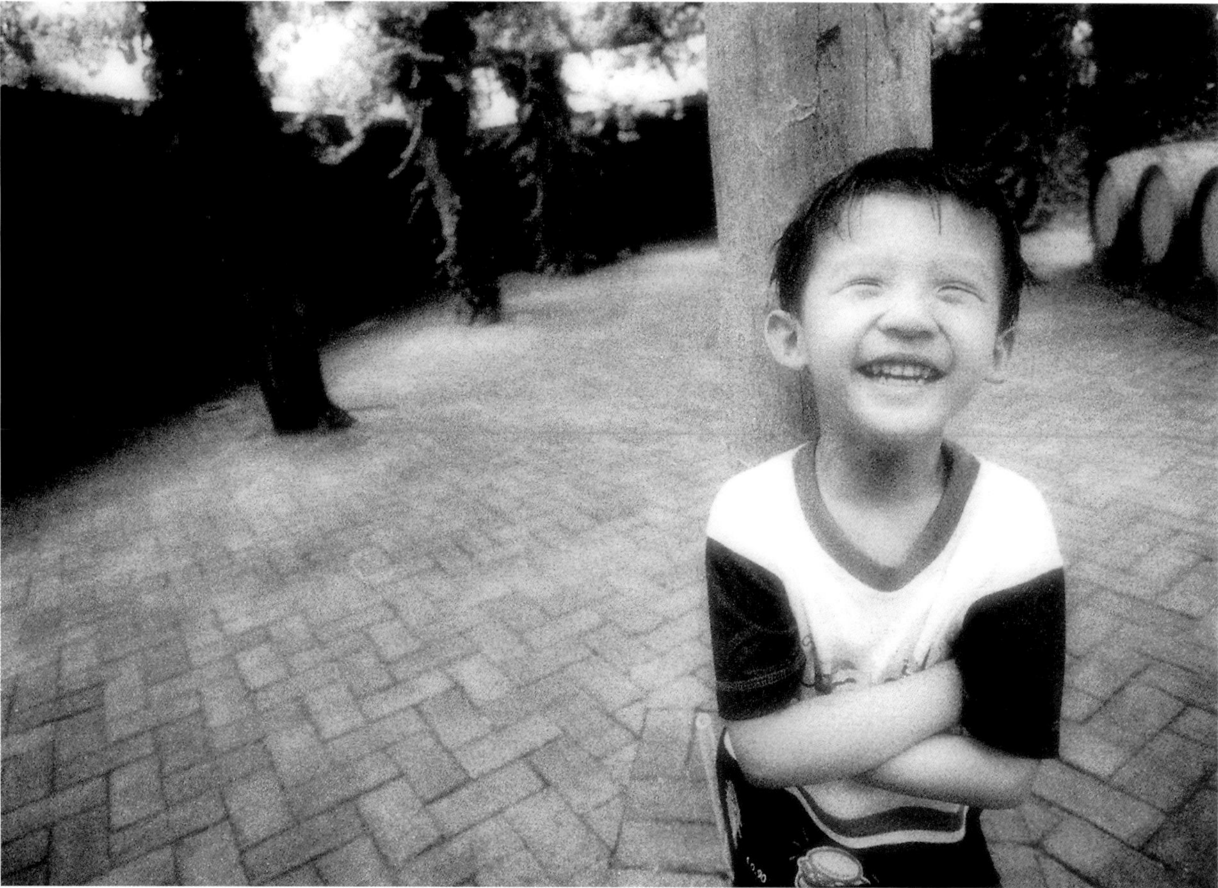

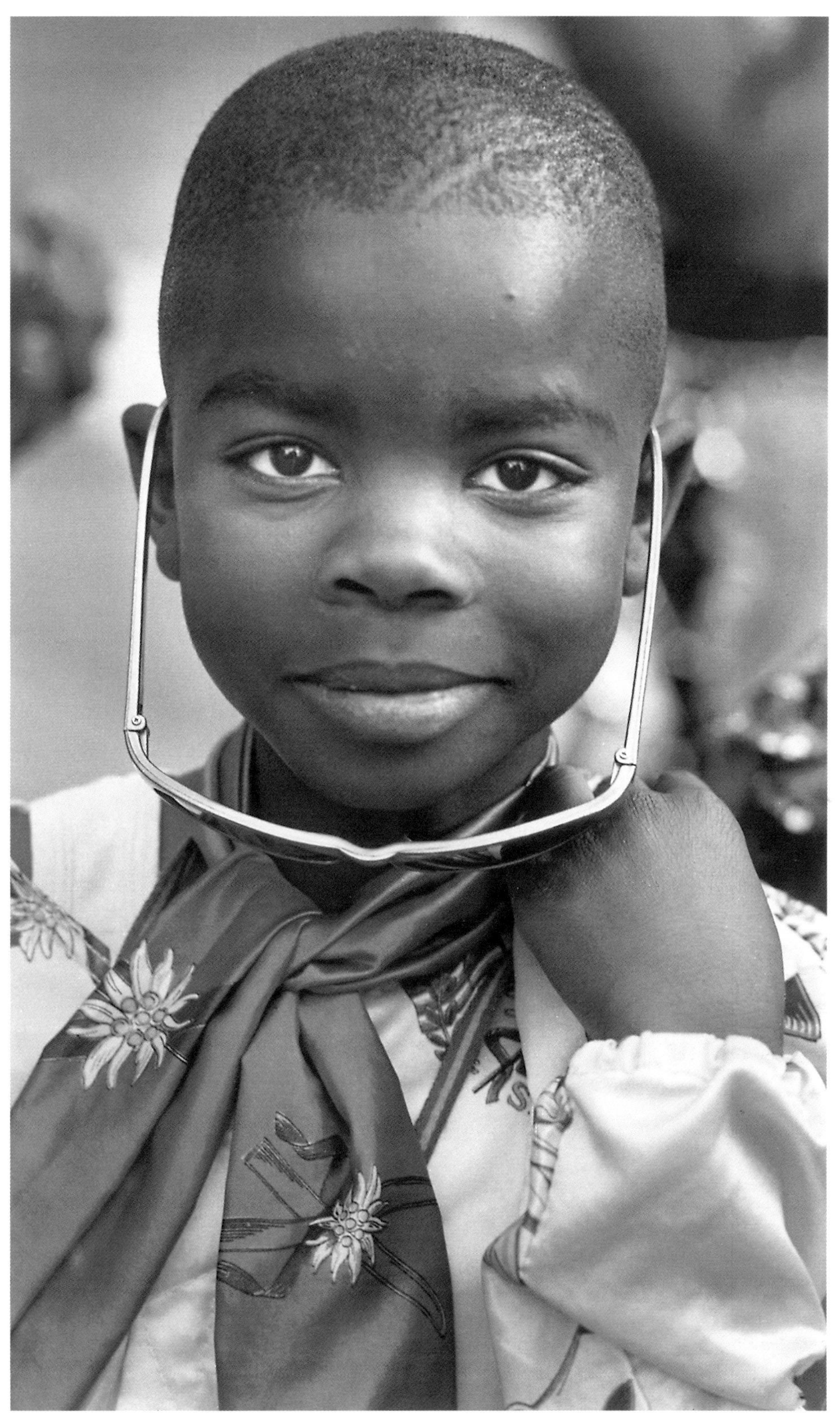

(opposite top left) 4 **Ari**, *Bob Marsdem*
(opposite top right) 5 **Jake**, *James Ngai*
(opposite bottom) 6 **Laughter**, *Luke Tan*
(above) 7 **Boy with sunglasses**, *Clive Harrison*

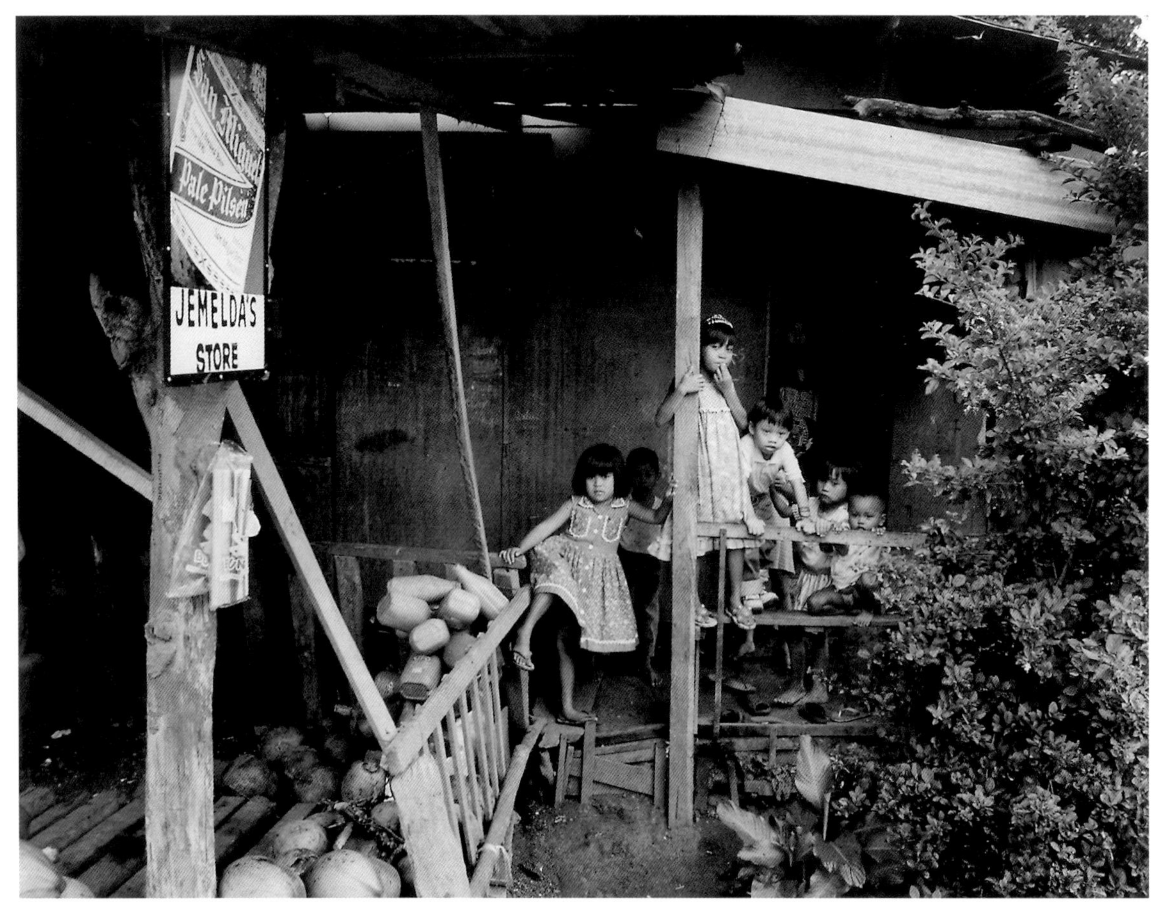
Pale Pilsen
JEMELDA'S
STORE

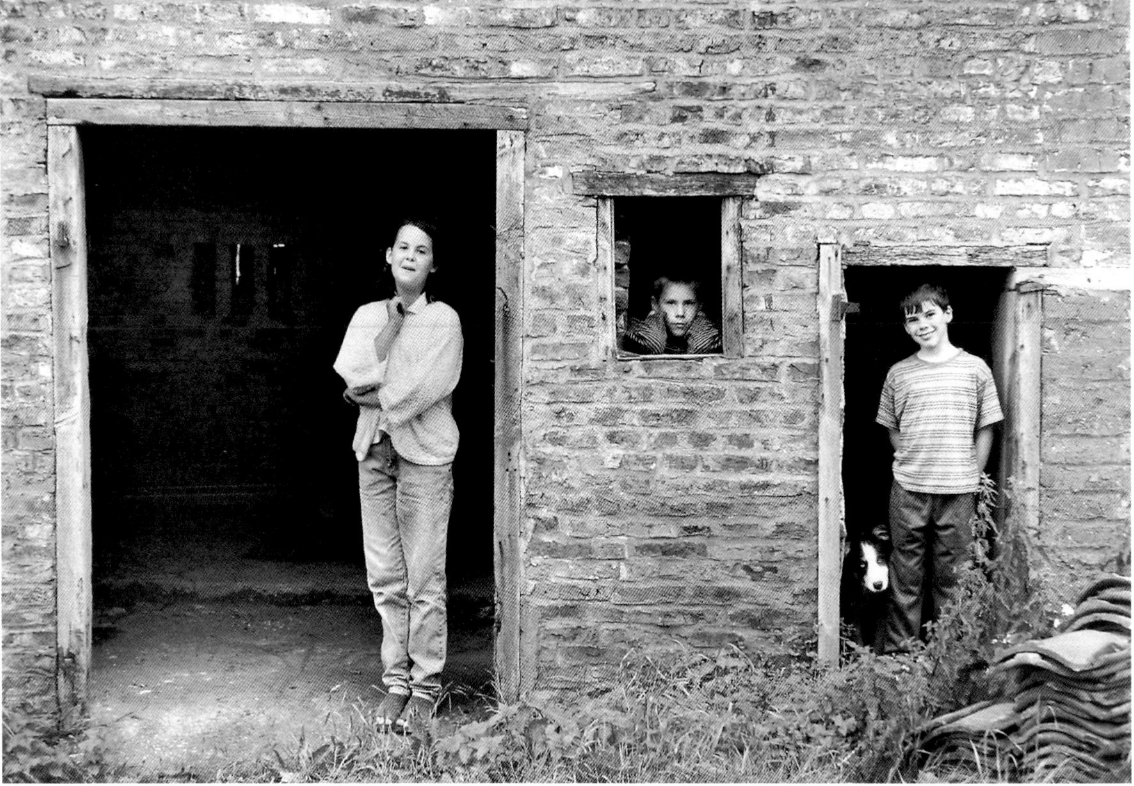

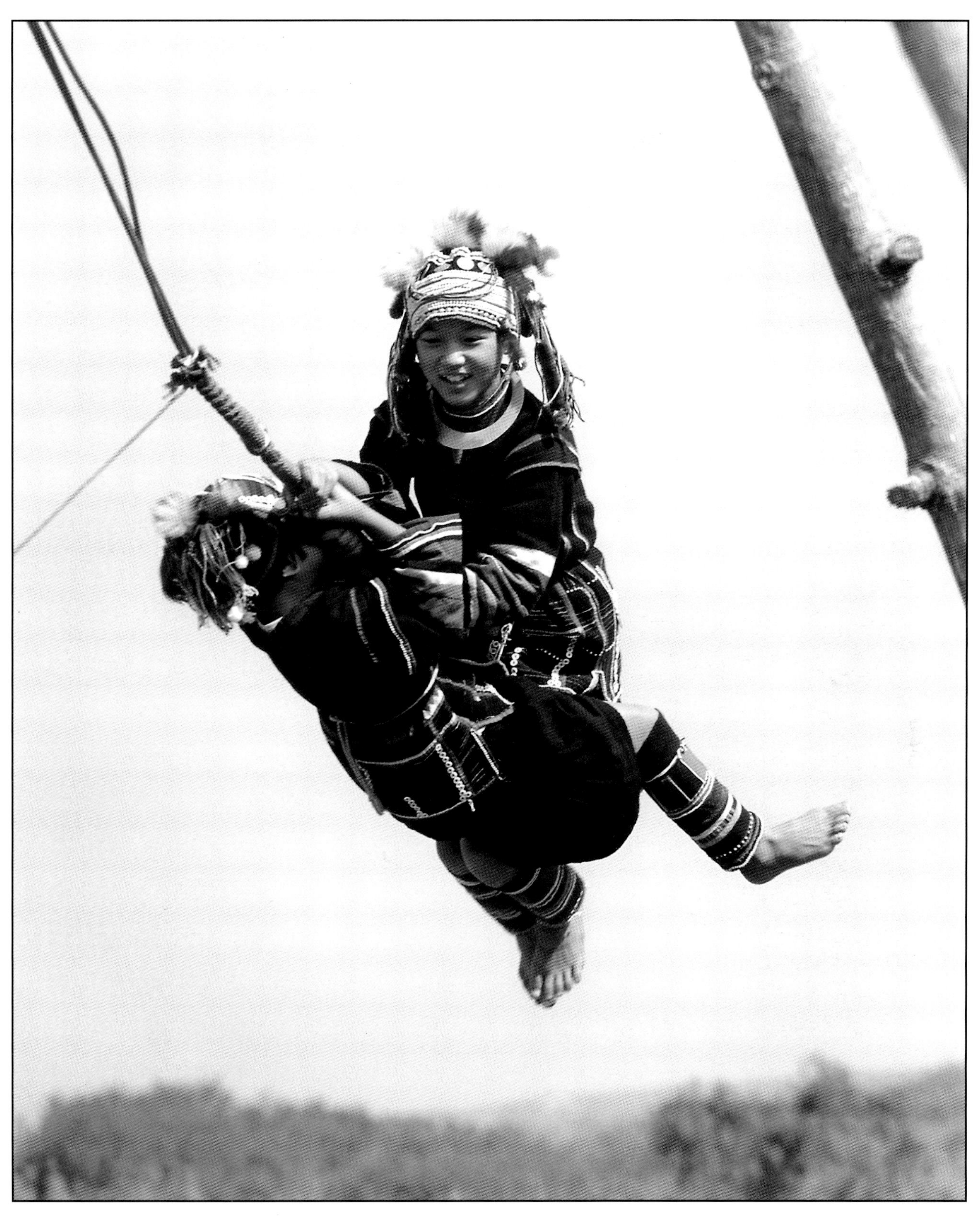

(opposite top) 8 **Jemelda's Store**, *Roy Frankland*
(opposite bottom) 9 **No title**, *Ken Baldwin*
(above) 10 **Fly now**, *Stephan Funke*

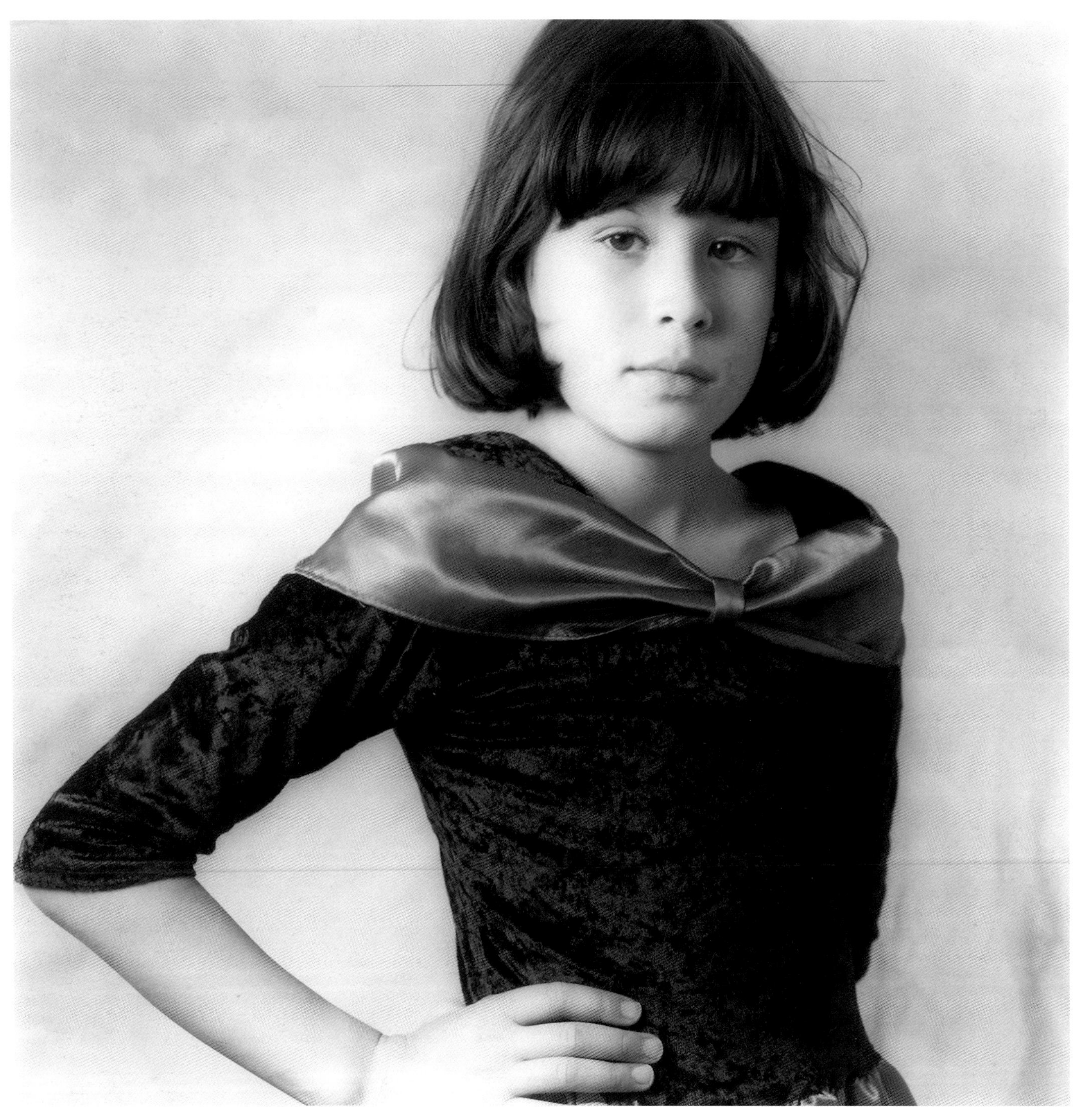

(above) 11 **Aaminah #1**, *Mark Snowdon*
(right) 12 **Alex**, *Nigel Surtees*

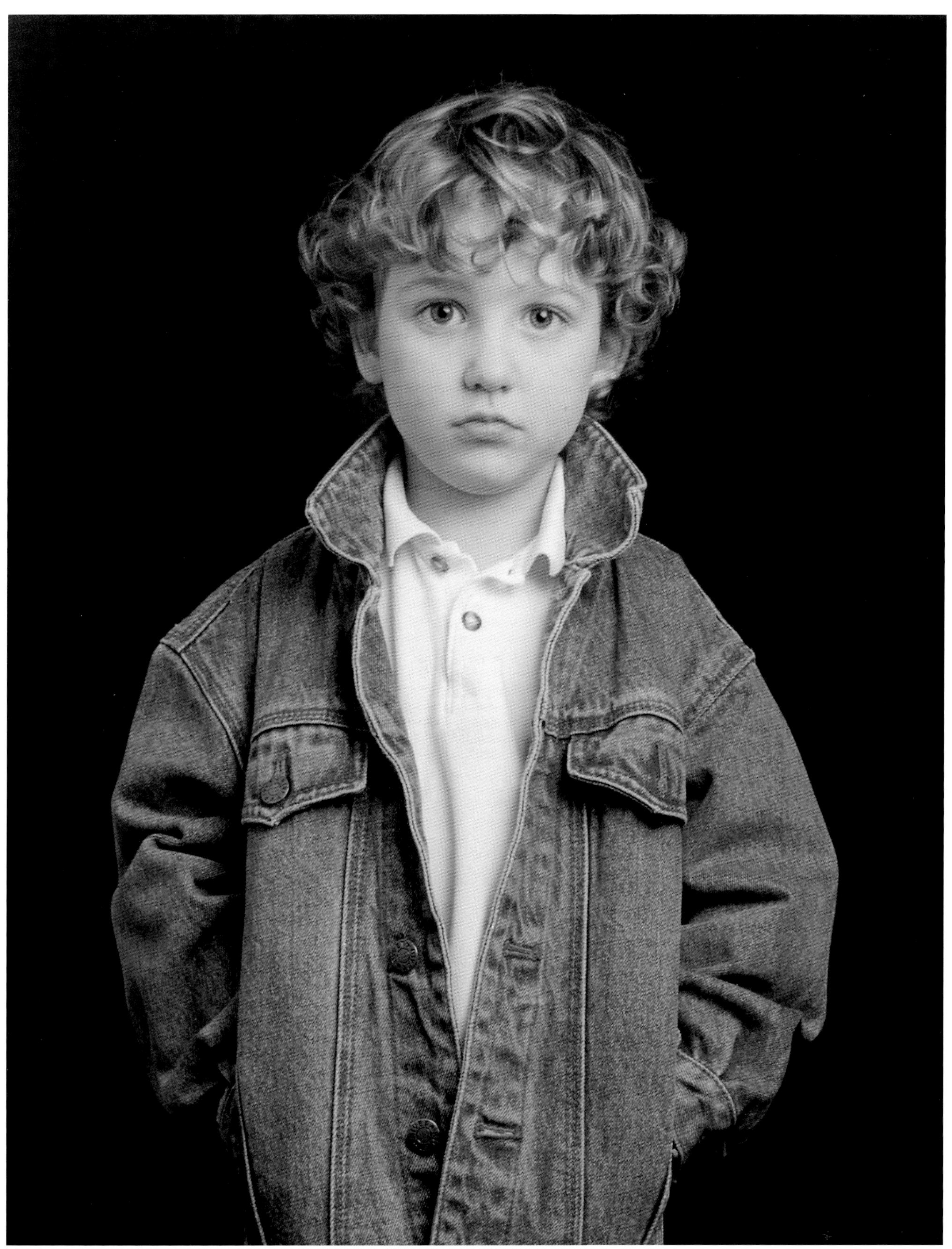

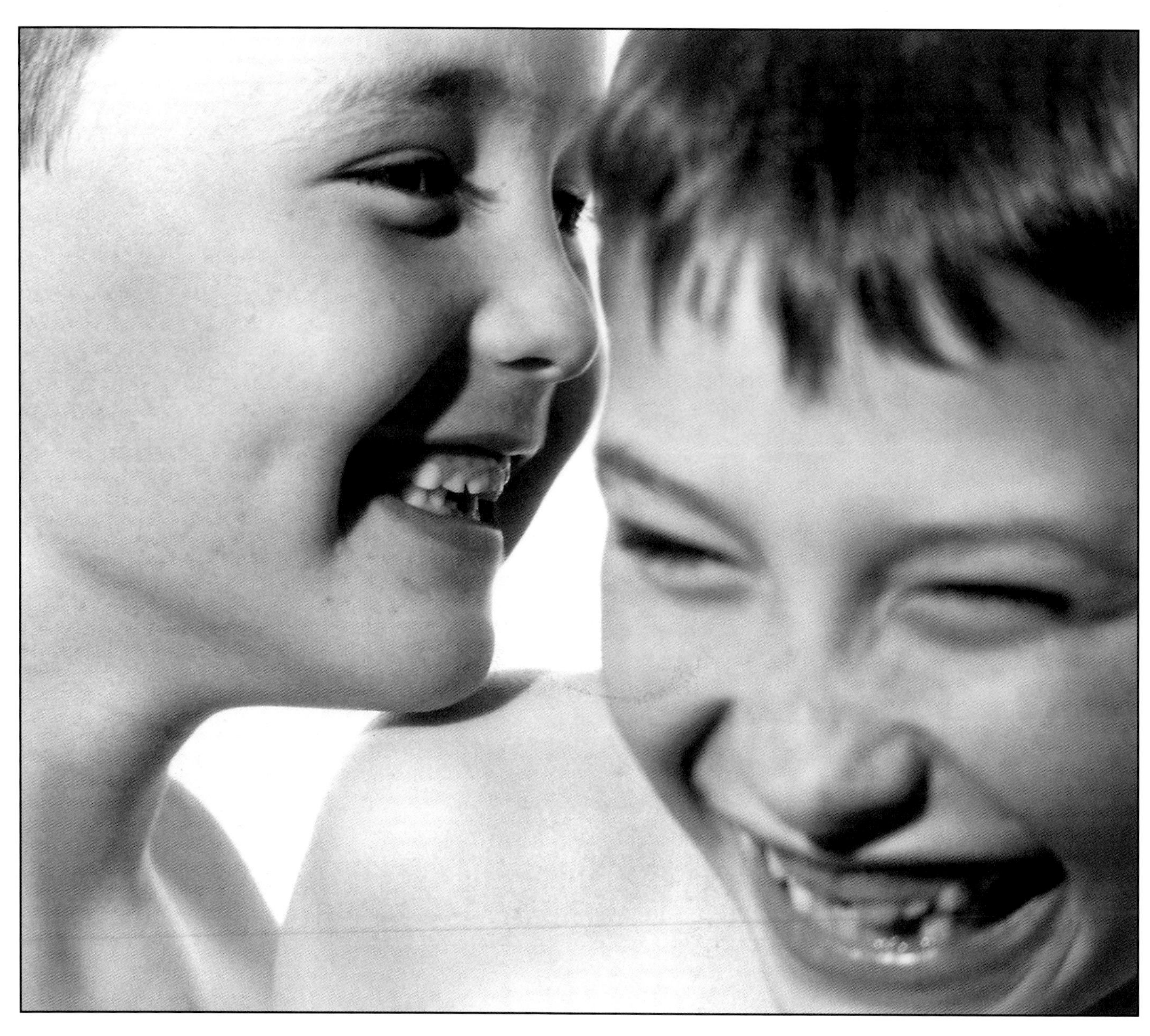

13
Punchline
Nigel Surtees

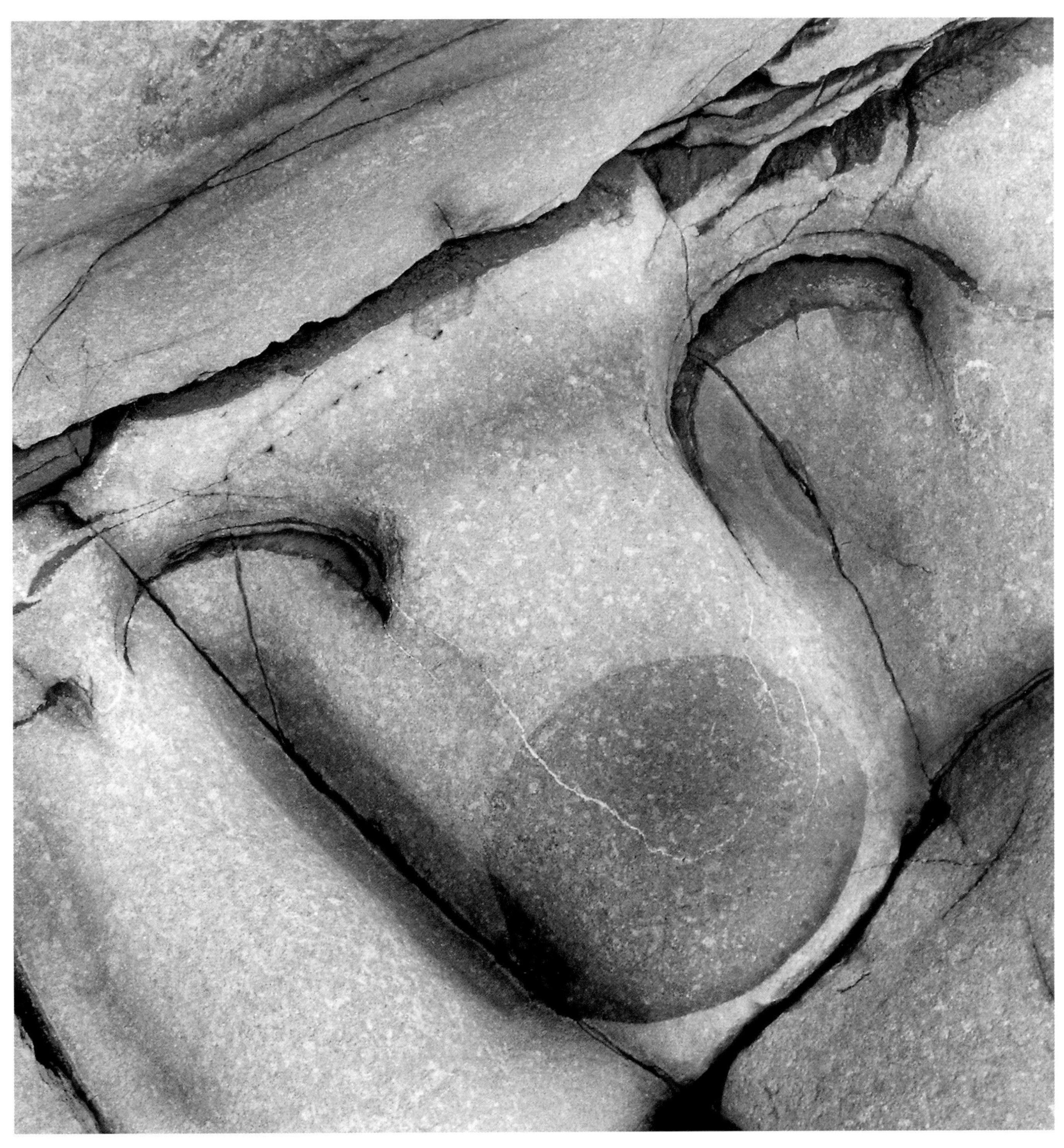

14
Rock face, North Cornwall
Anne Newell

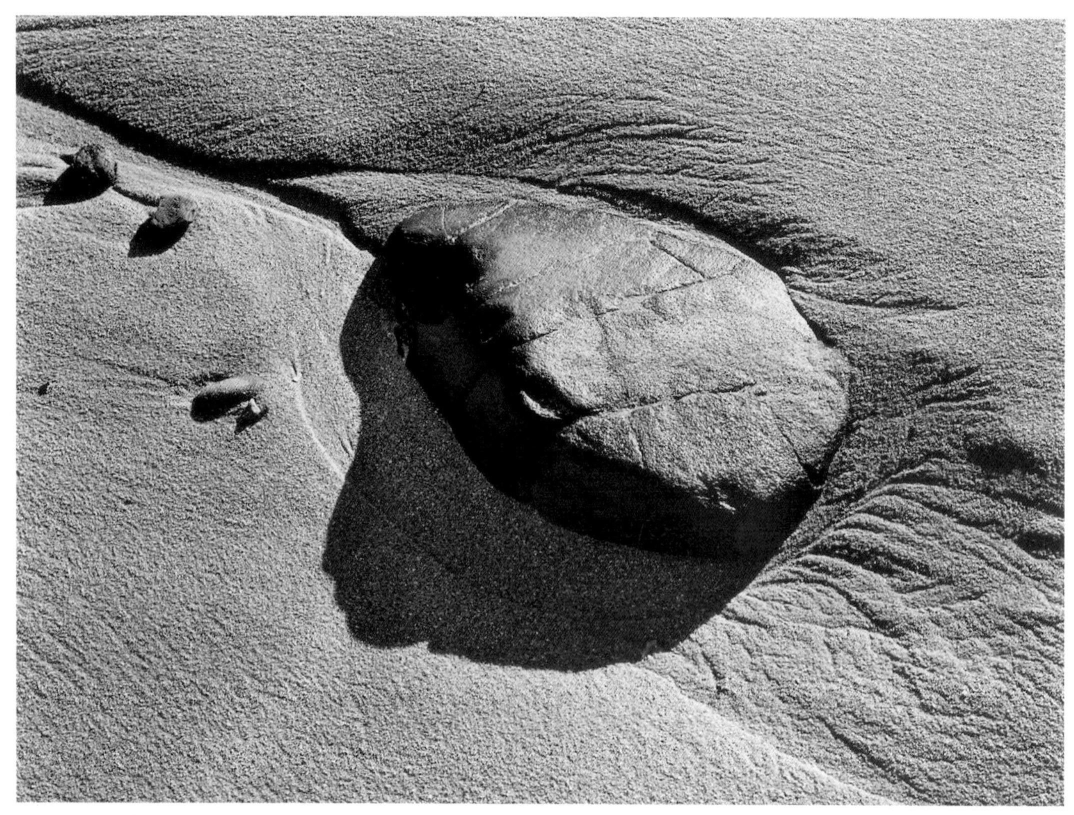

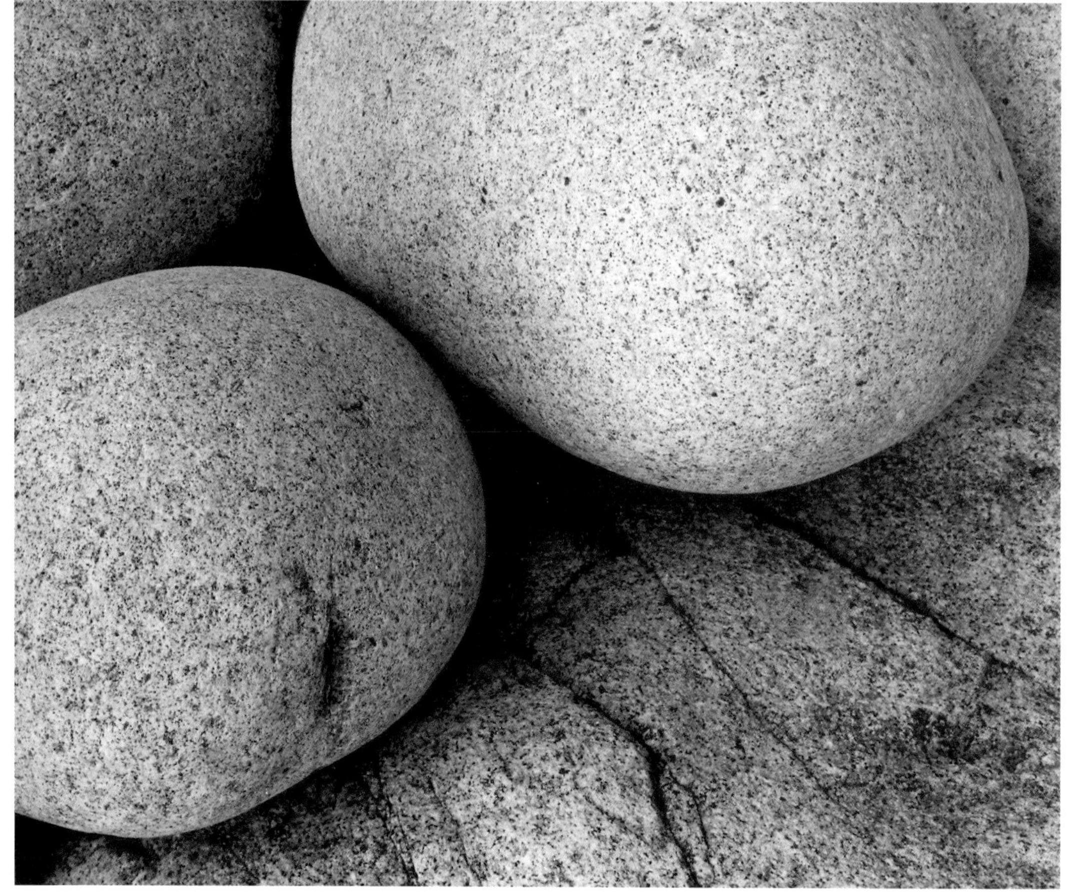

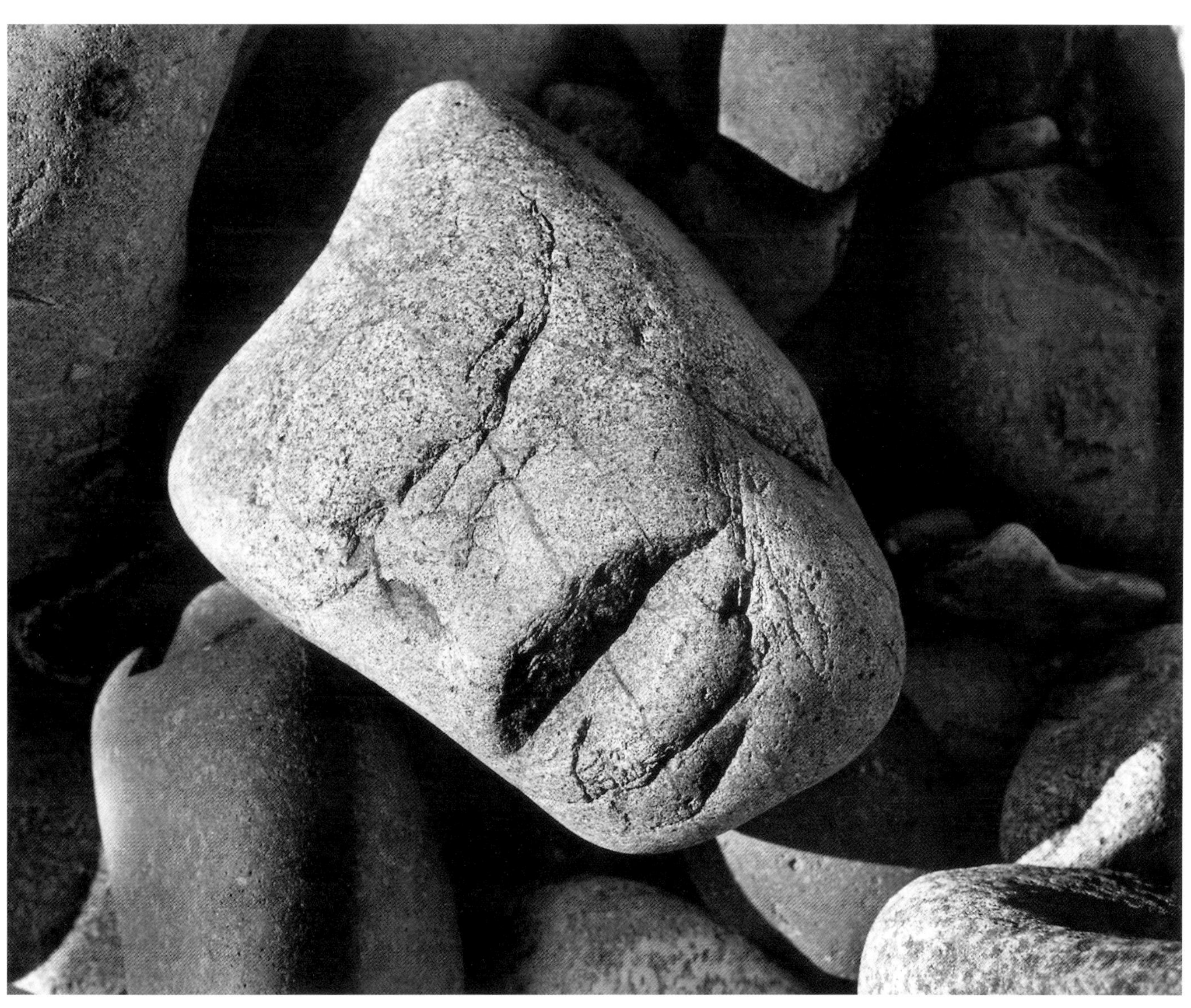

(opposite top) 15 **Seashore pattern**, *Jim Shipp*
(opposite bottom) 16 **Granite spheroids**, *Martin Rushworth*
(above) 17 **Stony face #2**, *John Day*

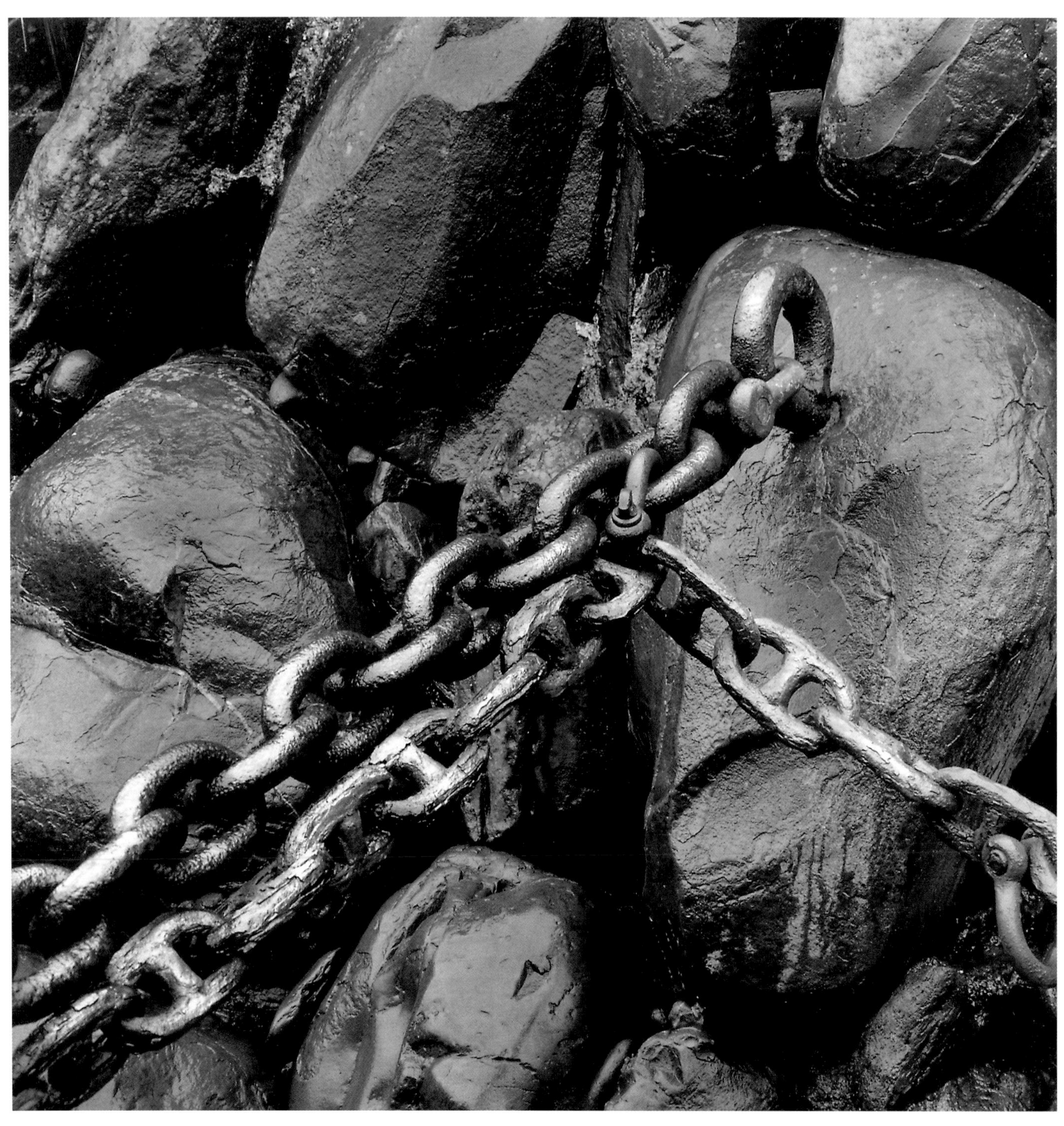

18
Harbour wall, Clovelly
Anne Newell

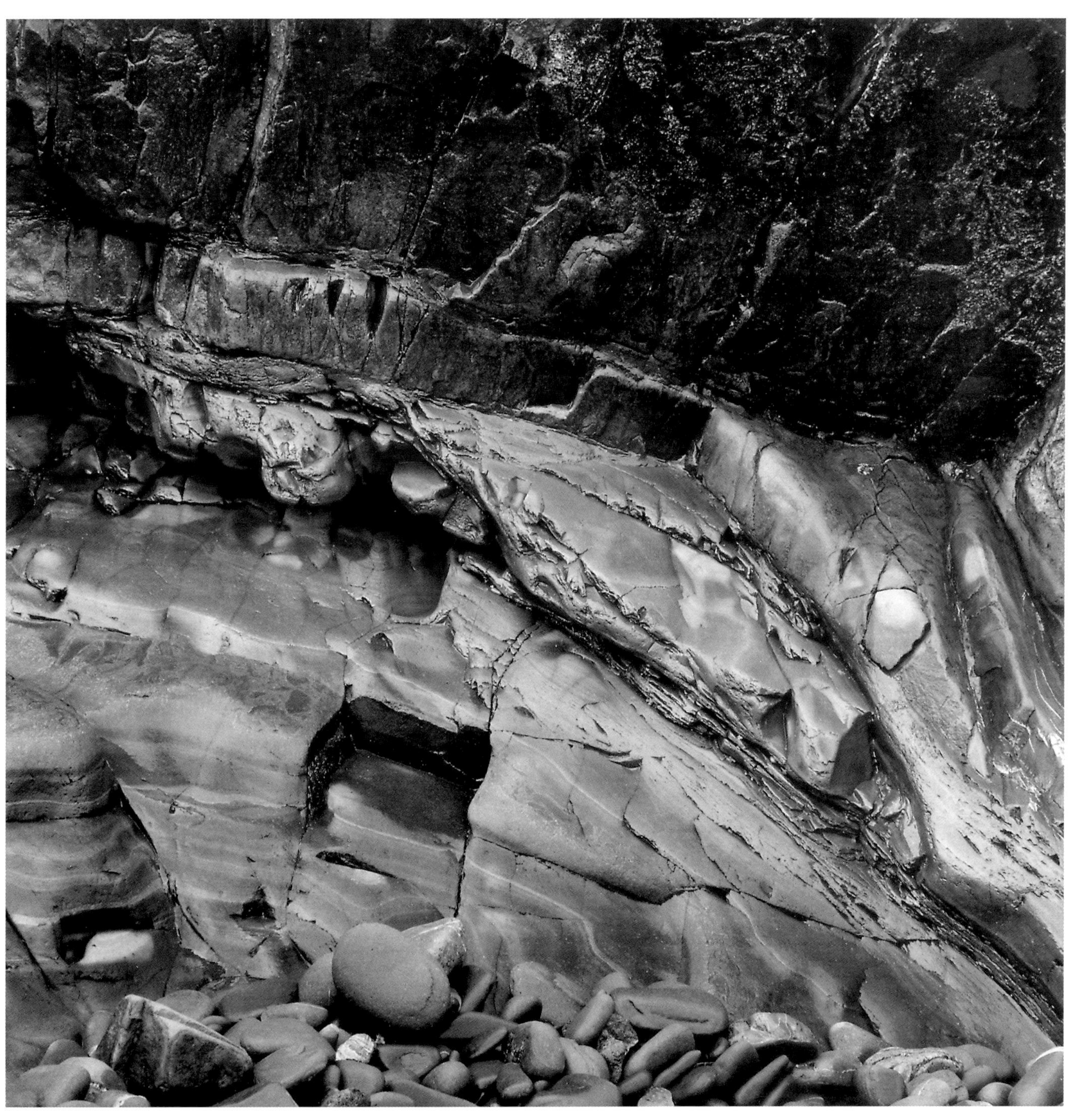

19
Rock series III, North Cornwall
Anne Newell

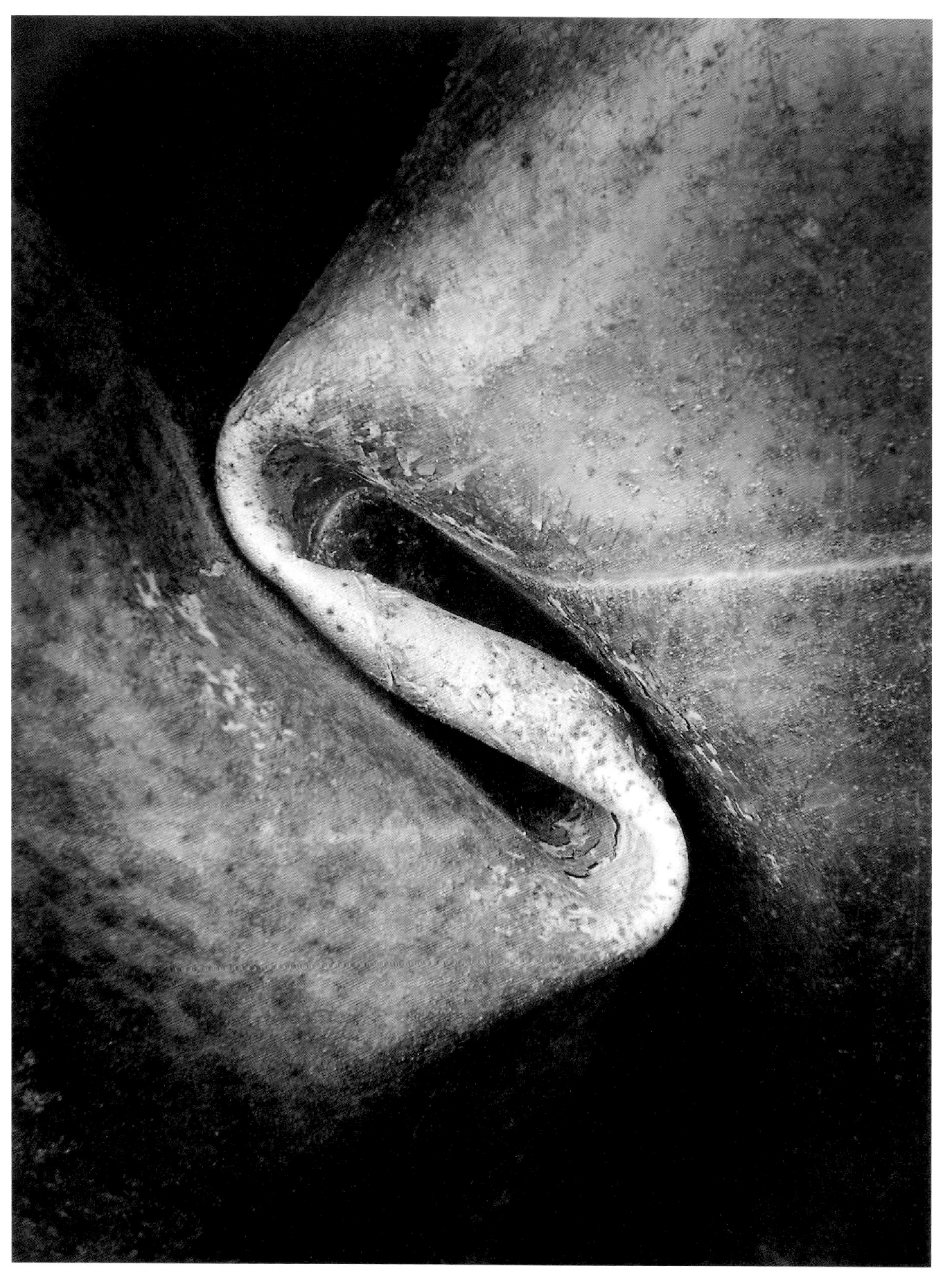

20
Twisted oil drum
Alan Walmsley

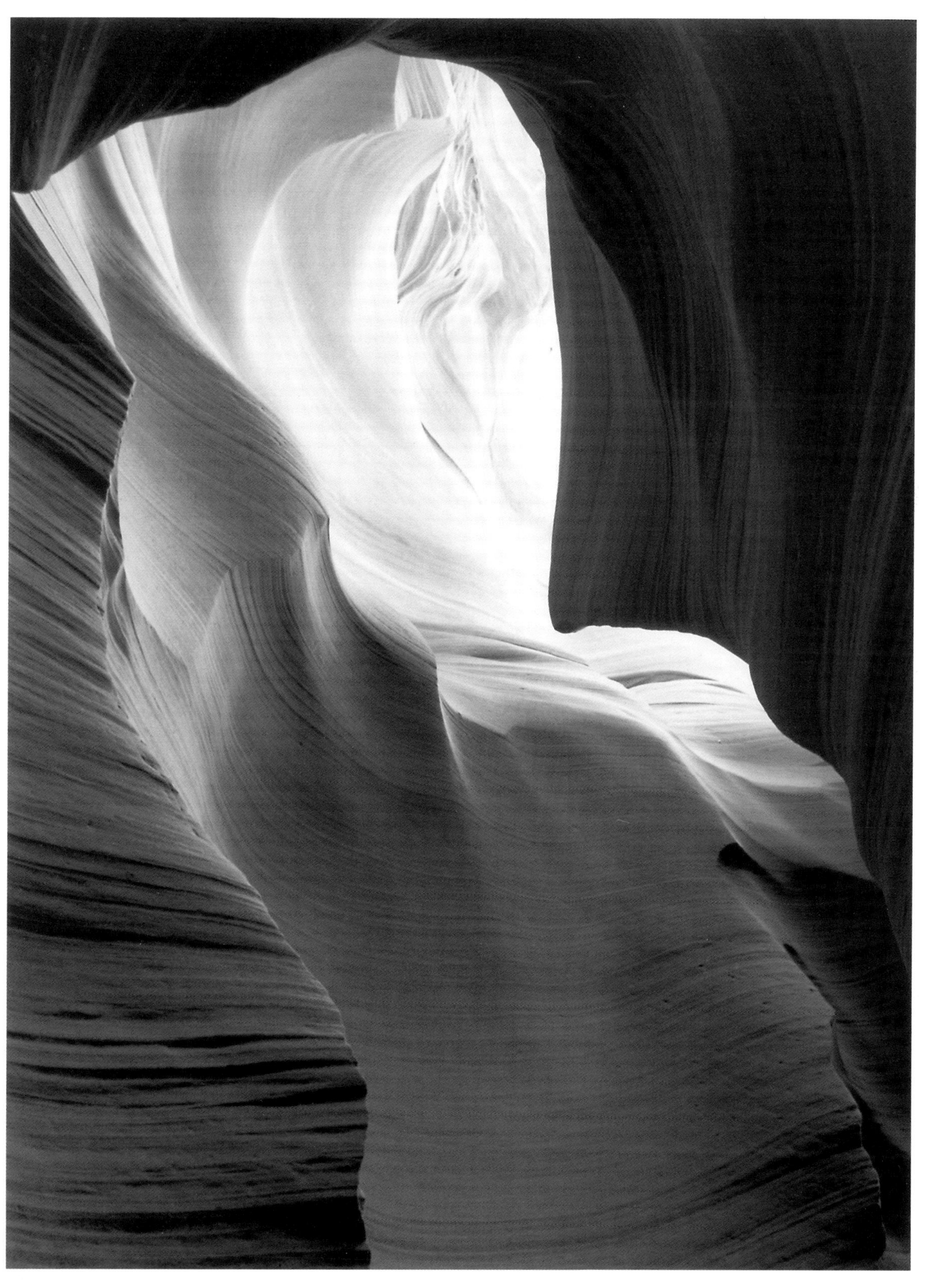

21
Lower Antelope Canyon #1
Peter Clark

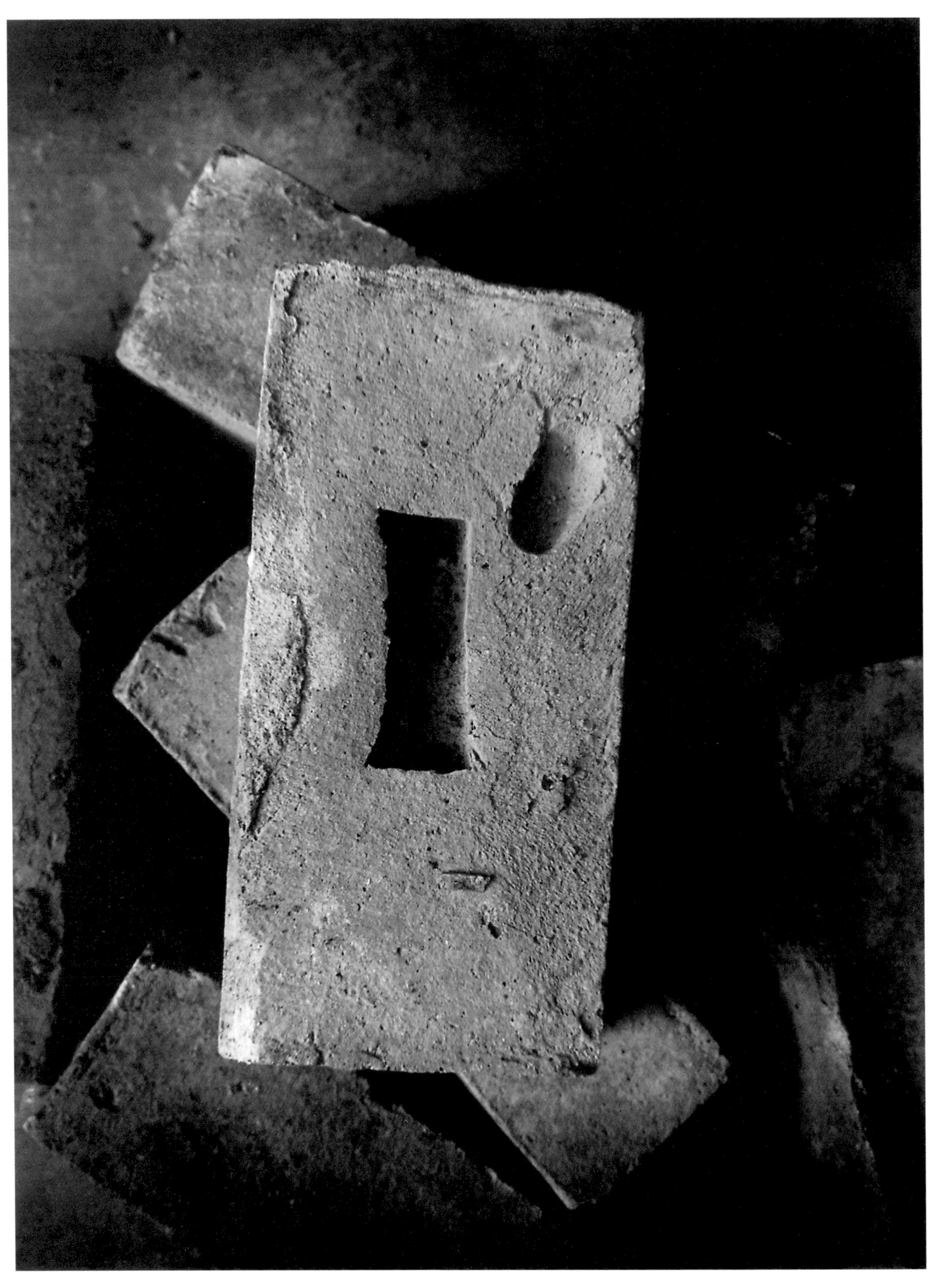

22
Butterknowle brick
Pat Maycroft

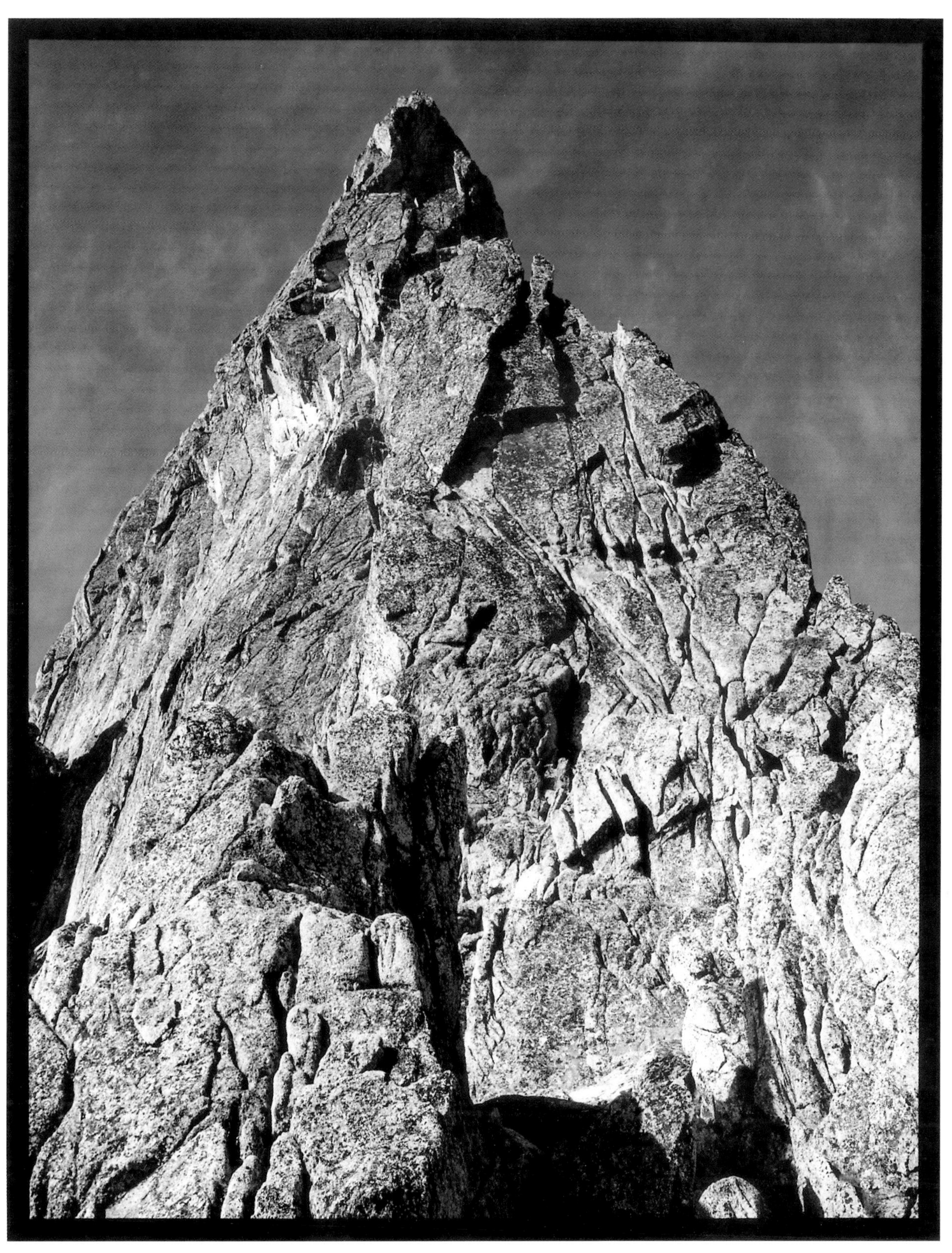

23
Rock wall at Fenetre D'Arpette
David Butcher

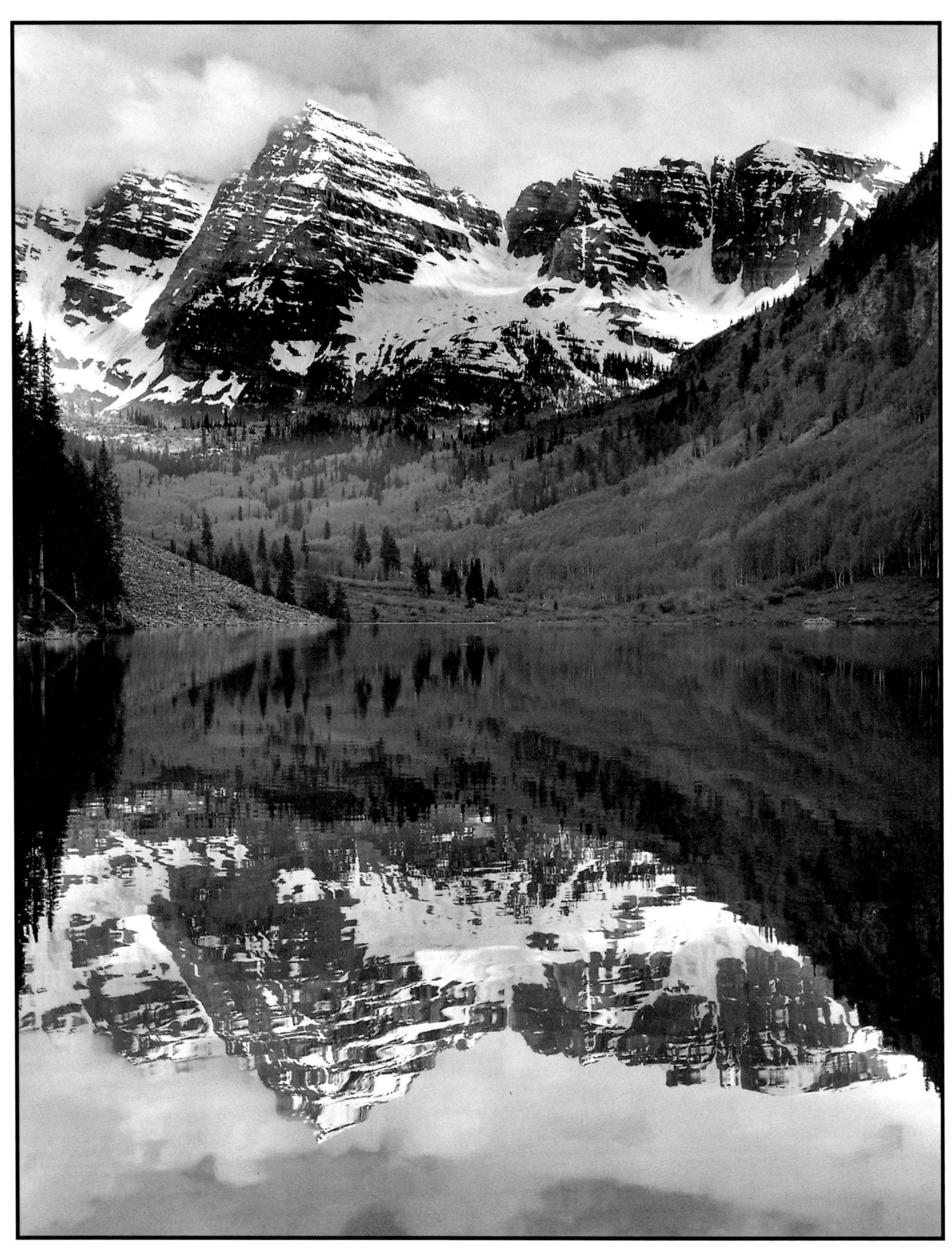

24
Maroon Bells reflection, Colorado Rockies
David Butcher

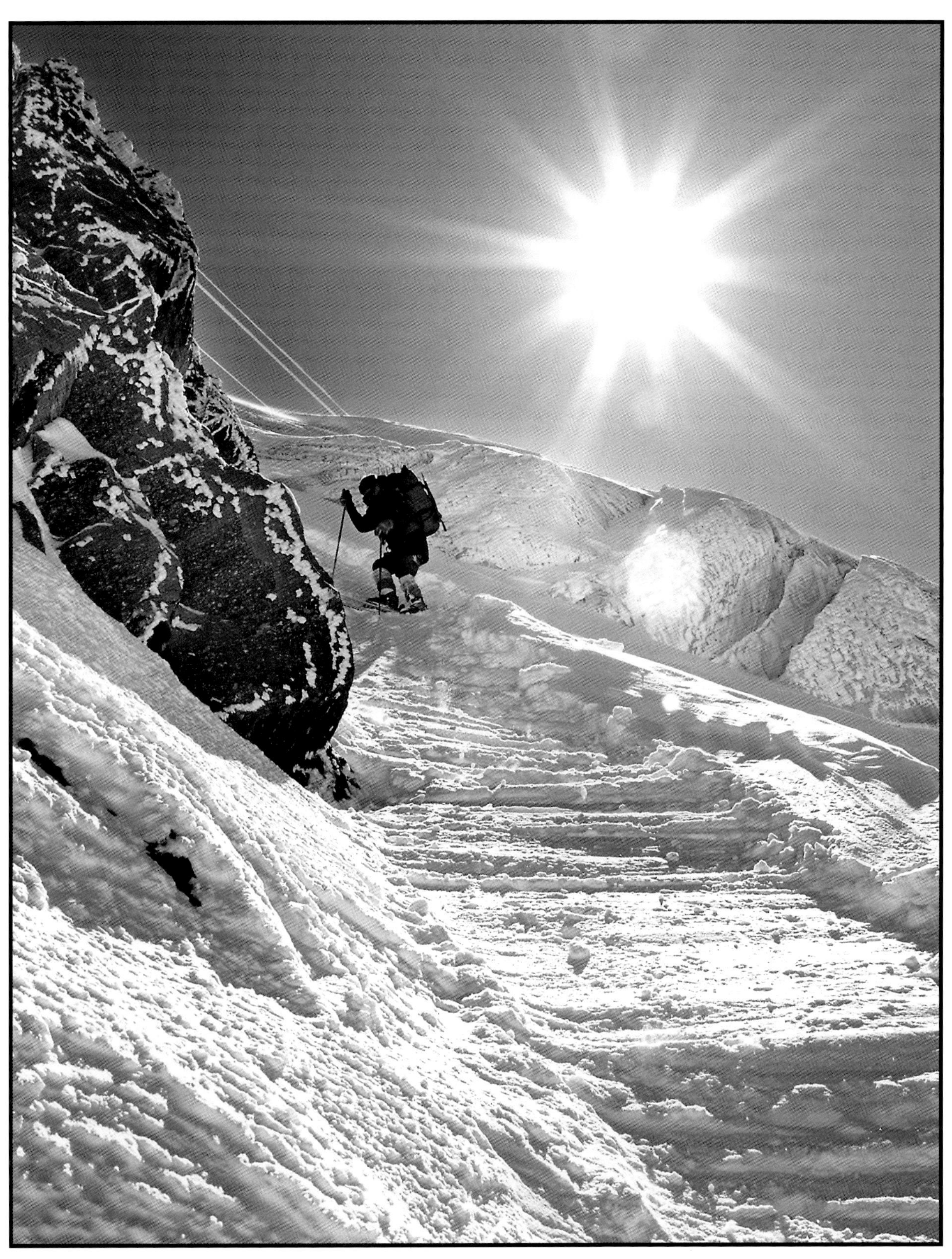

25
Careful descent, Otztal Alps
David Butcher

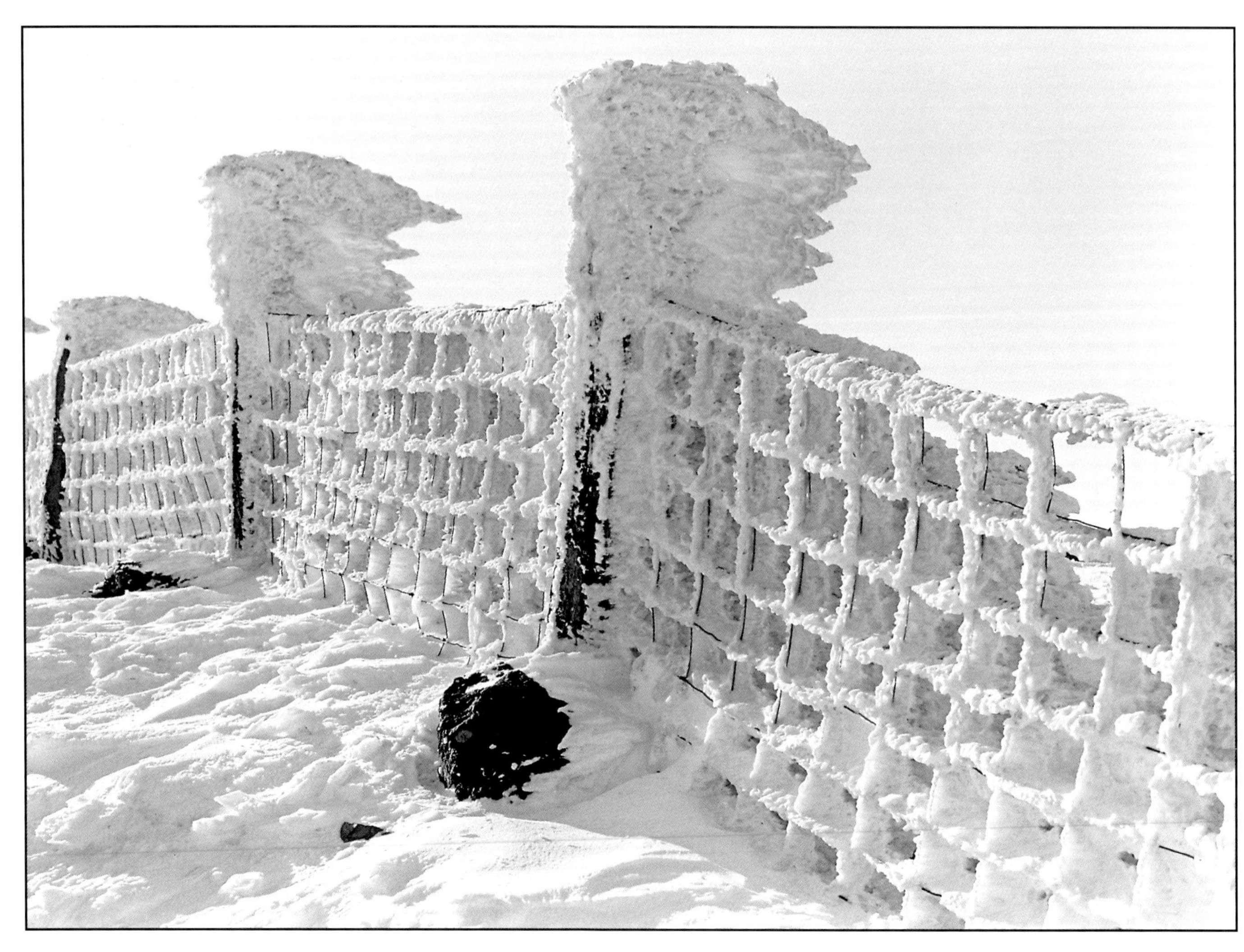

26
Ffens ar Arennig I
O Tudur Owen

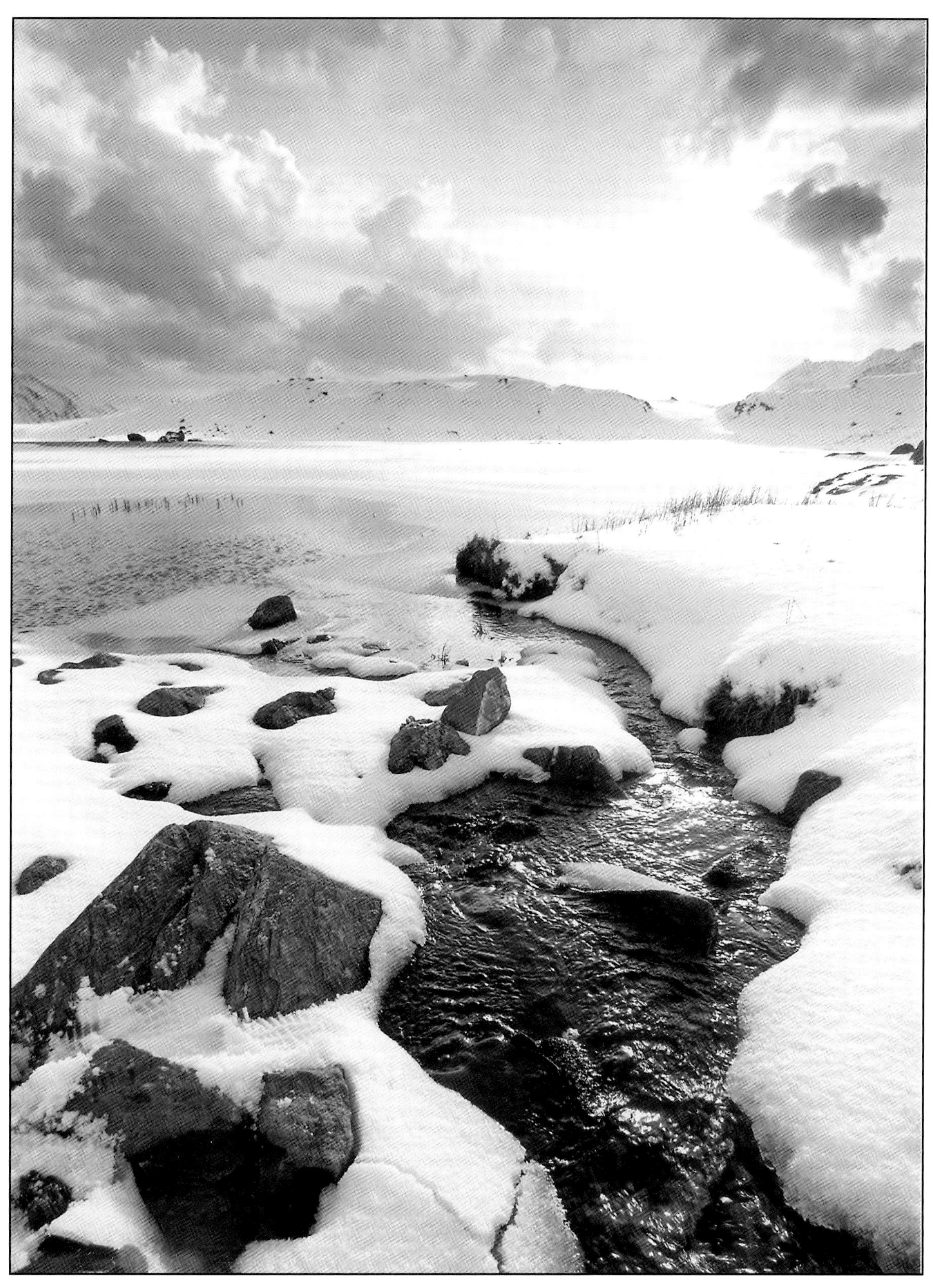

27
Llyn cwm Corsiog
O Tudur Owen

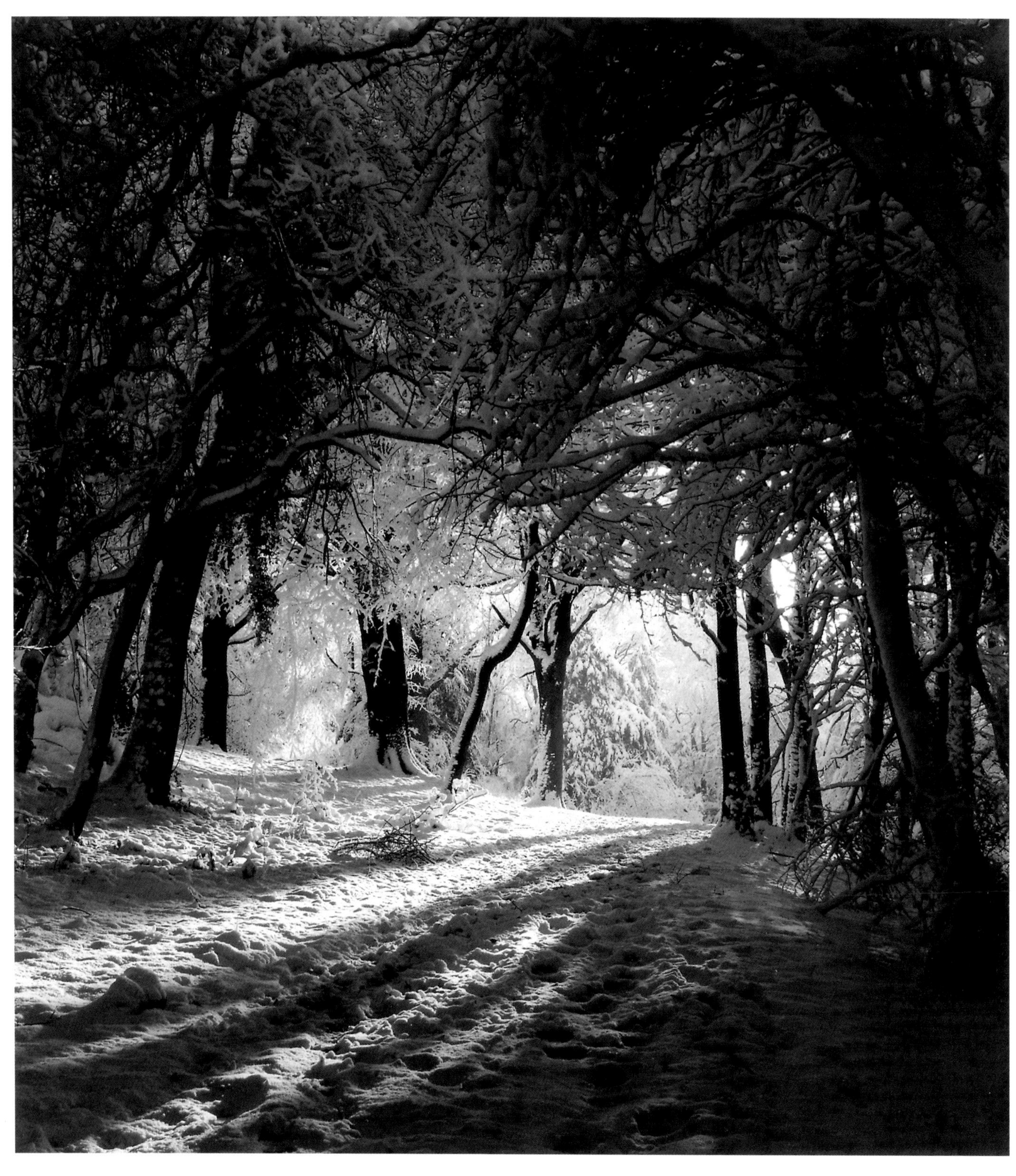

28
Snow, Viewpoint
Peter Rand

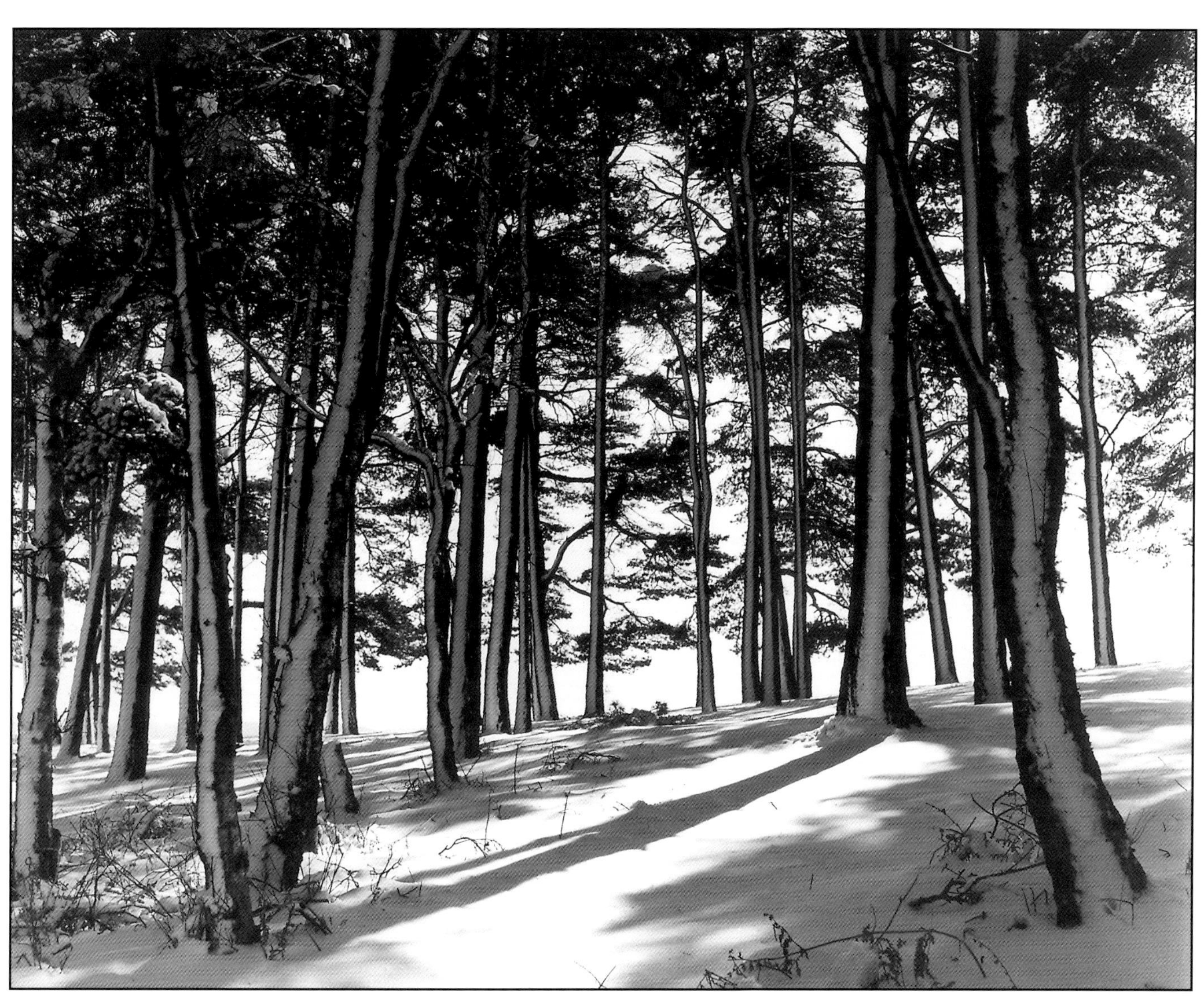

29
Snow shadows
Mike Preston

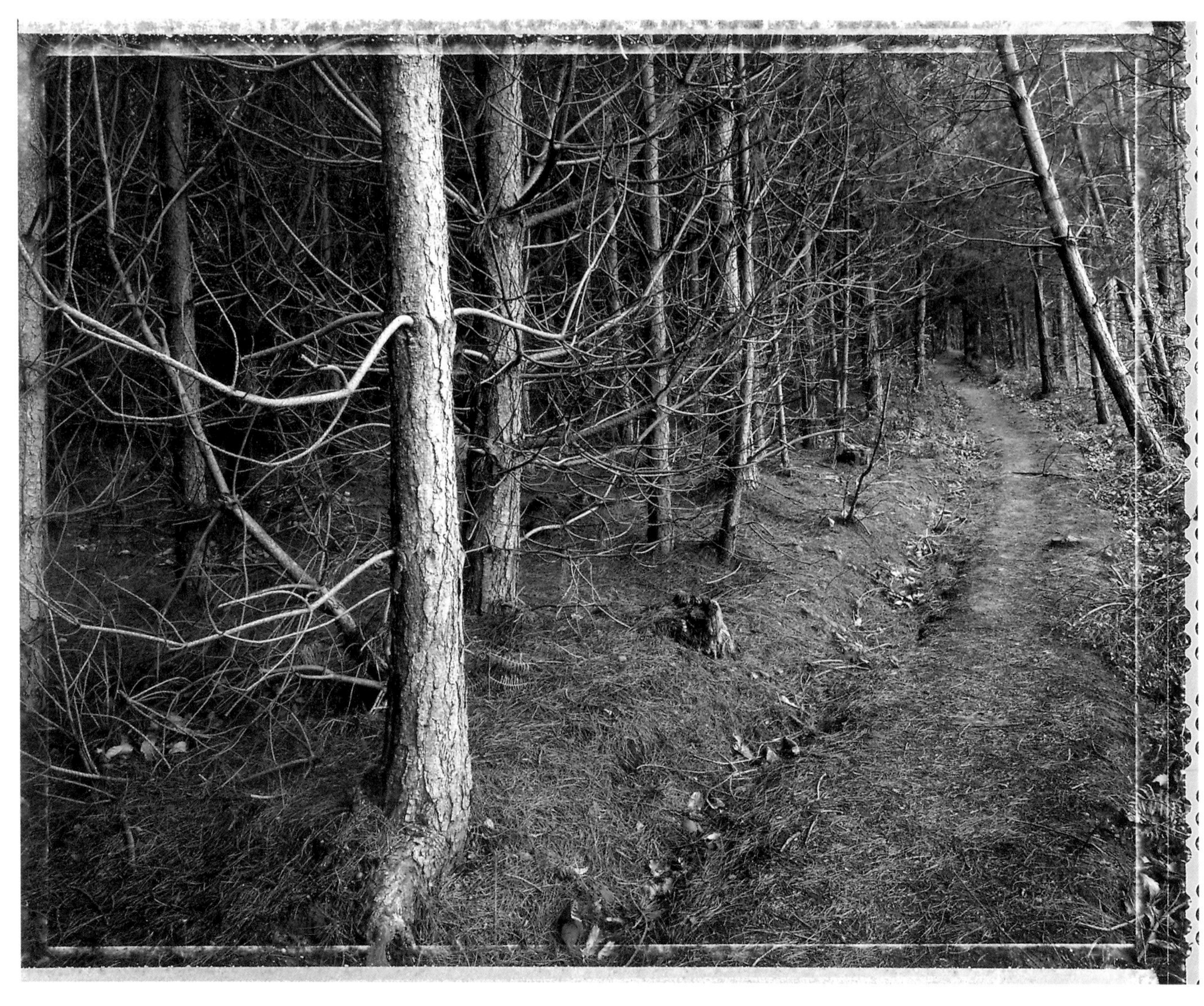

(above) 30 **Pines and path, West Blean Wood**, *Trevor Crone*
(opposite top) 31 **Standing alone**, *Jim Ainslie*
(opposite bottom) 32 **Dead tree**, *Arnold Hubbard*

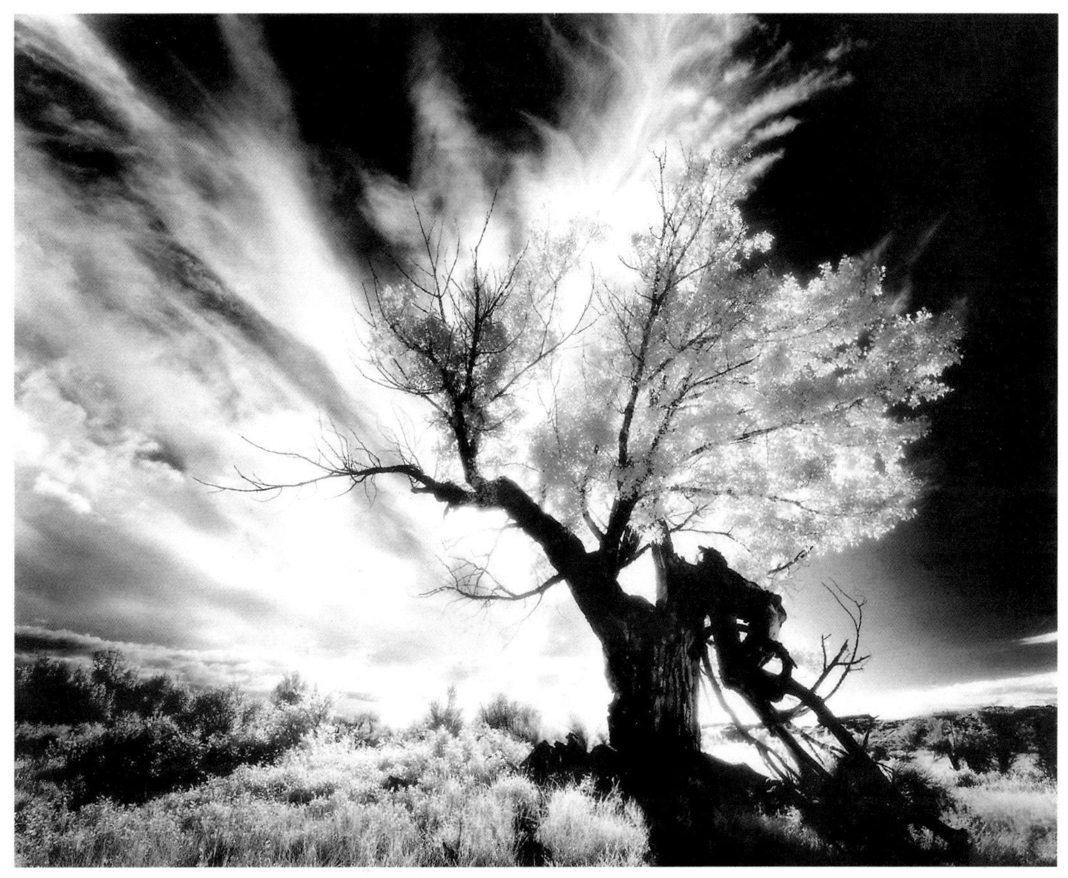

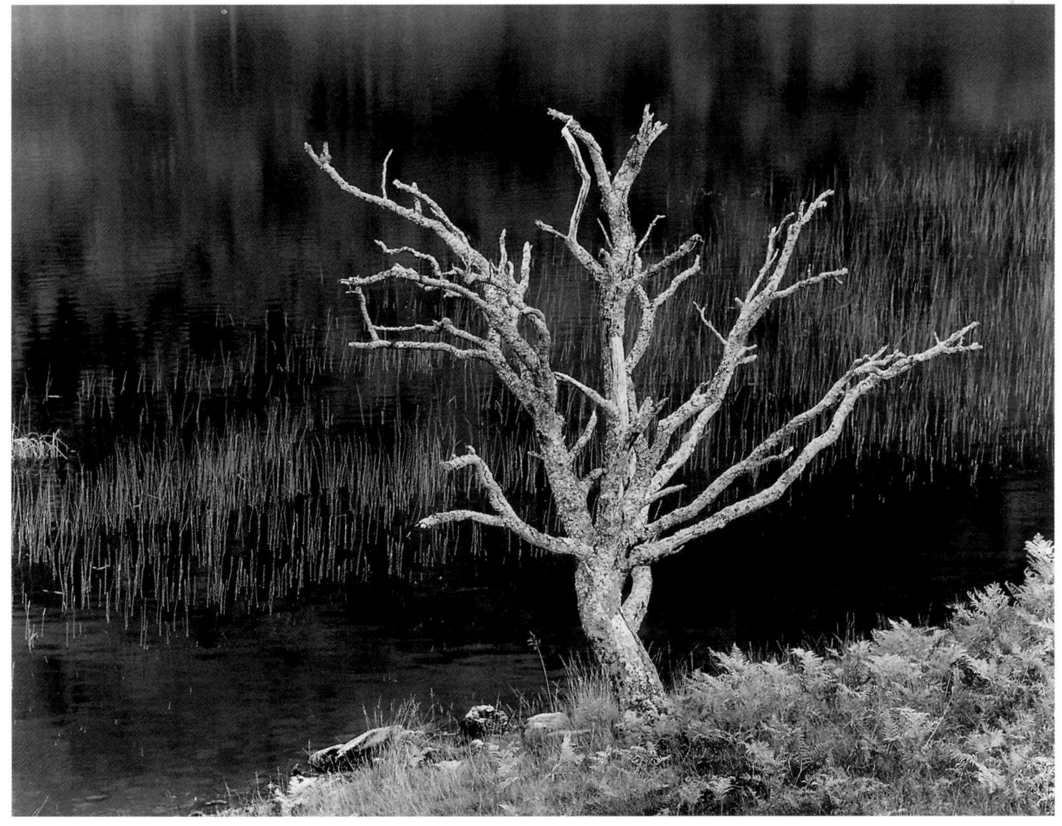

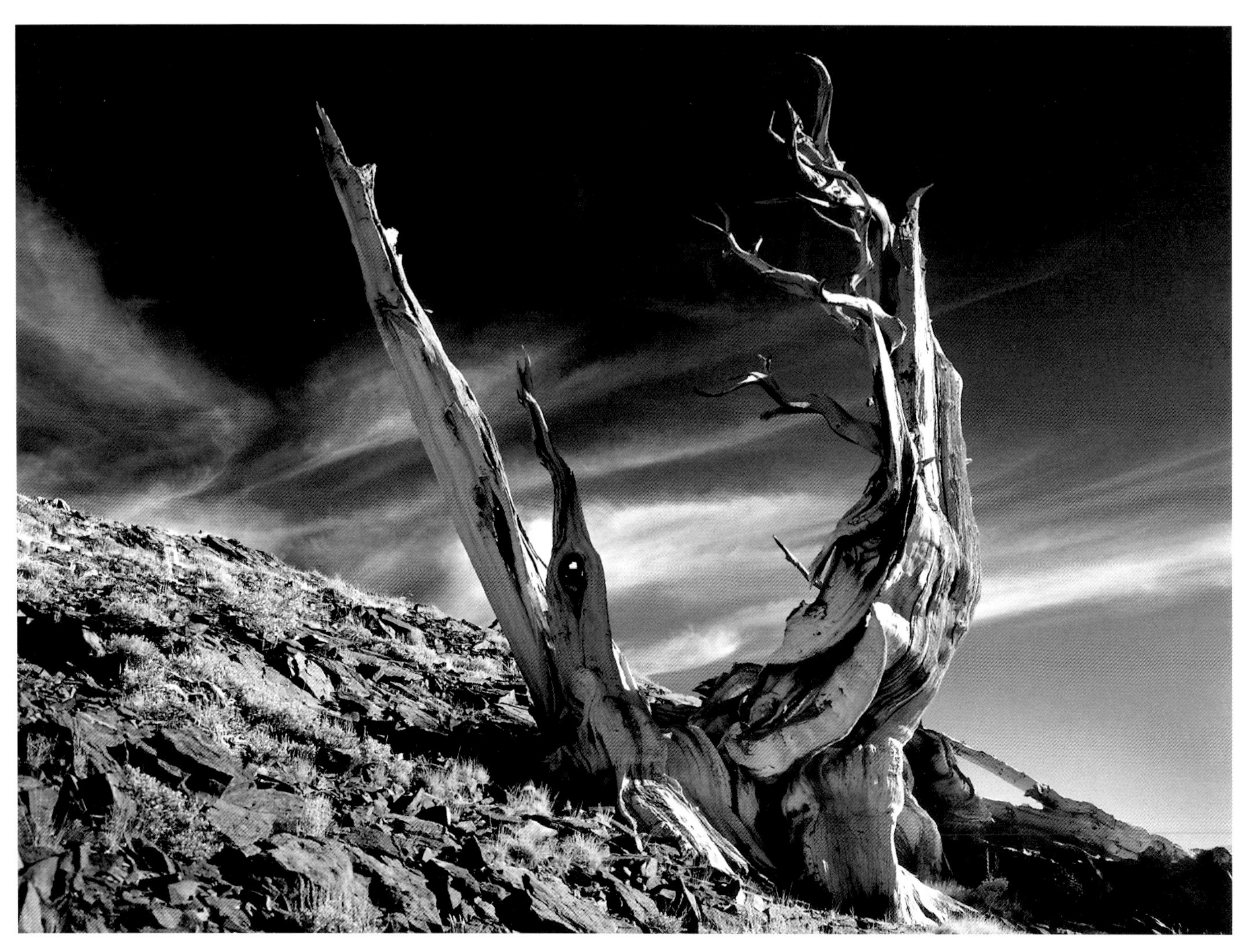

33
Bristlecone pine, California
Colin Westgate

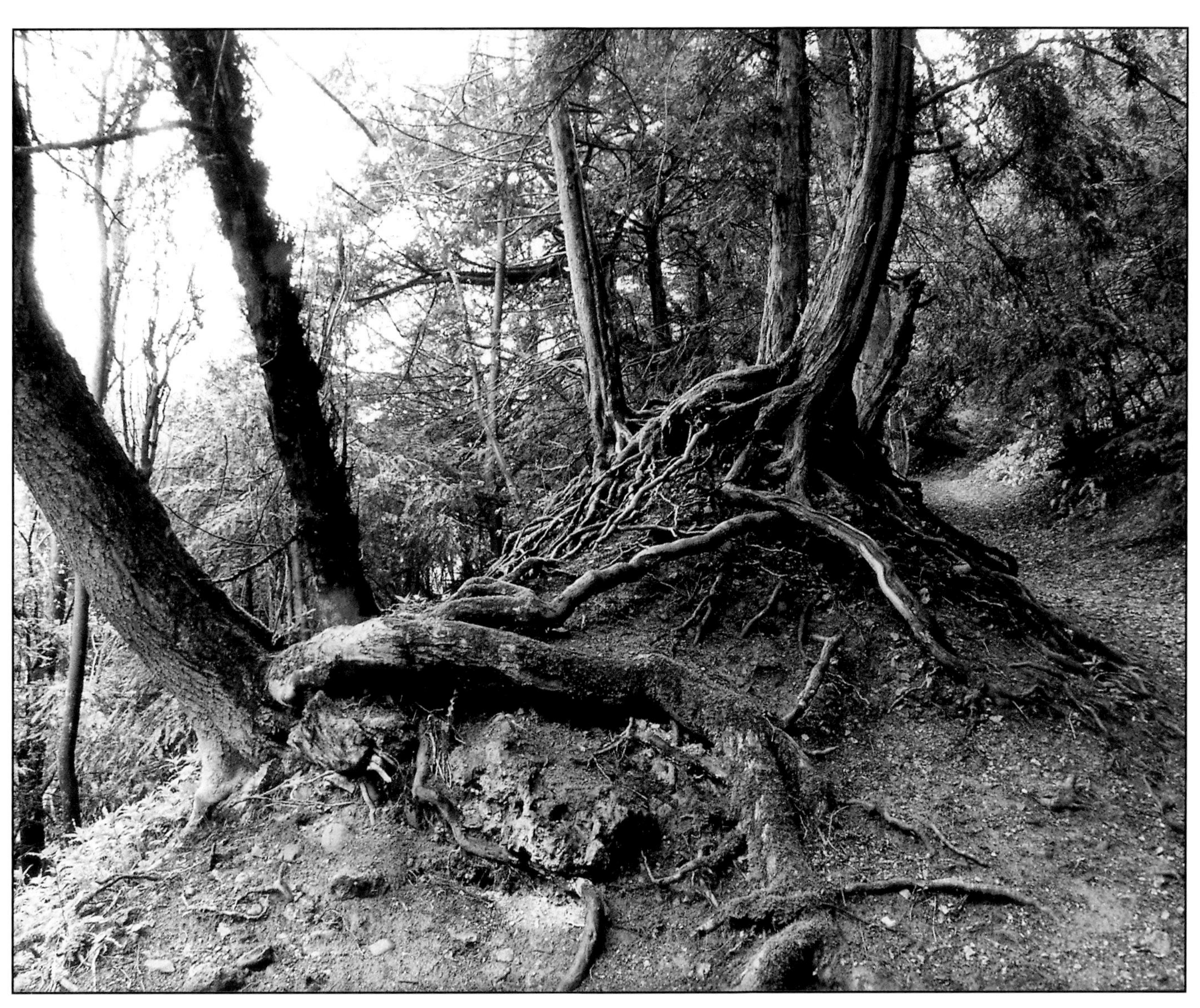

34
Castle Eden Dene
Gary Dixon

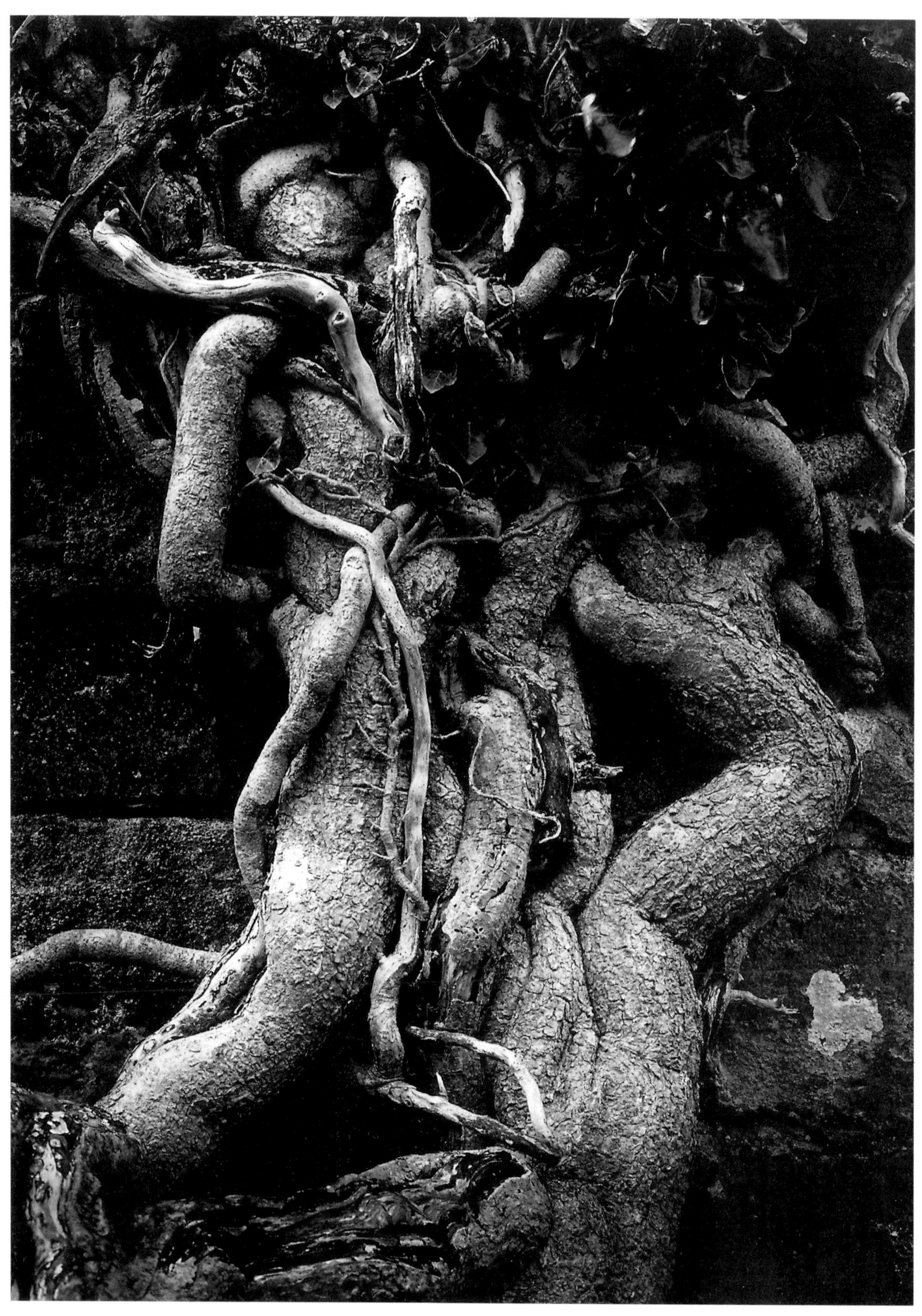

35
Entwined
Bob Marshall

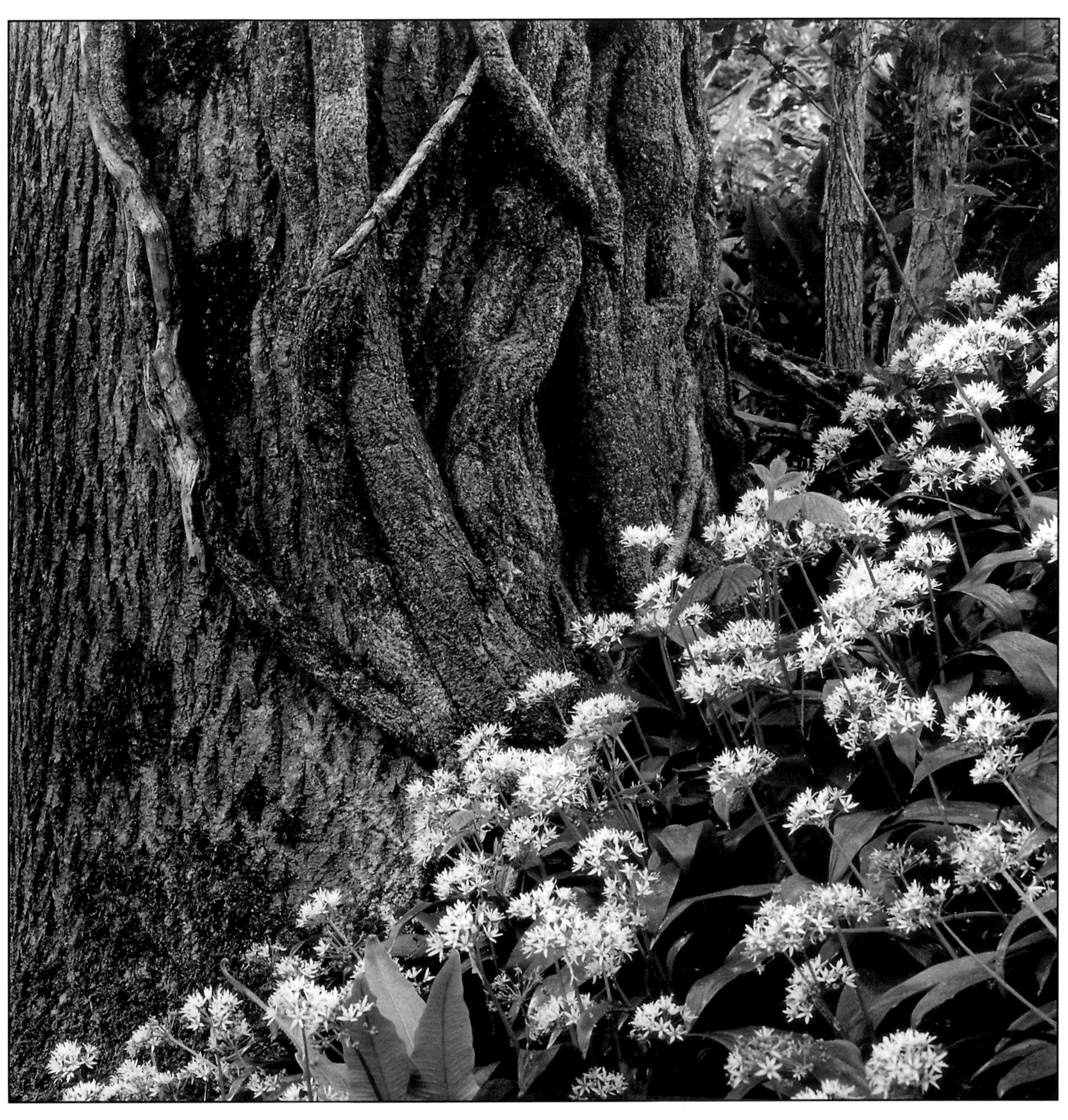

36
Ethy Wood, Lerryn
Anne Newell

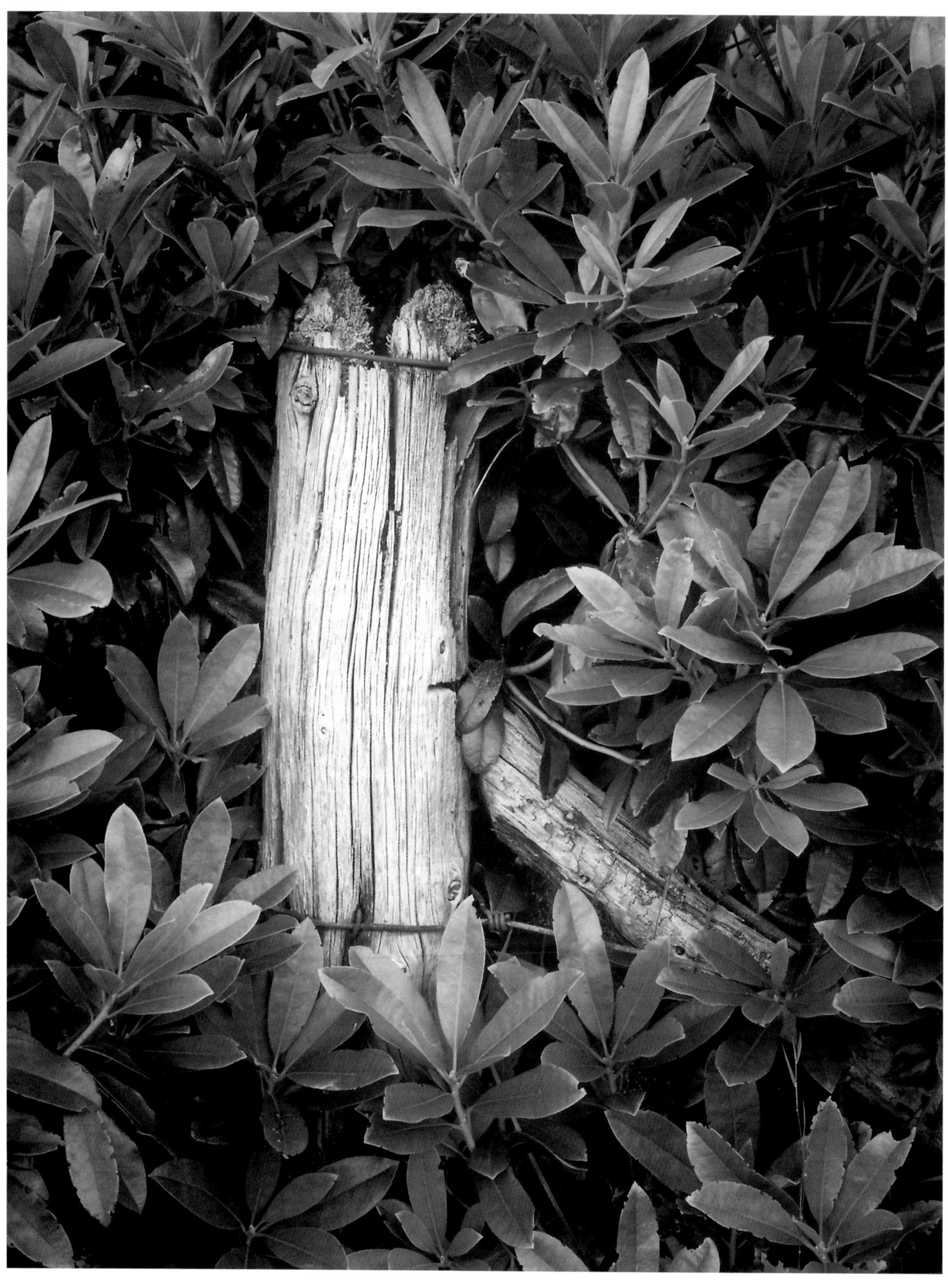

37
The post
Paul Damen

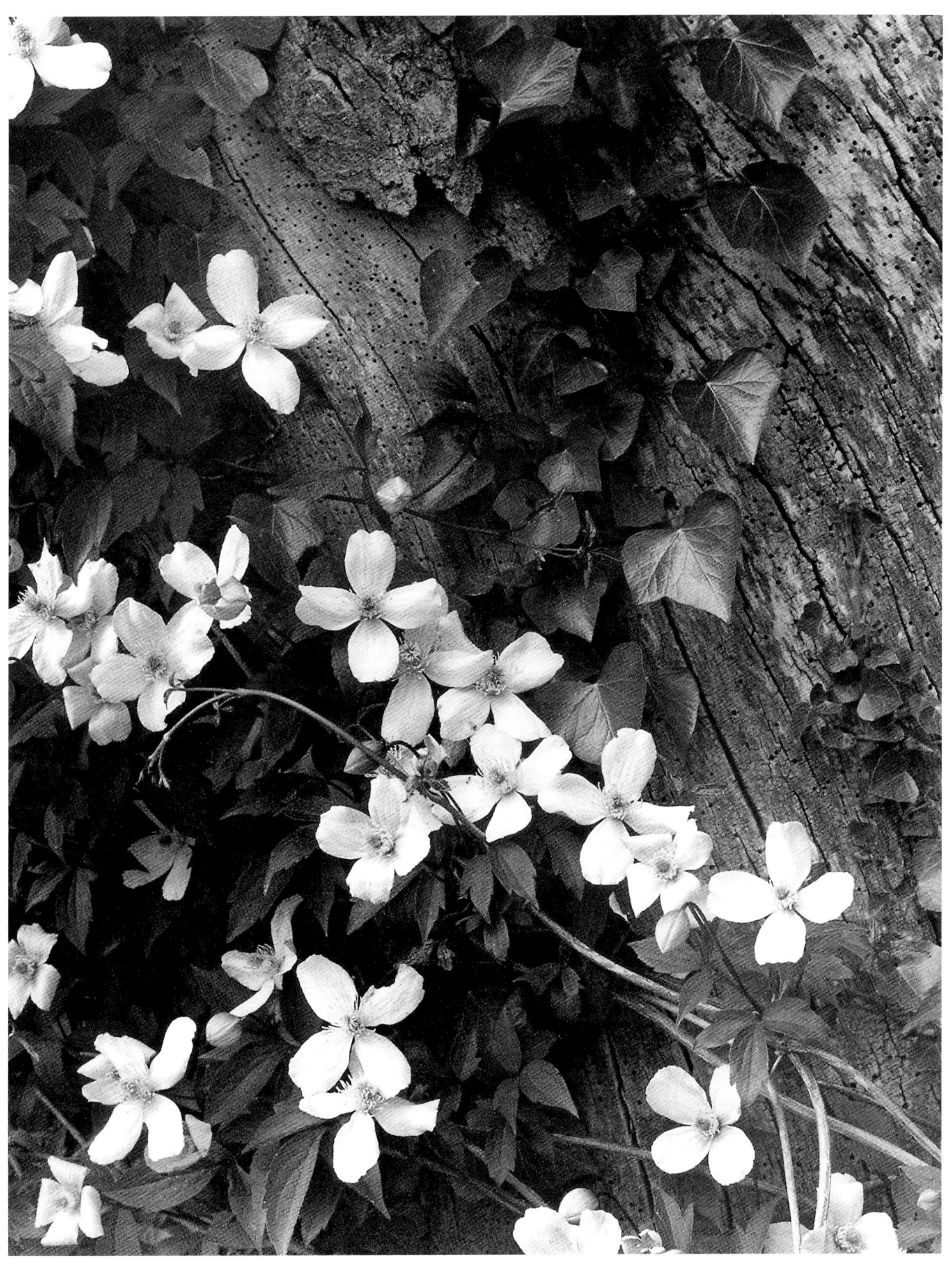

38
Clematis and ivy
Michael Cant

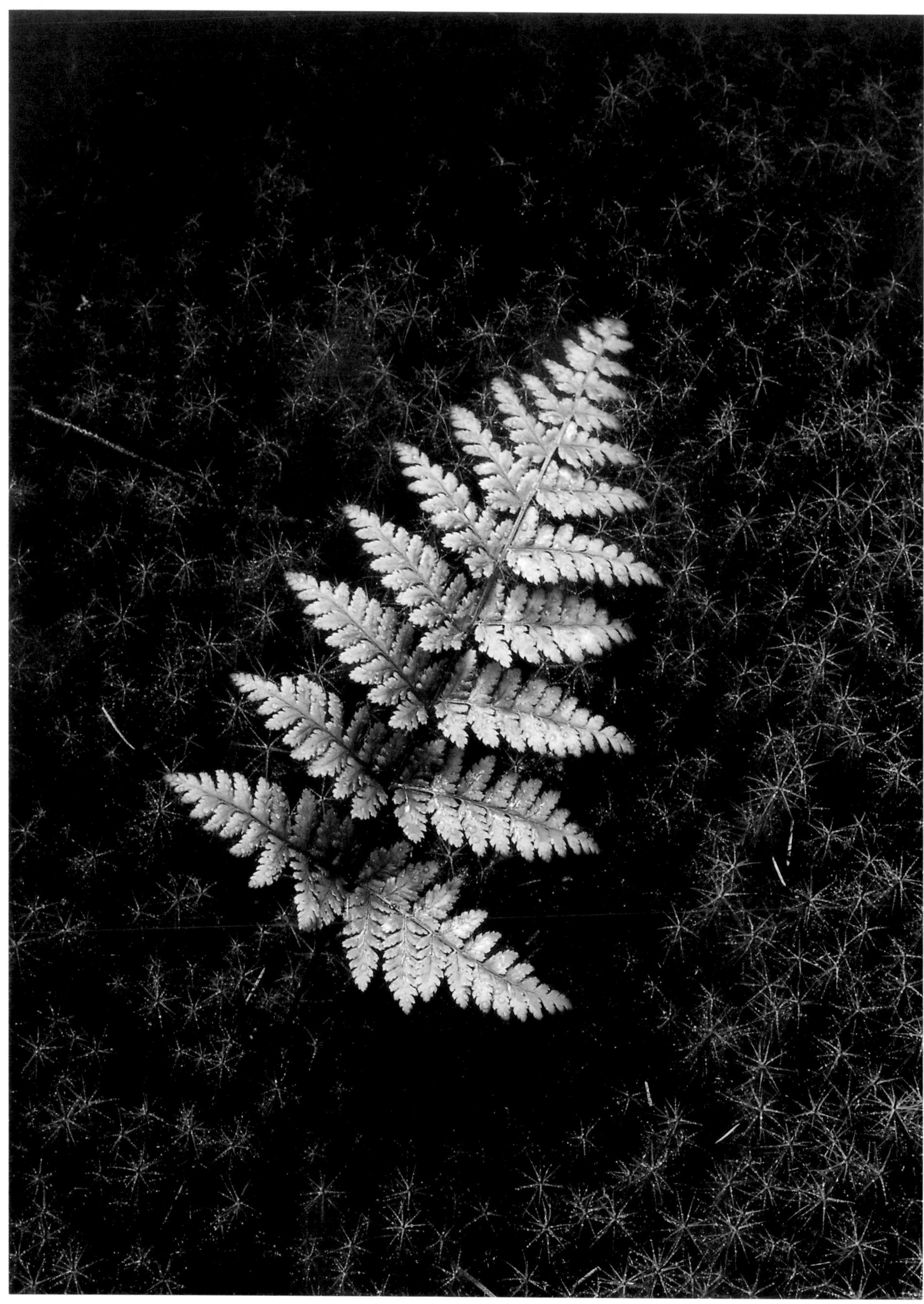

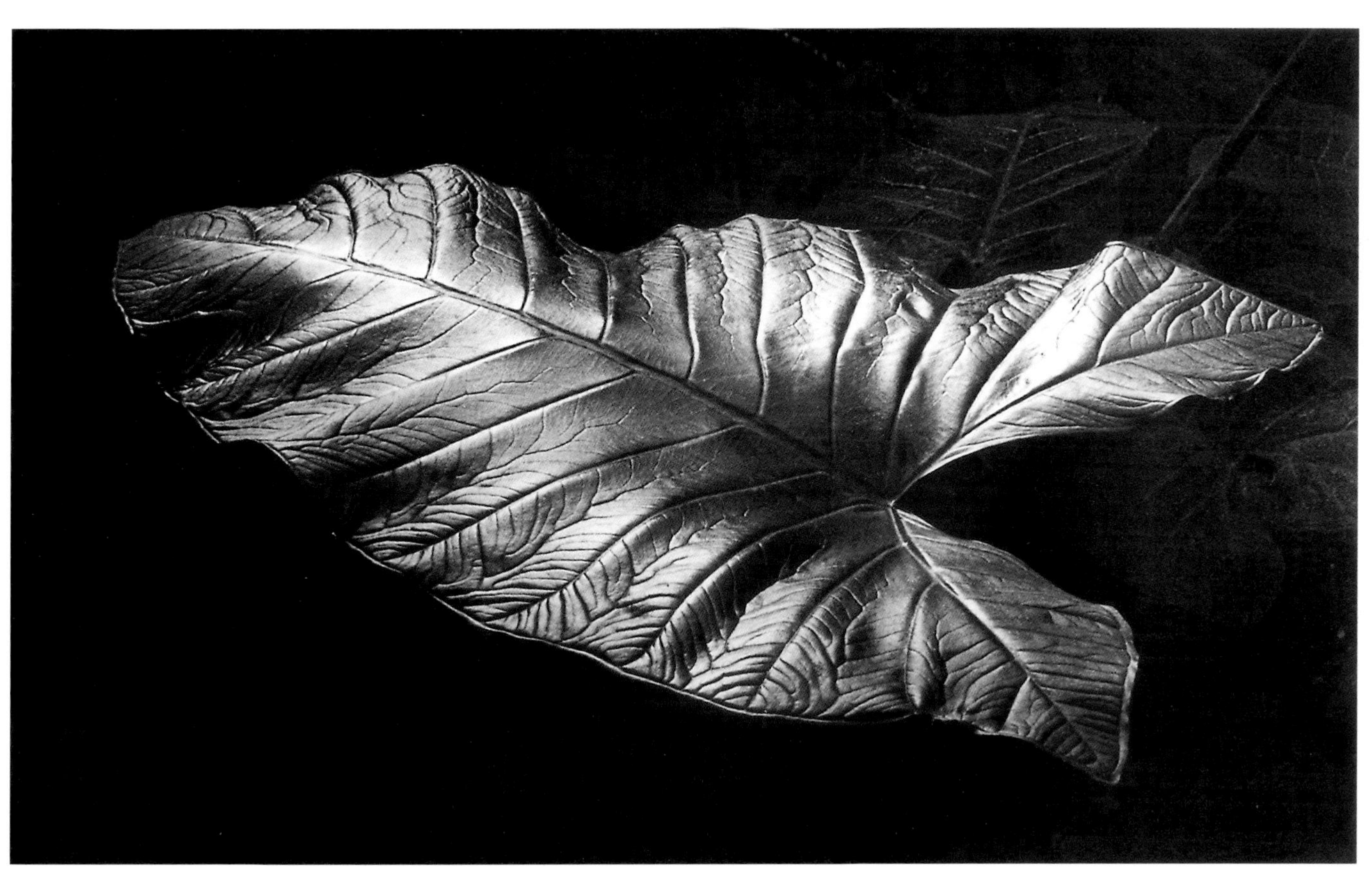

(left) 39 **Morning dew**, *Stephen Smith*
(above) 40 **Lone leaf**, *Peter Handford*

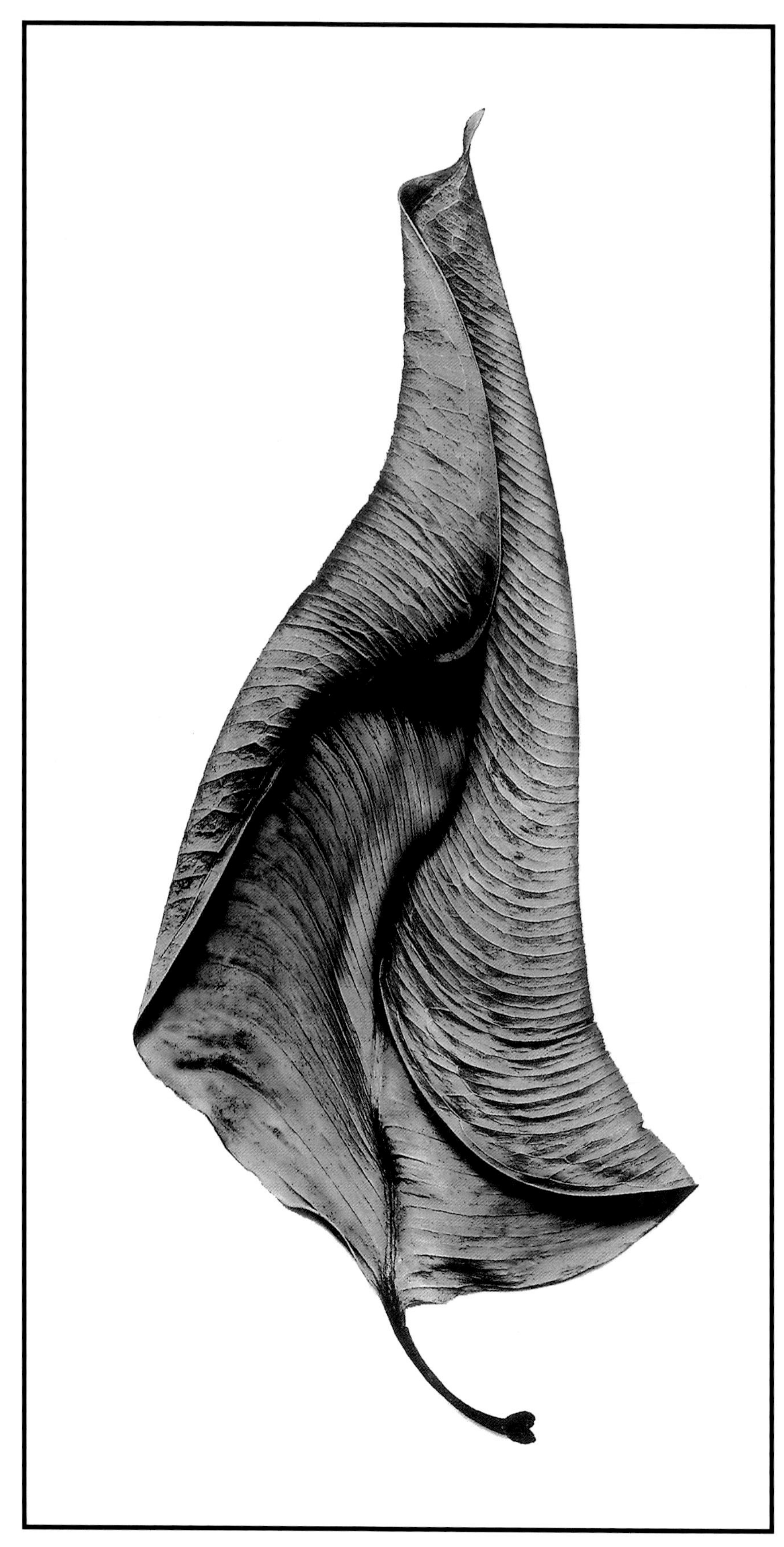

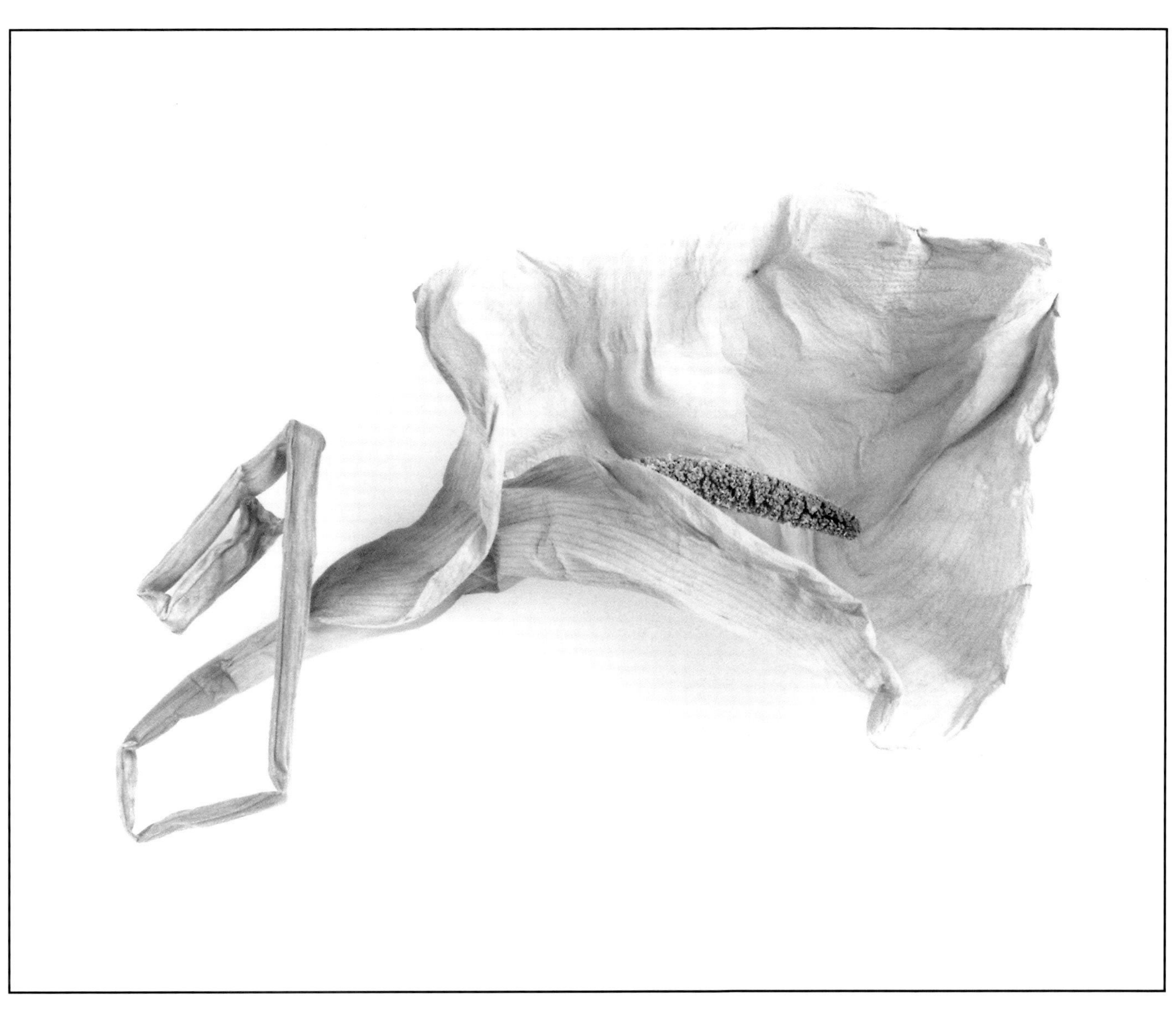

(left) 41 **Curled leaf**, *Rex Bamber*
(above) 42 **Calla lily**, *Caroline Taylor*

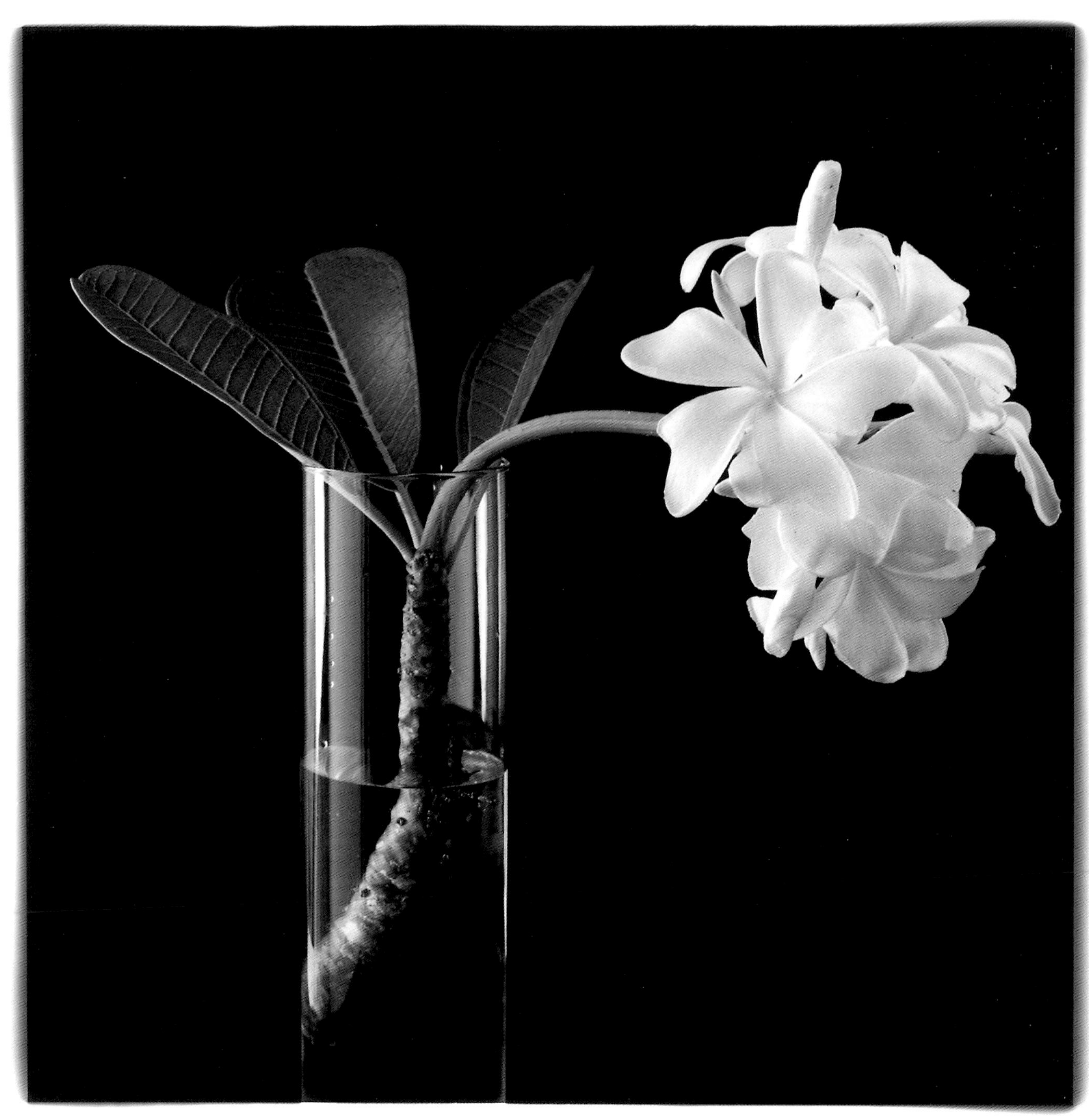

43
Frangi Pani I
Susanne Waldock

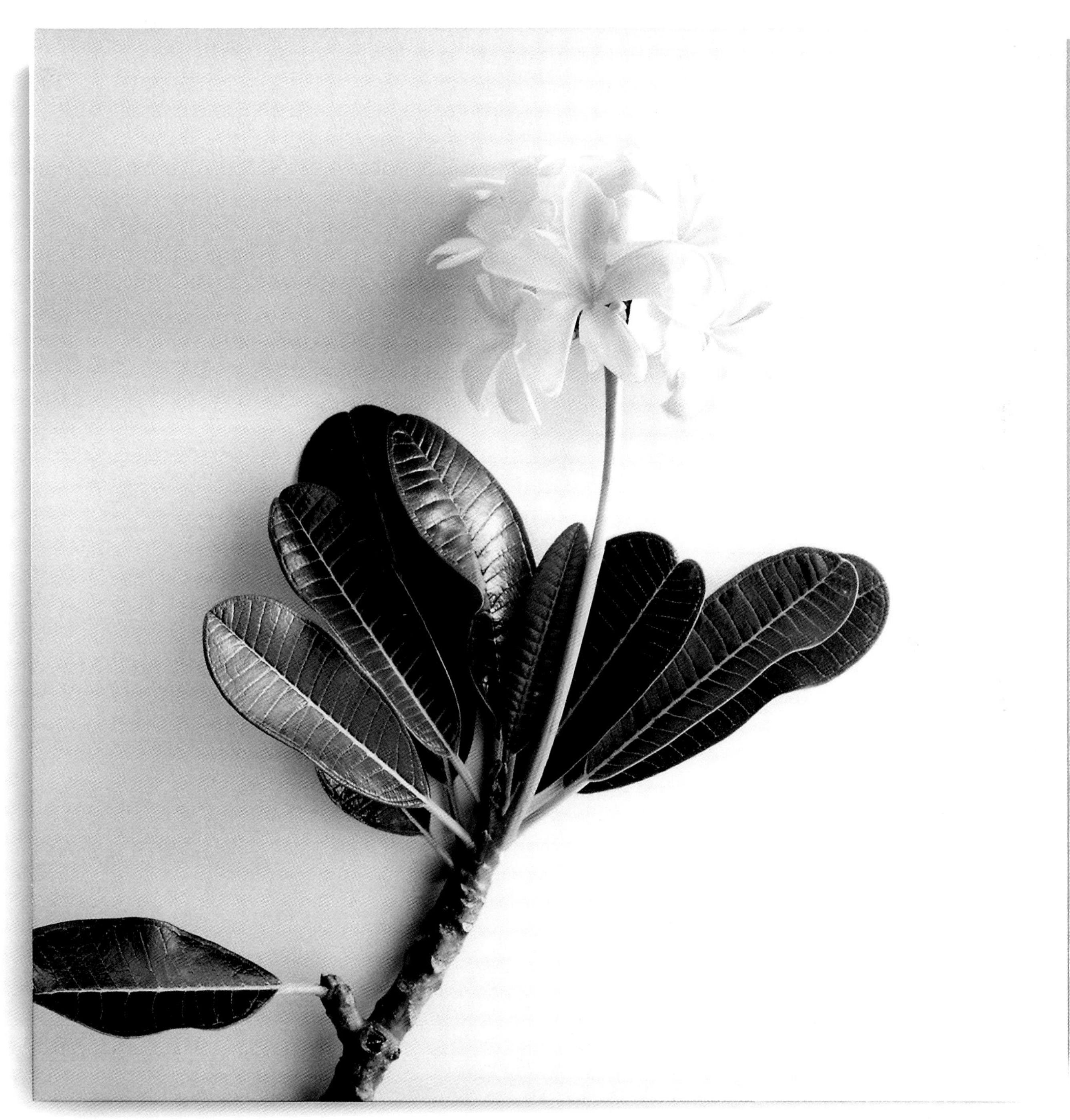

44
Frangi Pani II
Susanne Waldock

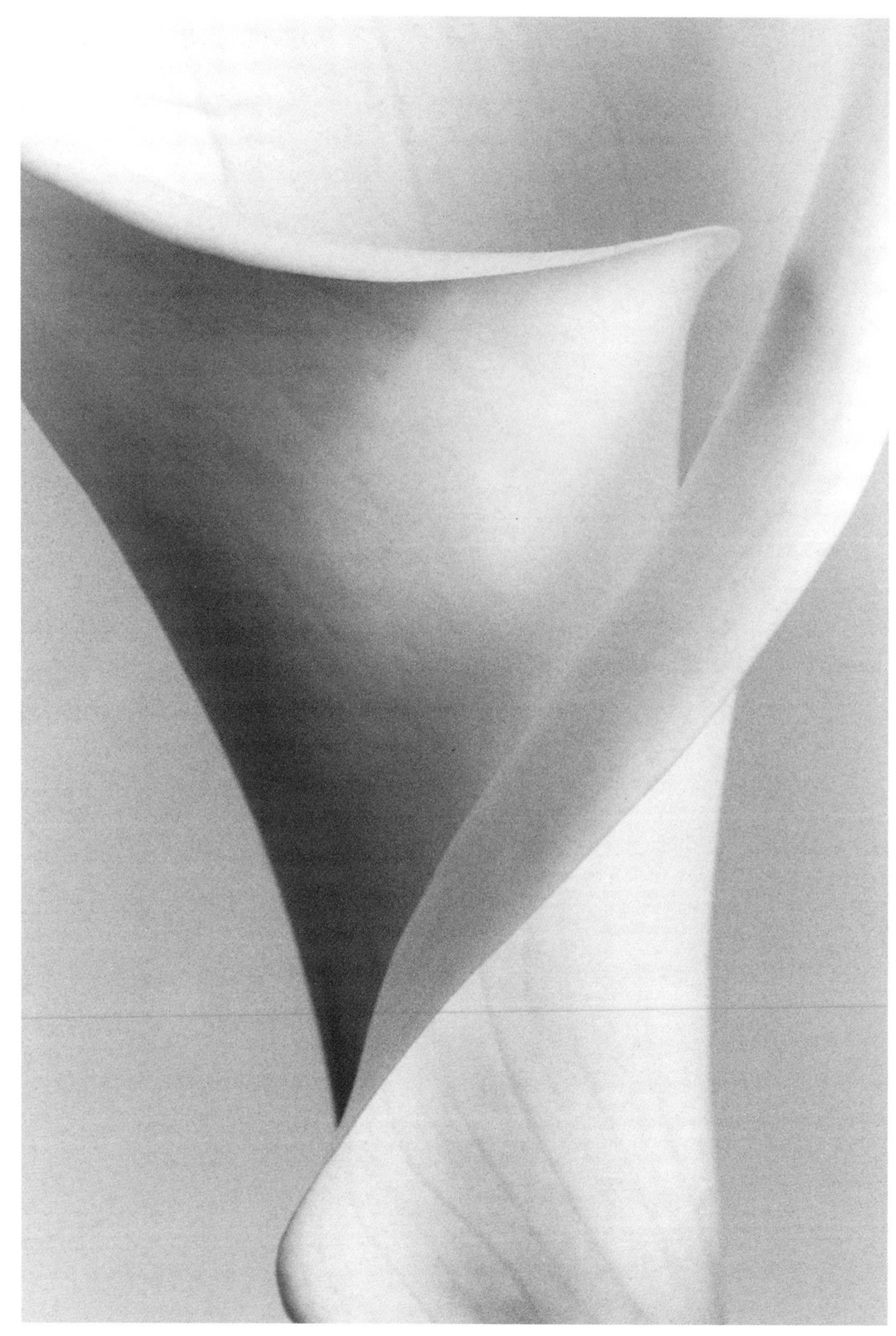

45
Arum lily
Gerry Coe

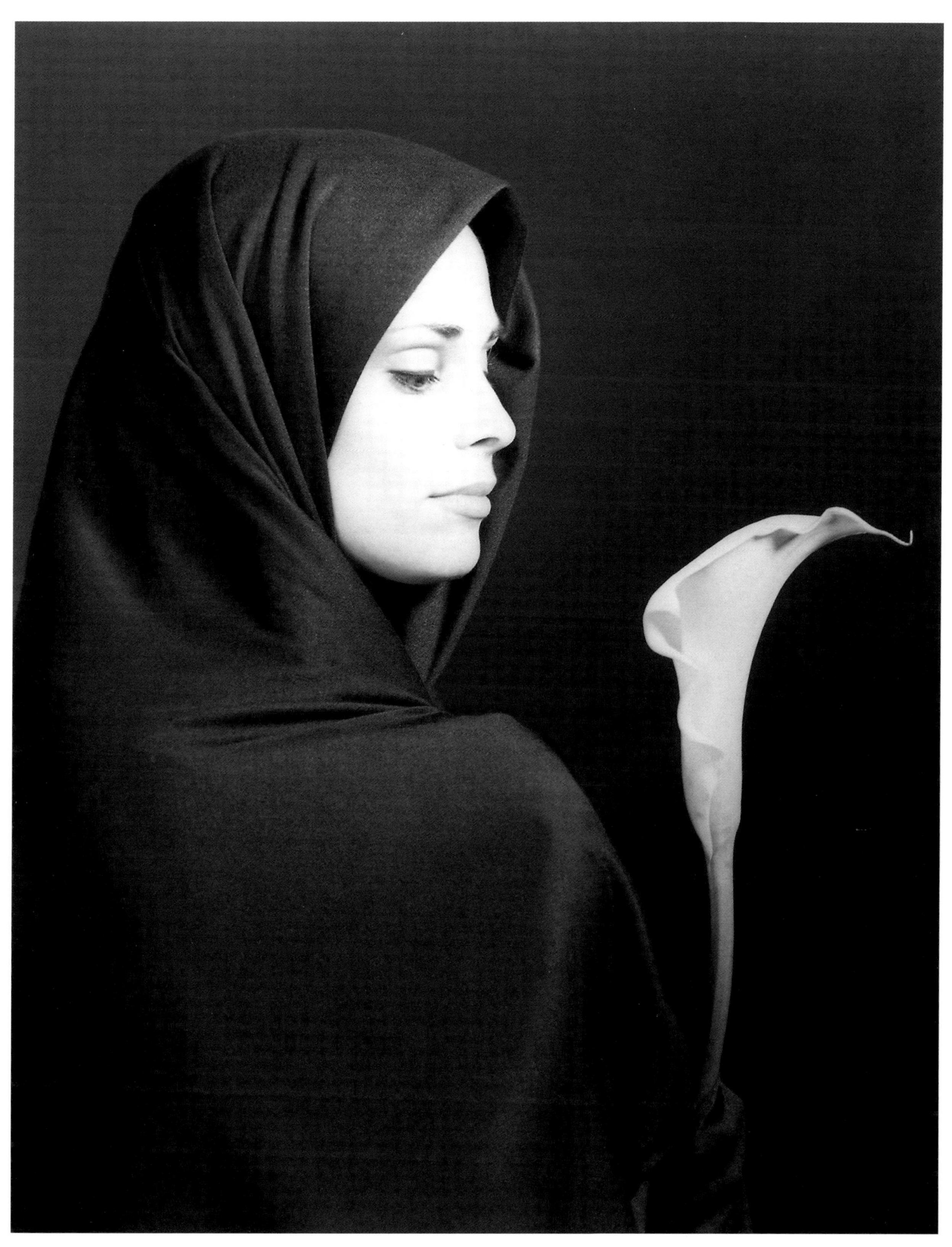

46
Lisa
Wolfgang Gilges

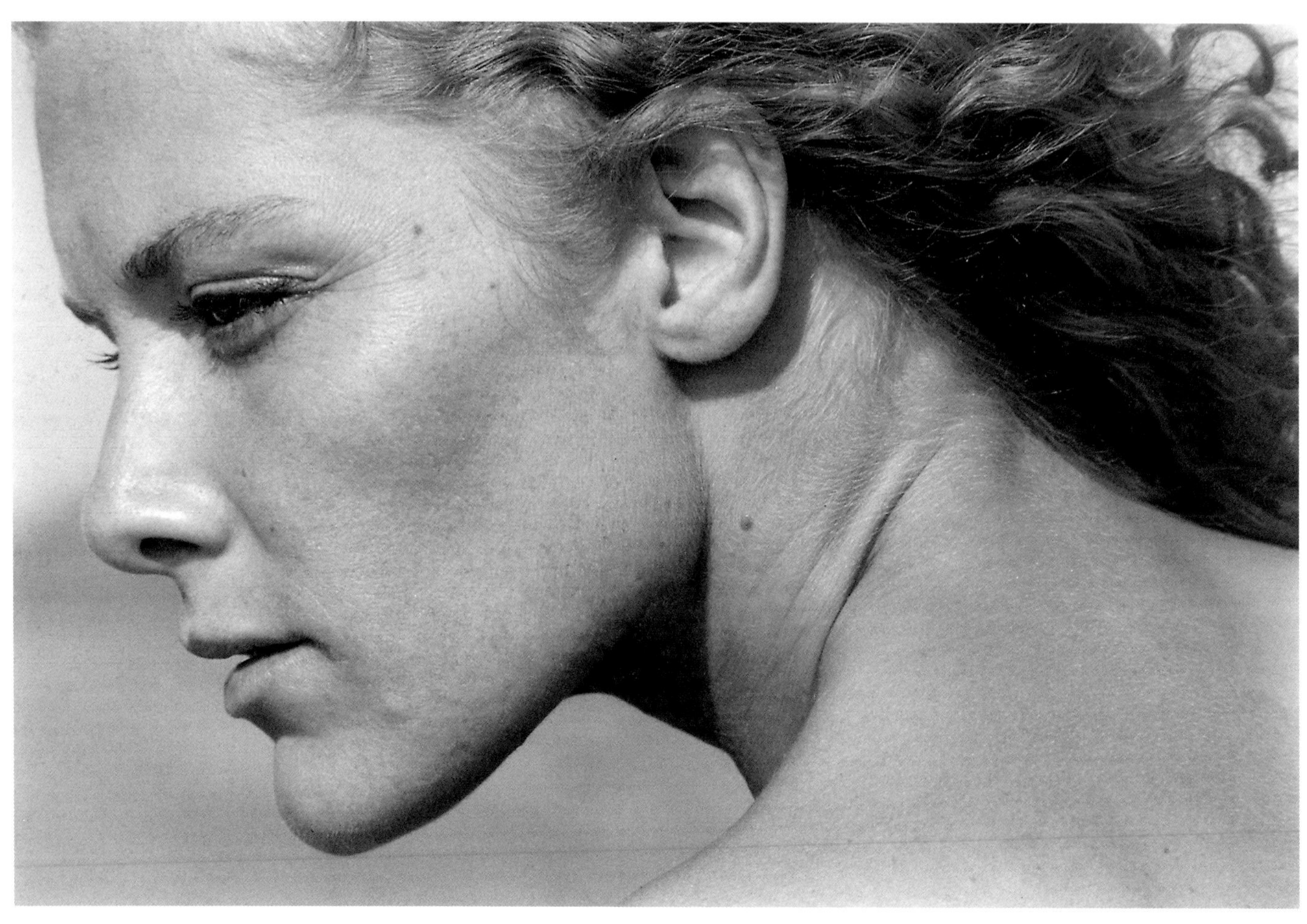

(above) 47 **Stephanie**, *Carolyn Bross*
(right) 48 **Carol**, *Christopher Read*

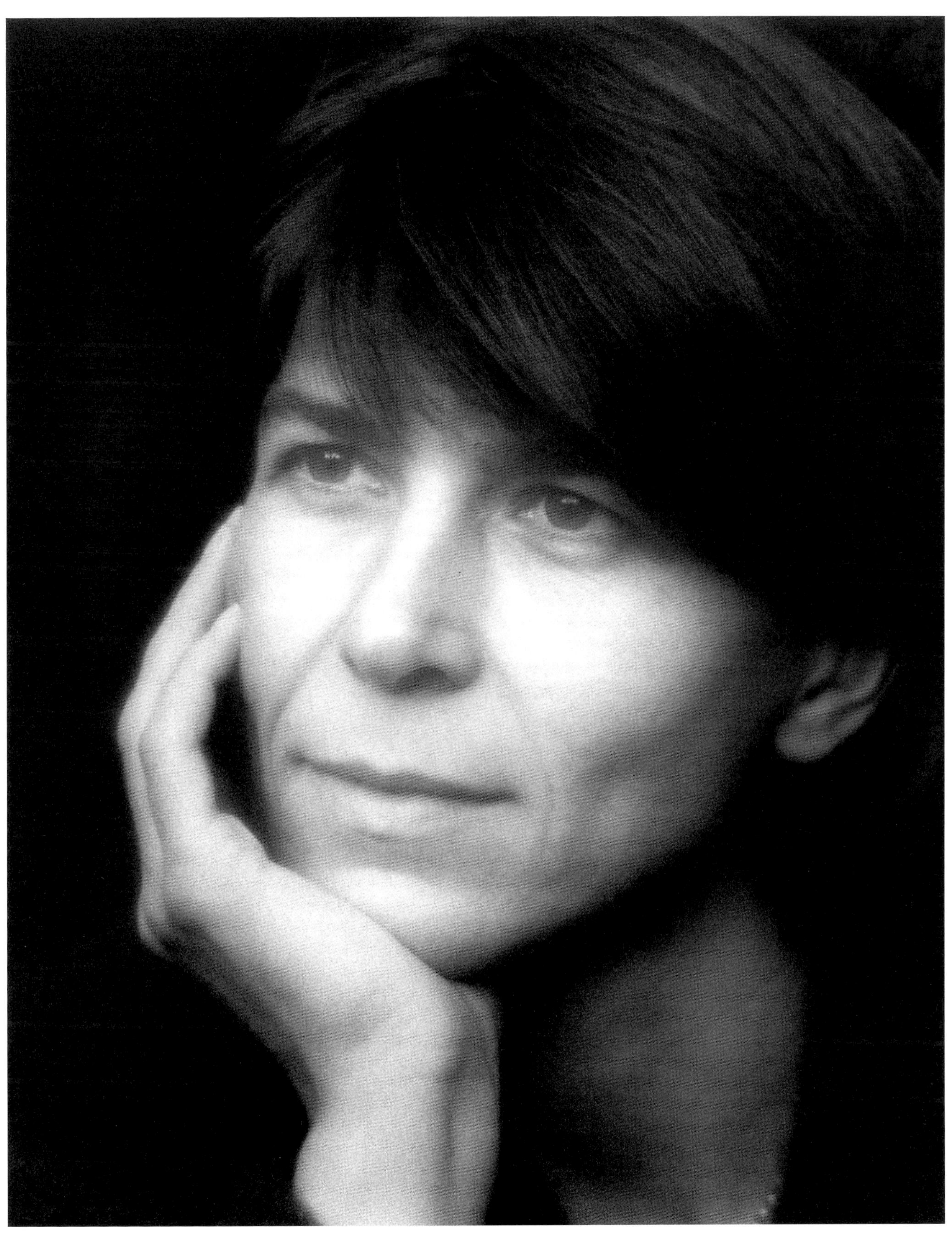

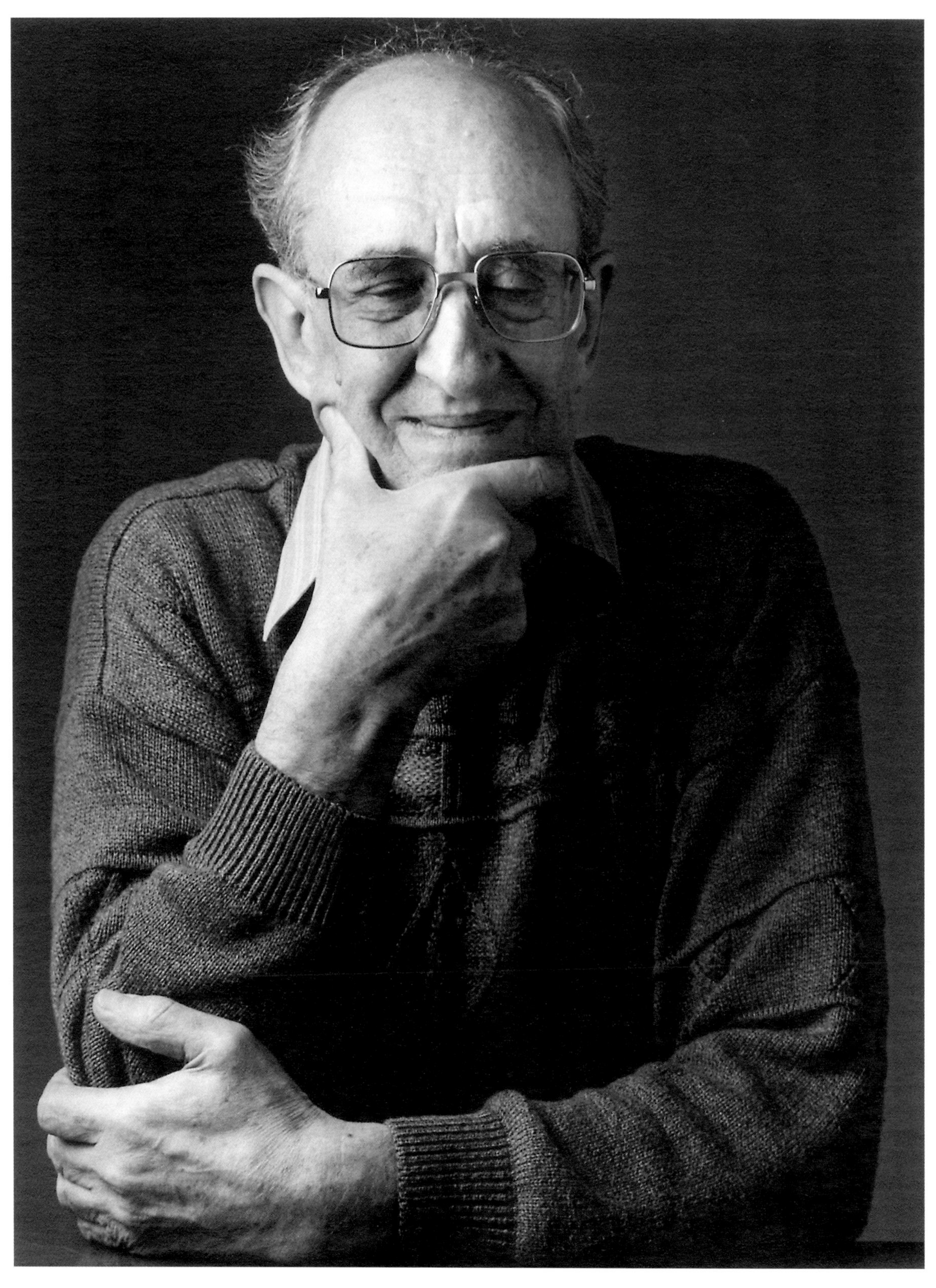

49
Hugh Milsom
Ronnie Bennett

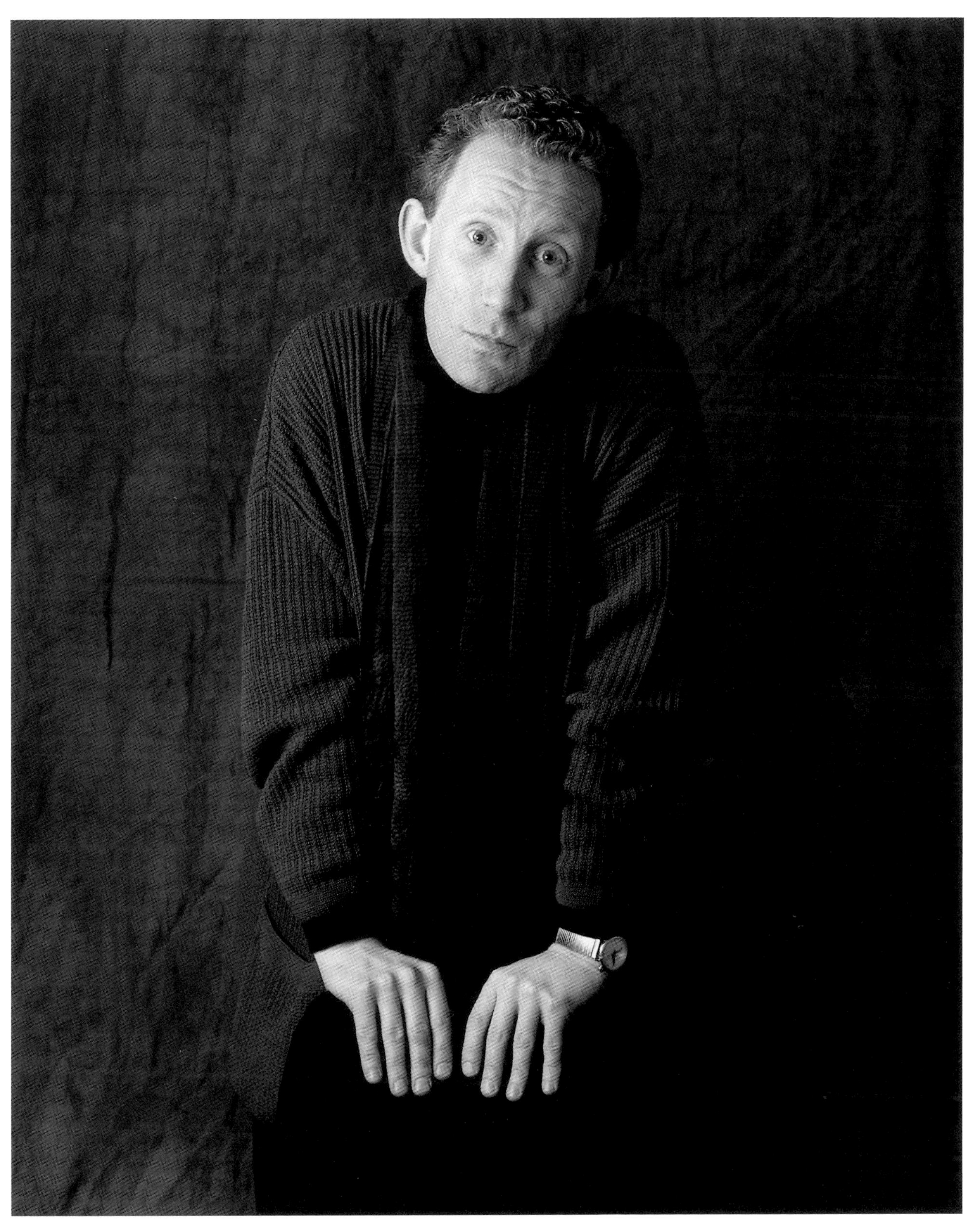

50
Portrait Wilhelm R
Klaus Peters

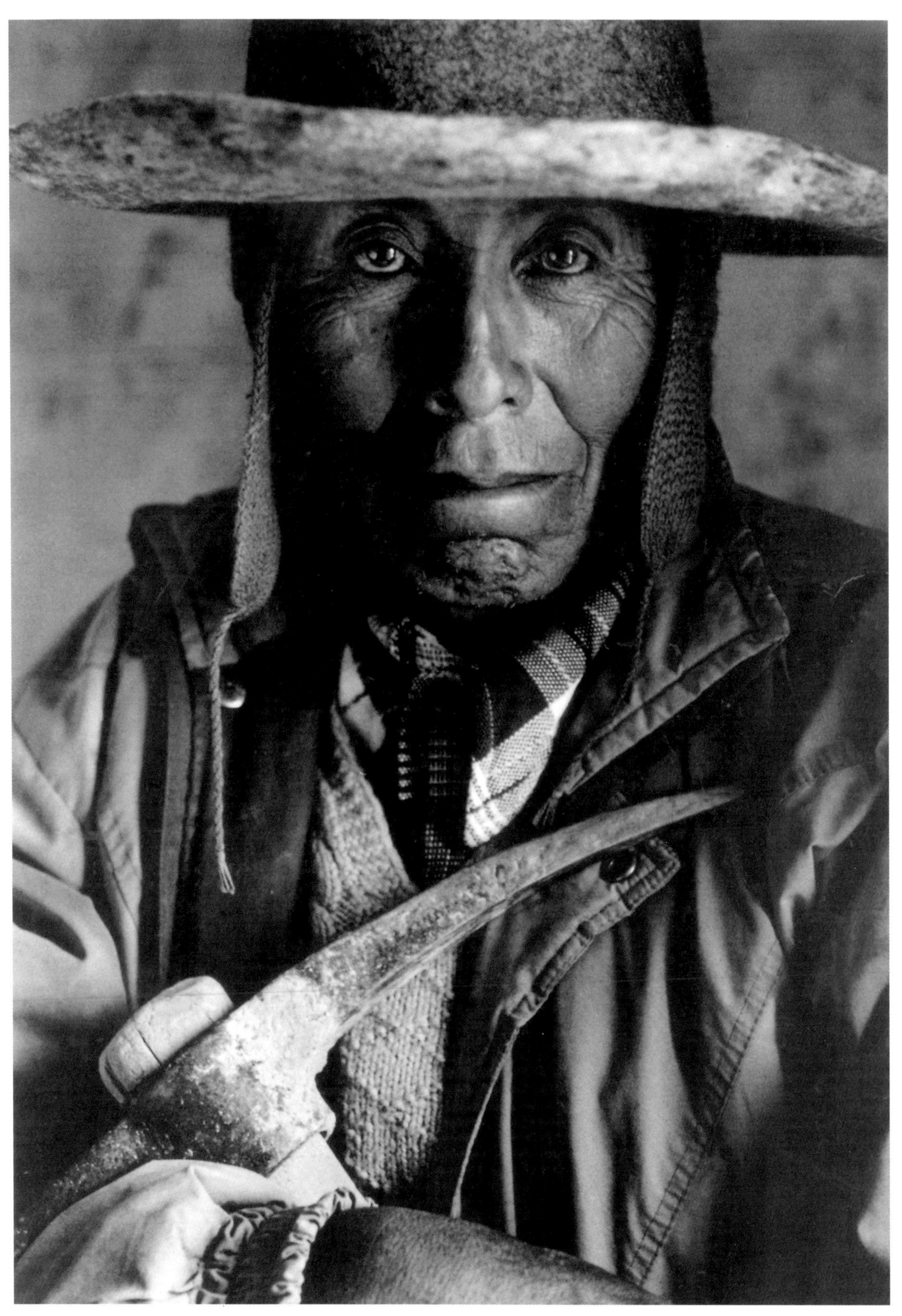

51
Mr Mamani and pick
Marj Clayton

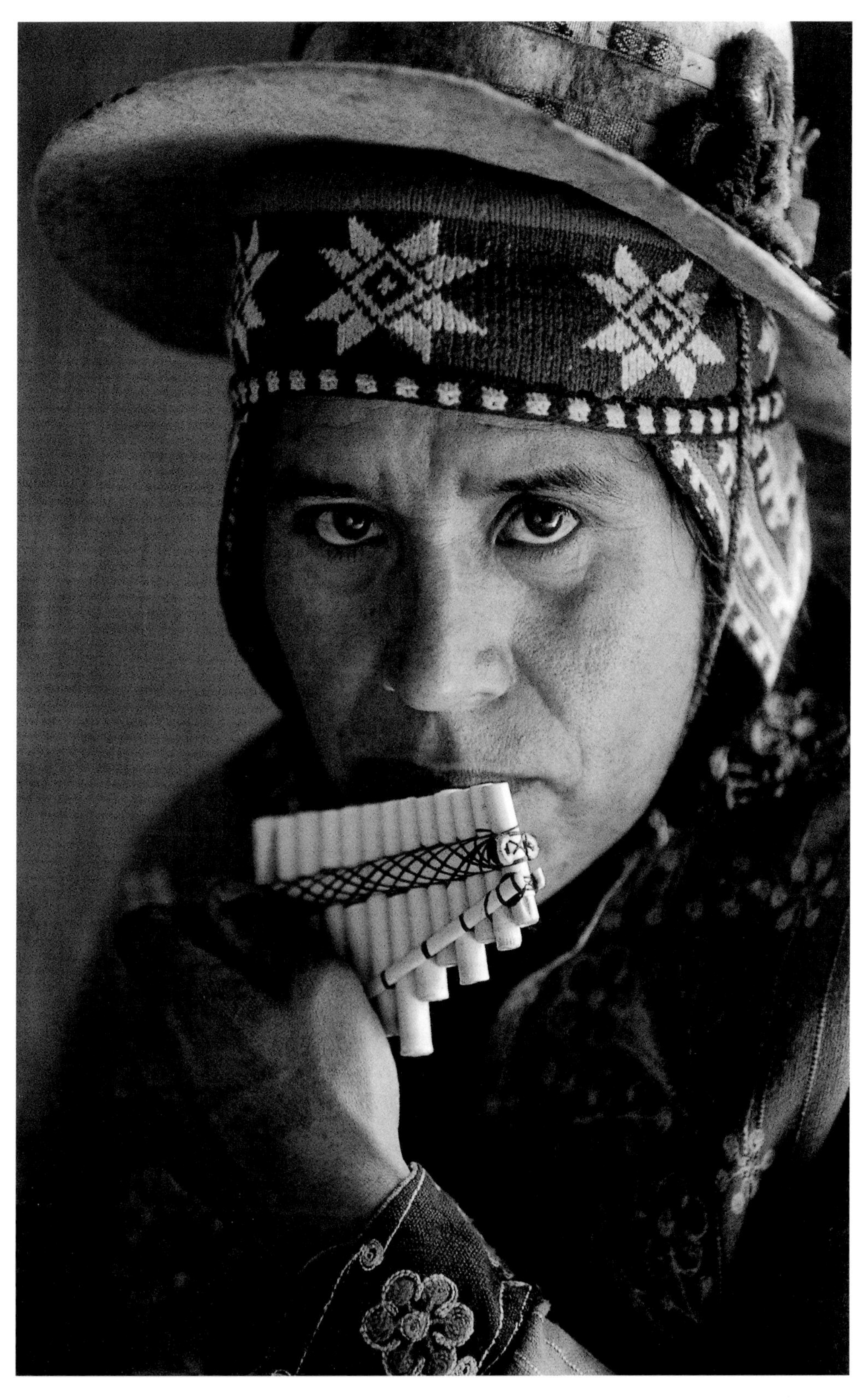

52
Quirki
Marj Clayton

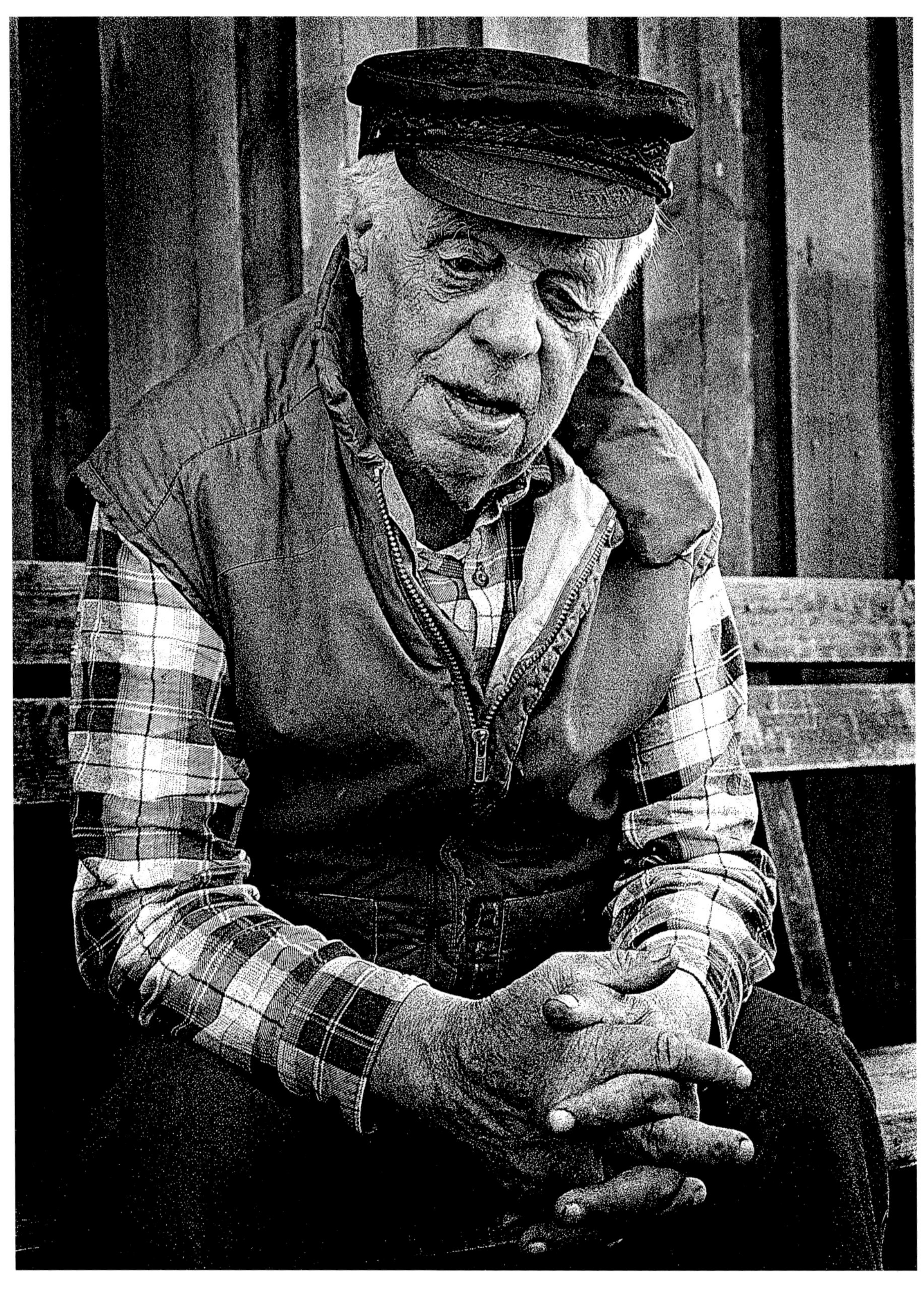

53
Memory time
Signe Drevsjø

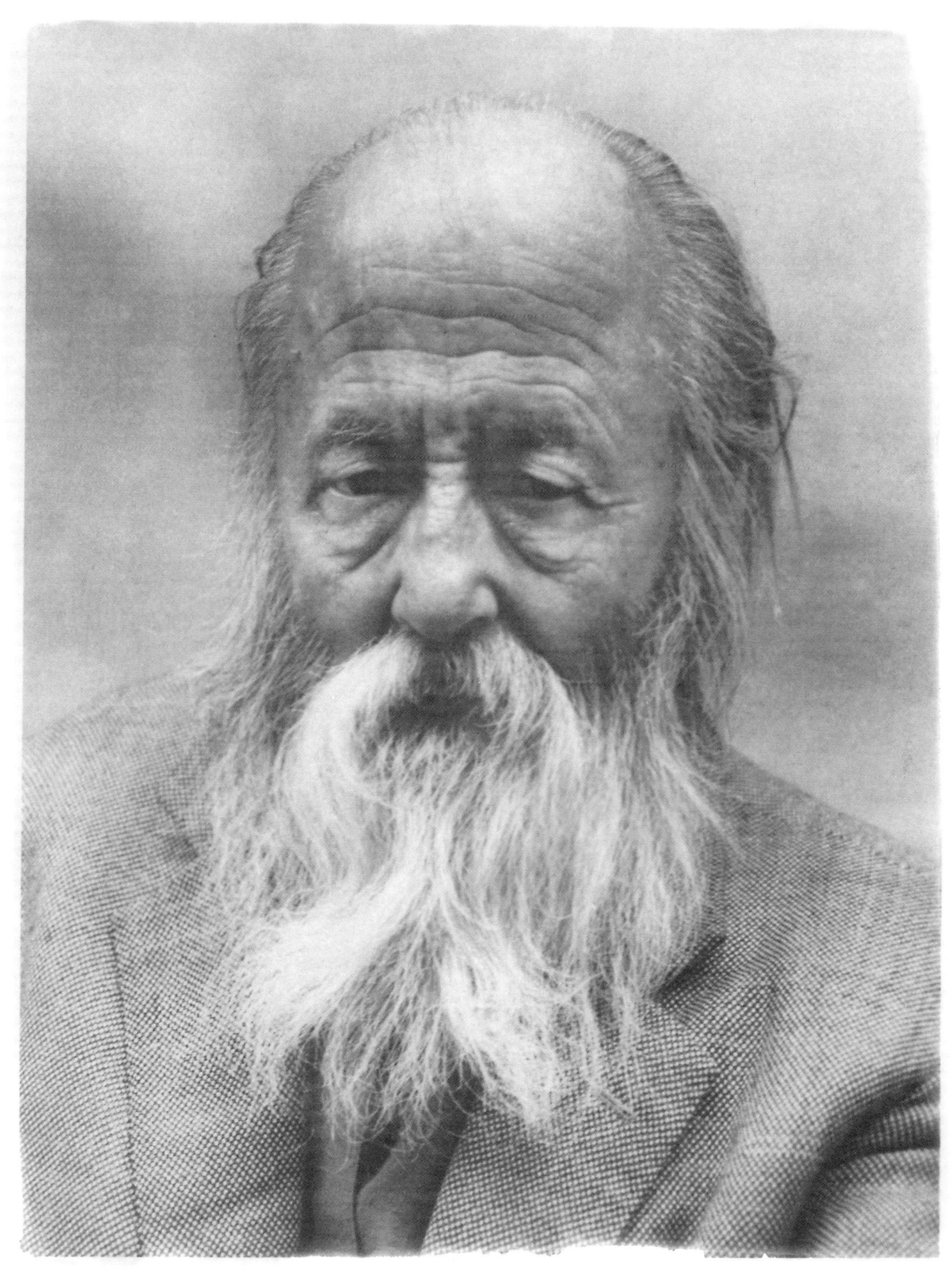

54
Old man of Prague
Jim Bennett

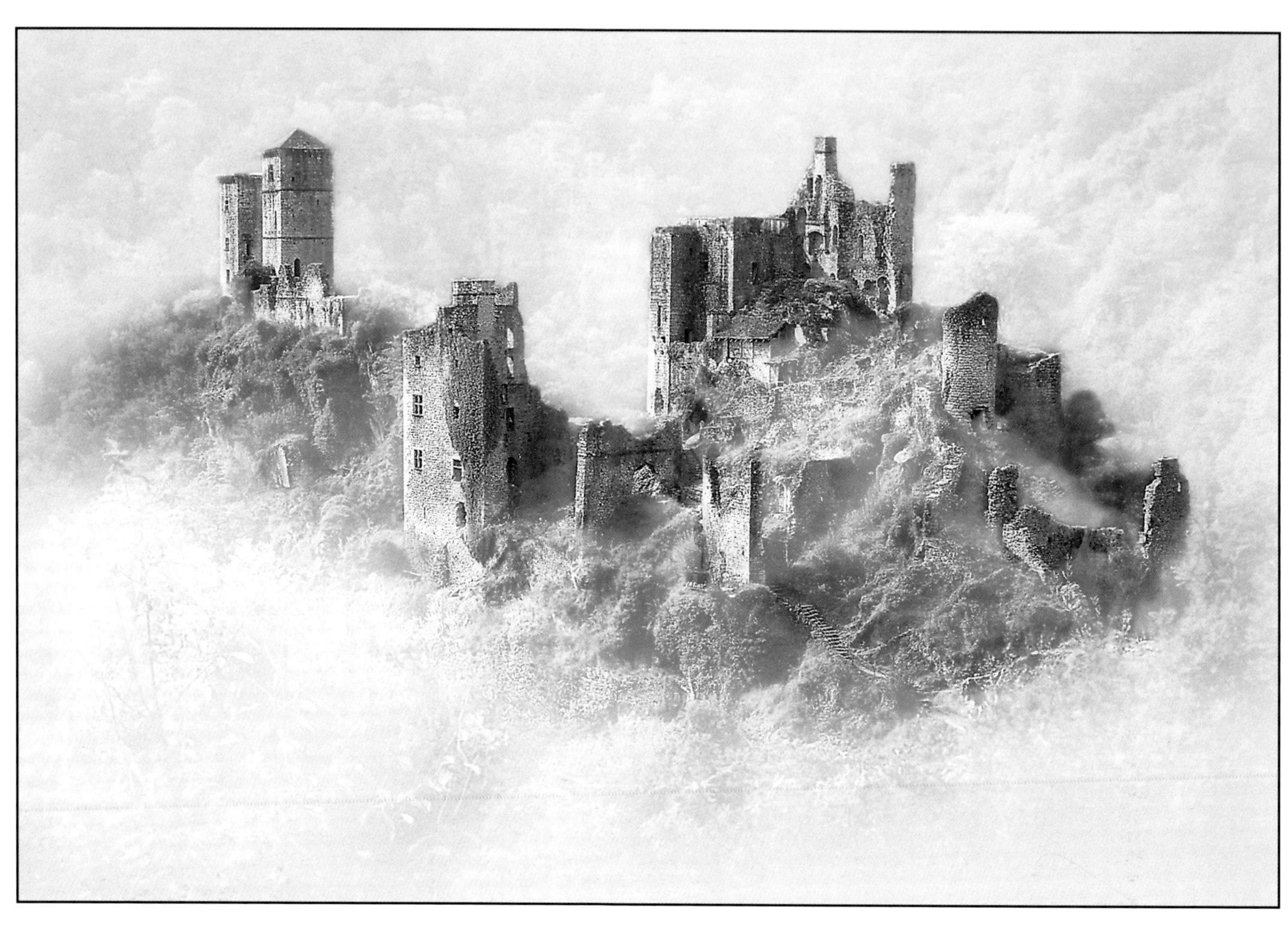

(above) 55 **Lifting morning mist, Les Tours de Merles**, *Gaston Alziary*
(right) 56 **The Great Wall**, *Guy Cheeseman*

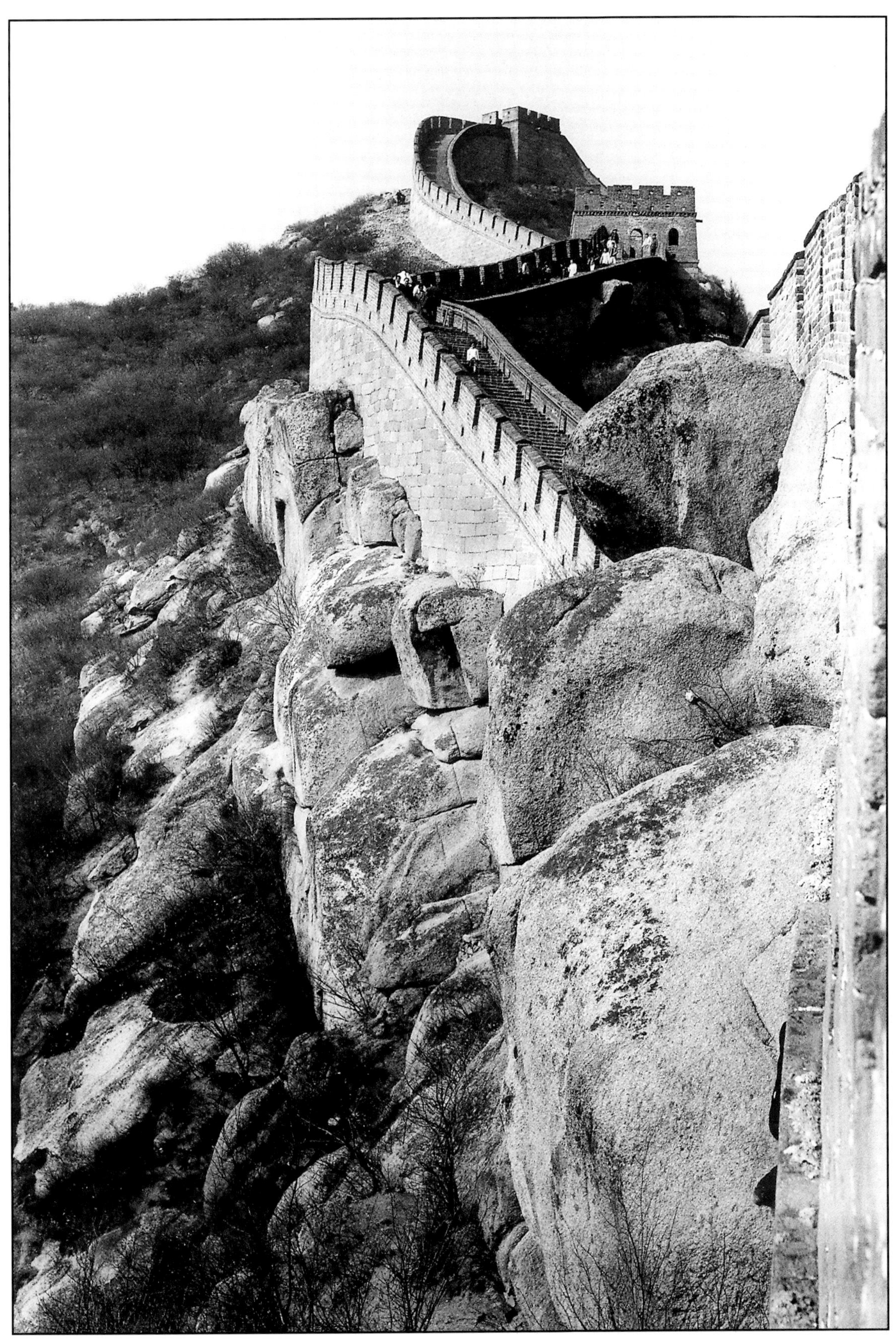

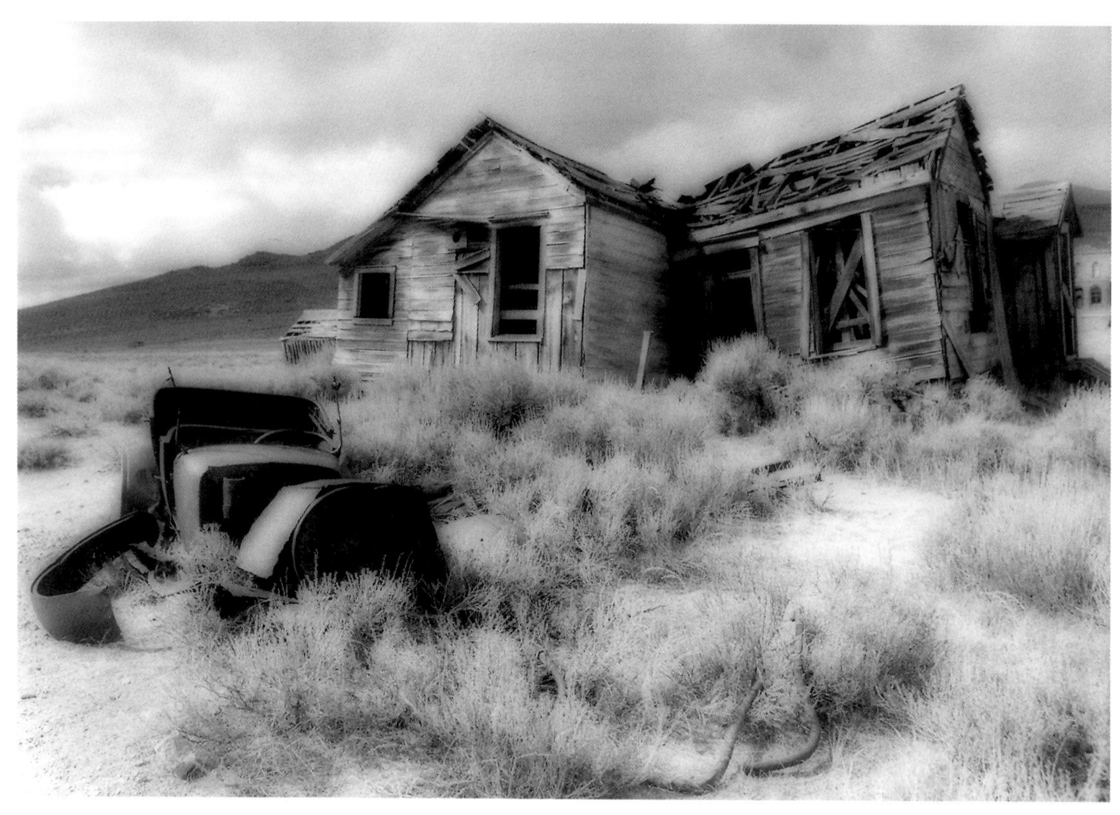

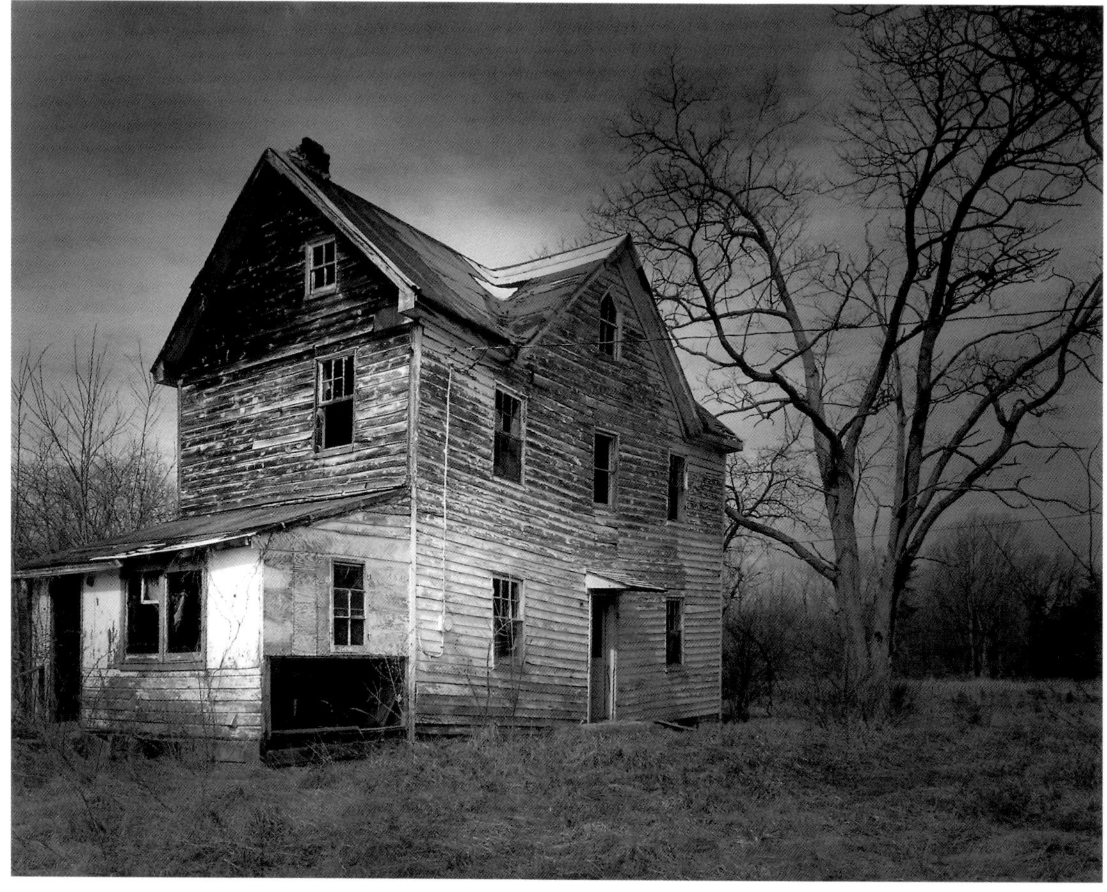

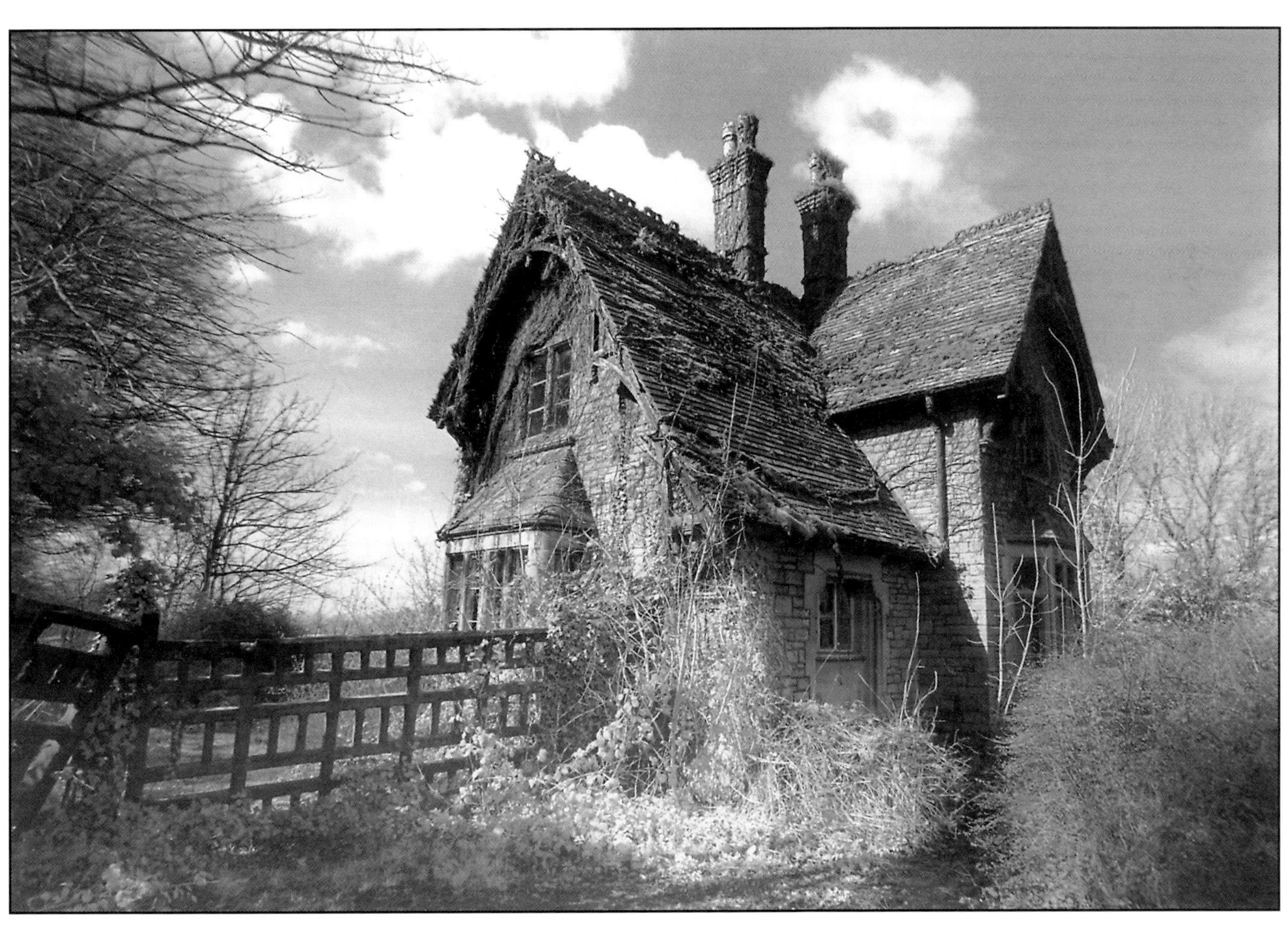

(left) 57 **A life that once was – Bodie**, *Peter Clark*
(above top) 58 **Desres, Maryland**, *Colin Conway*
(bottom) 59 **Deserted**, *Clifford Brown*

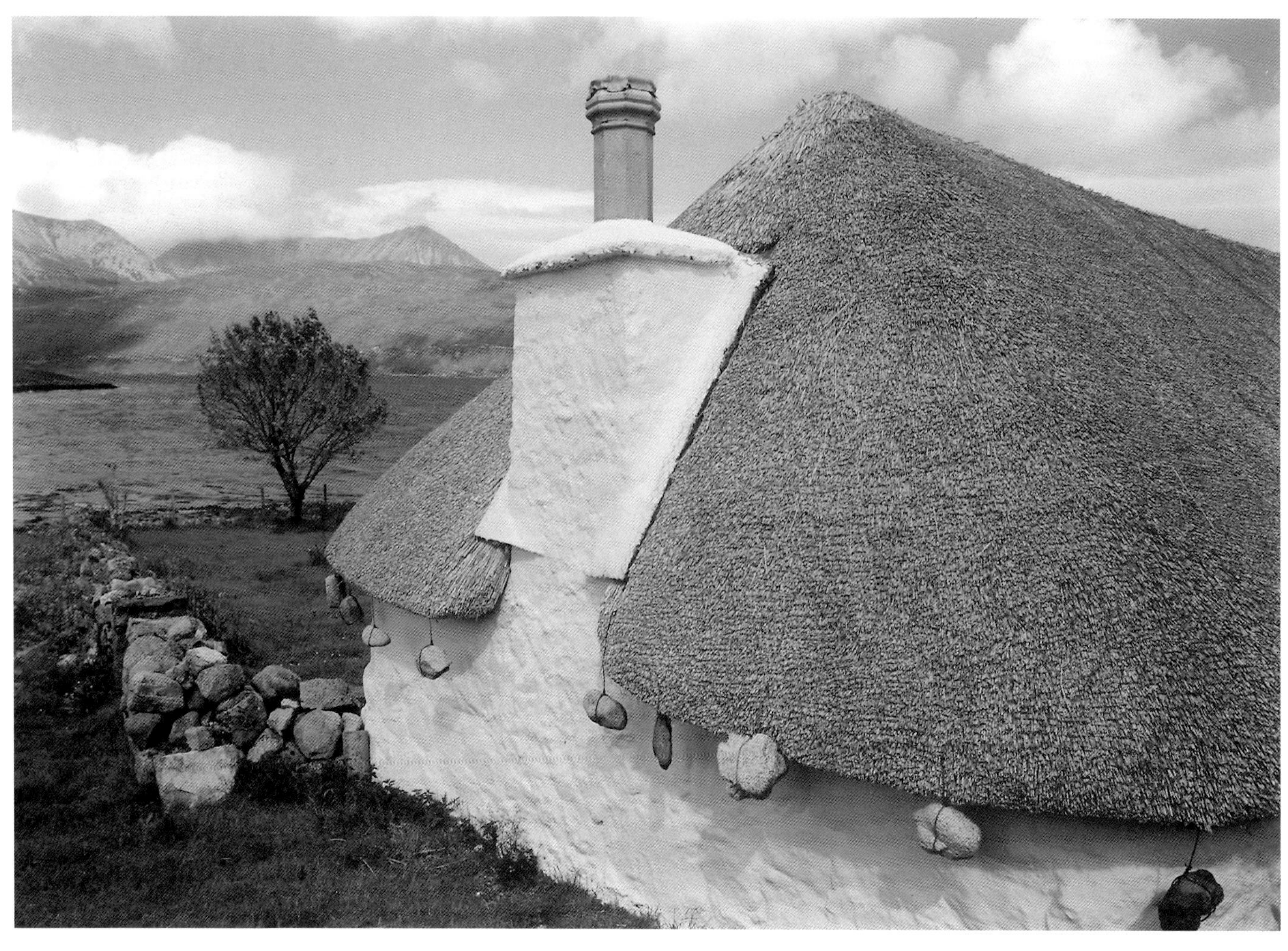

(above) 60 **Luib crofthouse**, *Caroline Mockett*
(top right) 61 **Sky sculpture#9**, *Alan Brown*
(bottom right) 62 **Chimney pots**, *Andy Hanson*

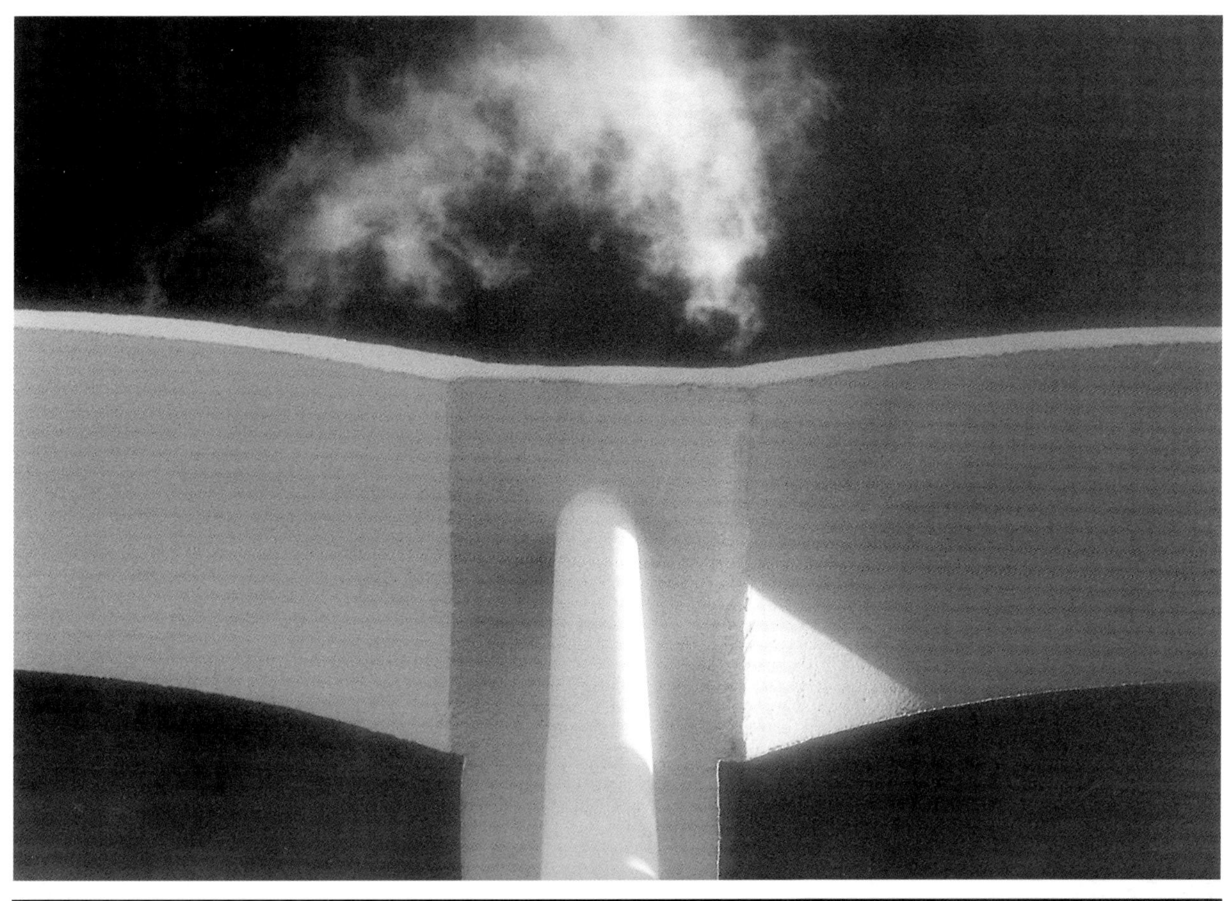

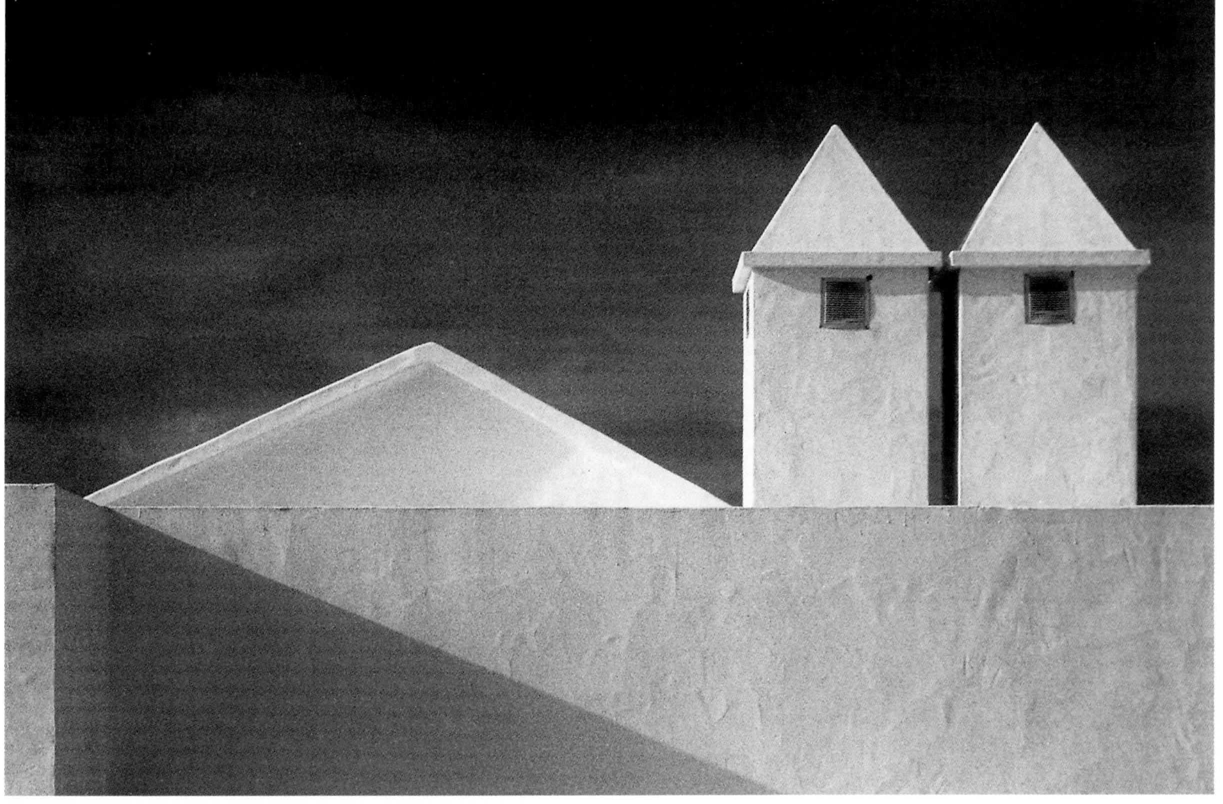

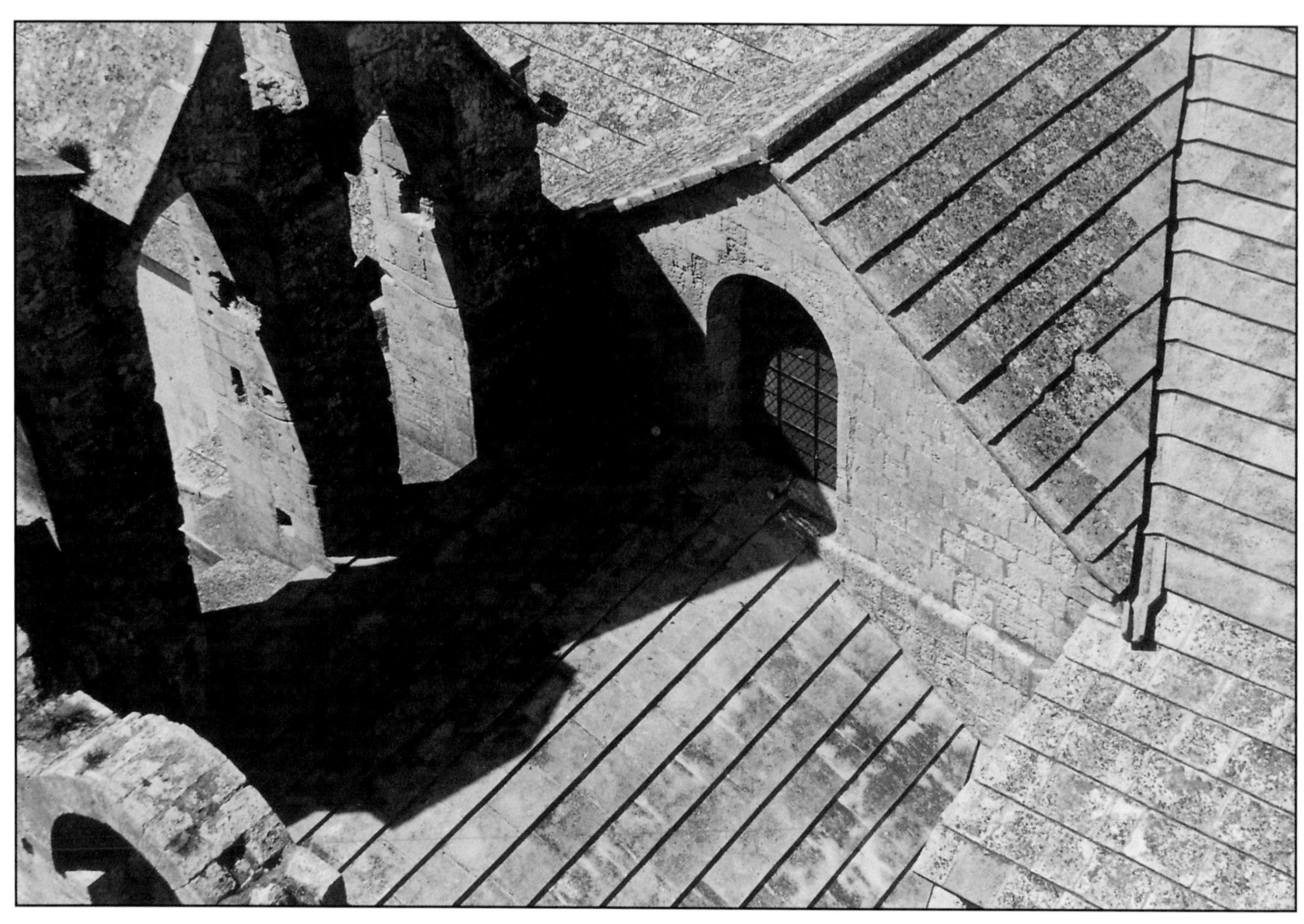

63
Rooftops
Nick Stout

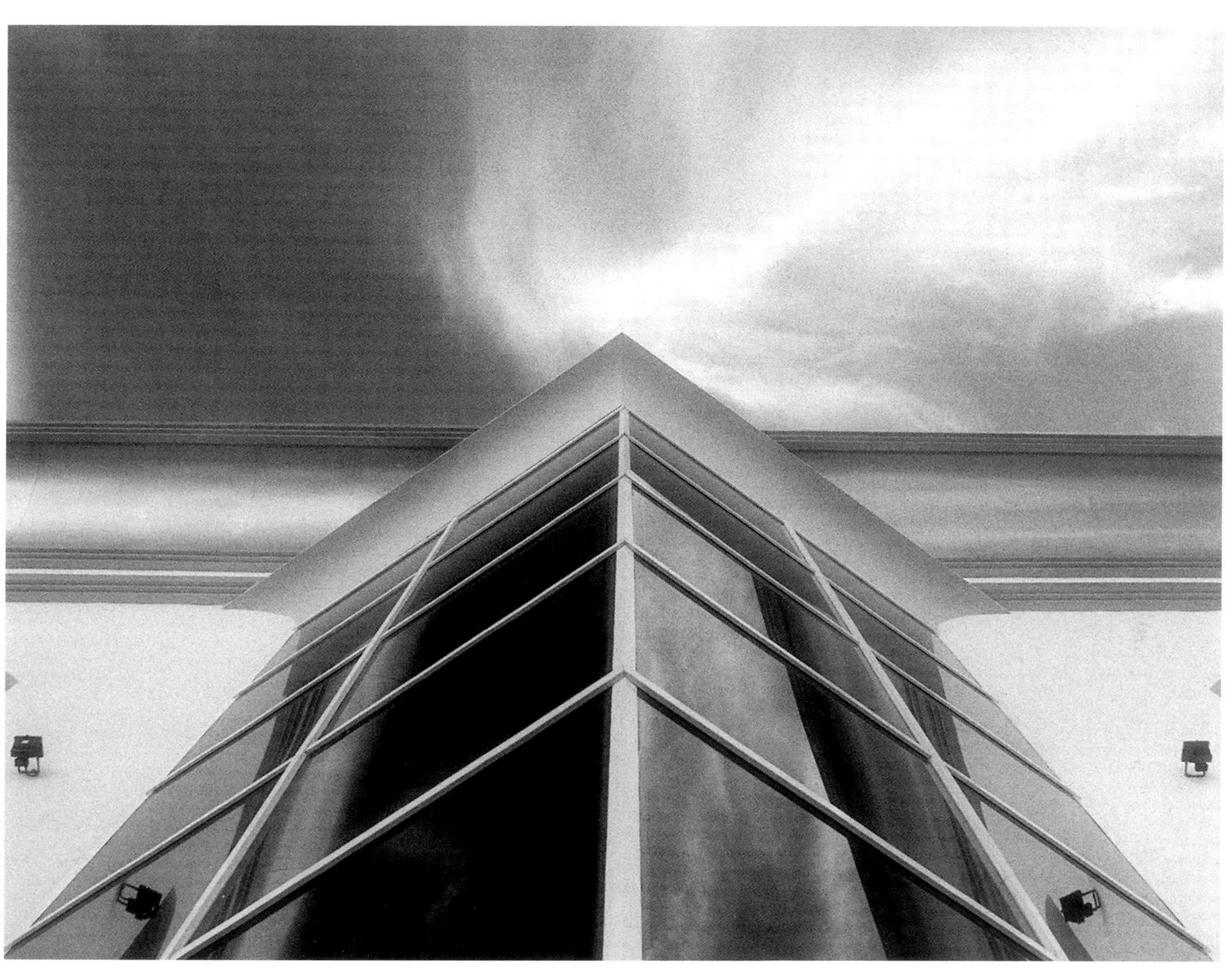

64
Glass angles
Alan Brown

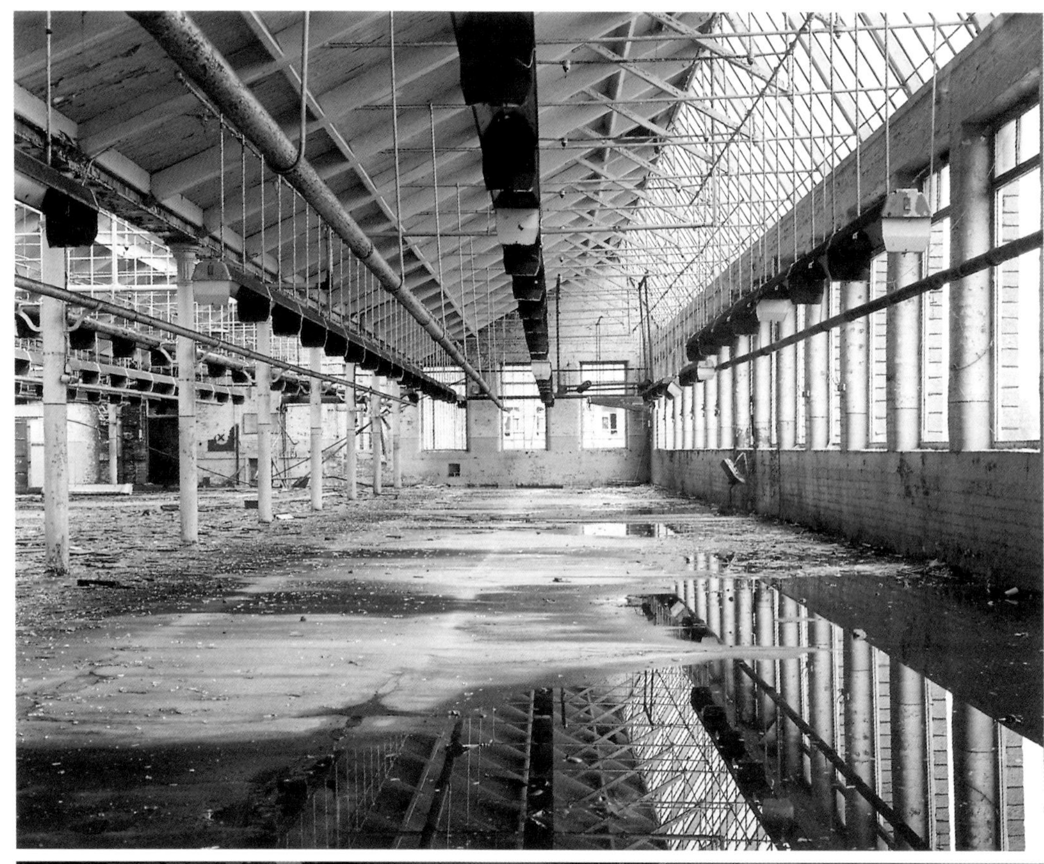

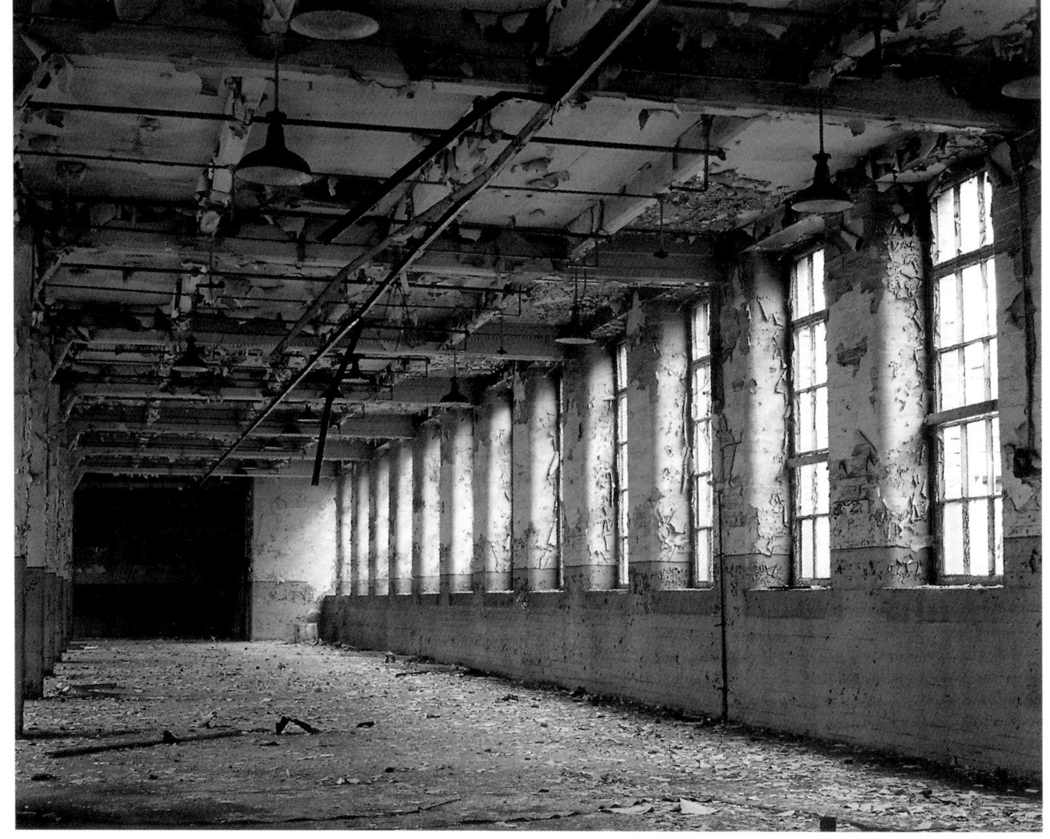

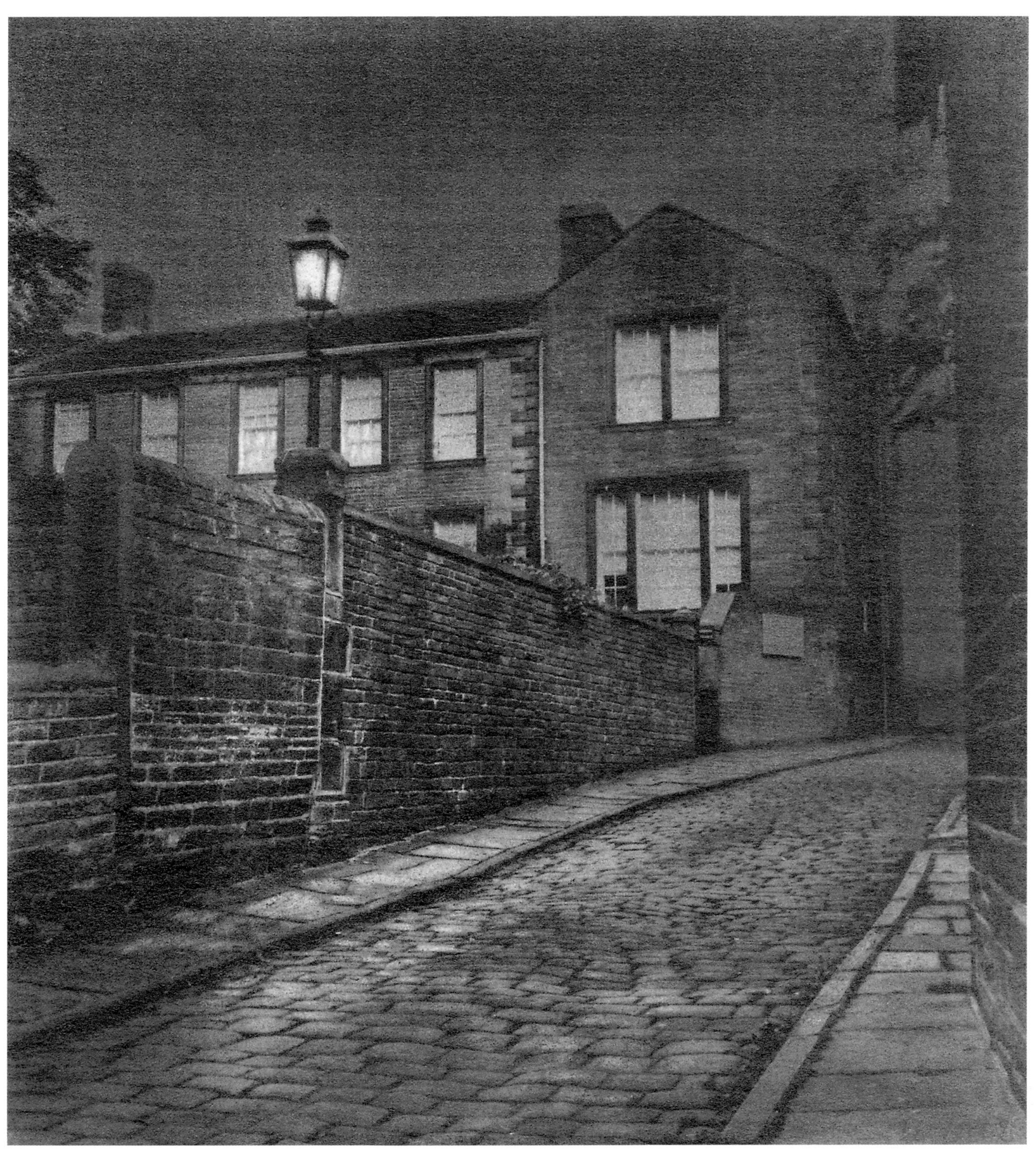

(top left) 65 **Derelict mill #2**, *David Turlow*
(bottom left) 66 **Derelict mill #3**, *David Thurlow*
(above) 67 **Haworth**, *Kirk Toft*

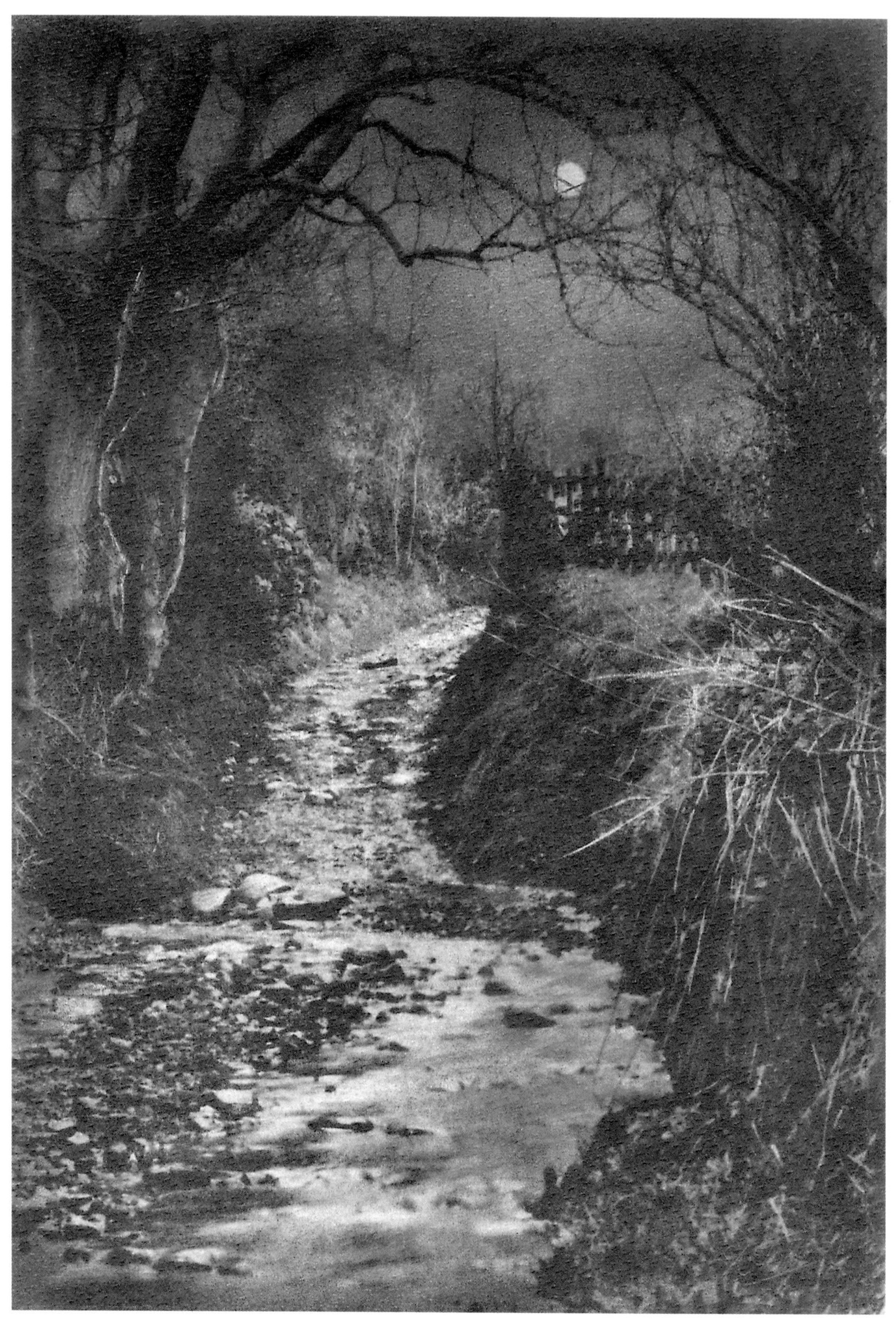

(above) 68 **Winter nocturne**, *Kirk Toft*
(top right) 69 **Landscape near Euerdorf**, *Johannes Müller*
(bottom right) 70 **One tree road**, *Steve Terry*

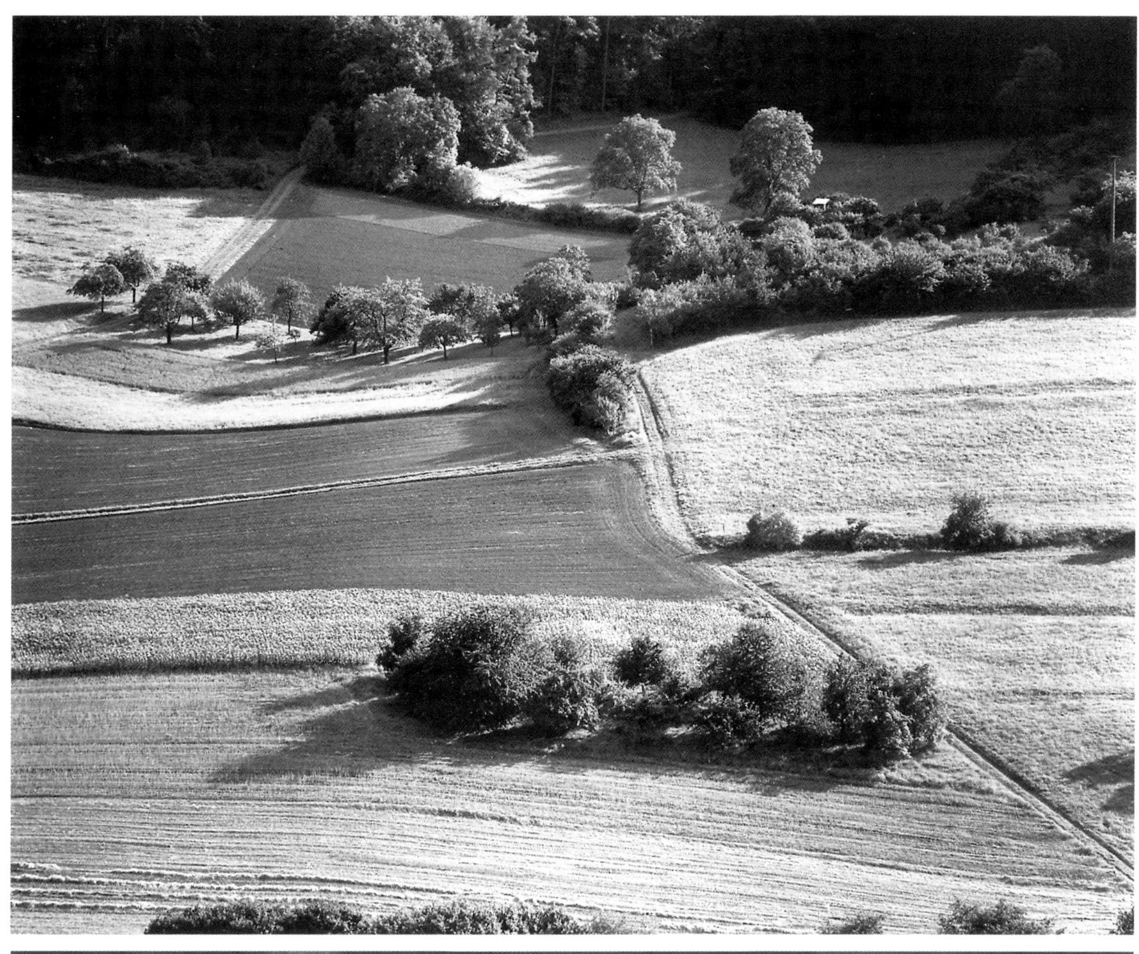

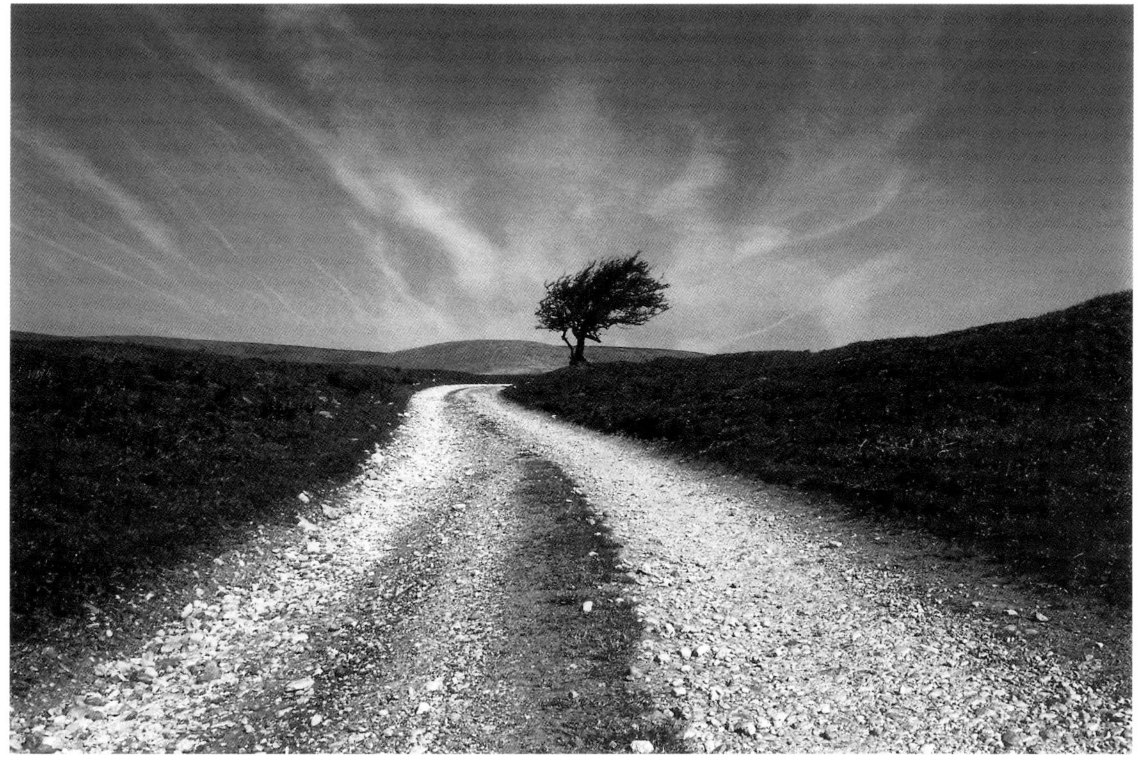

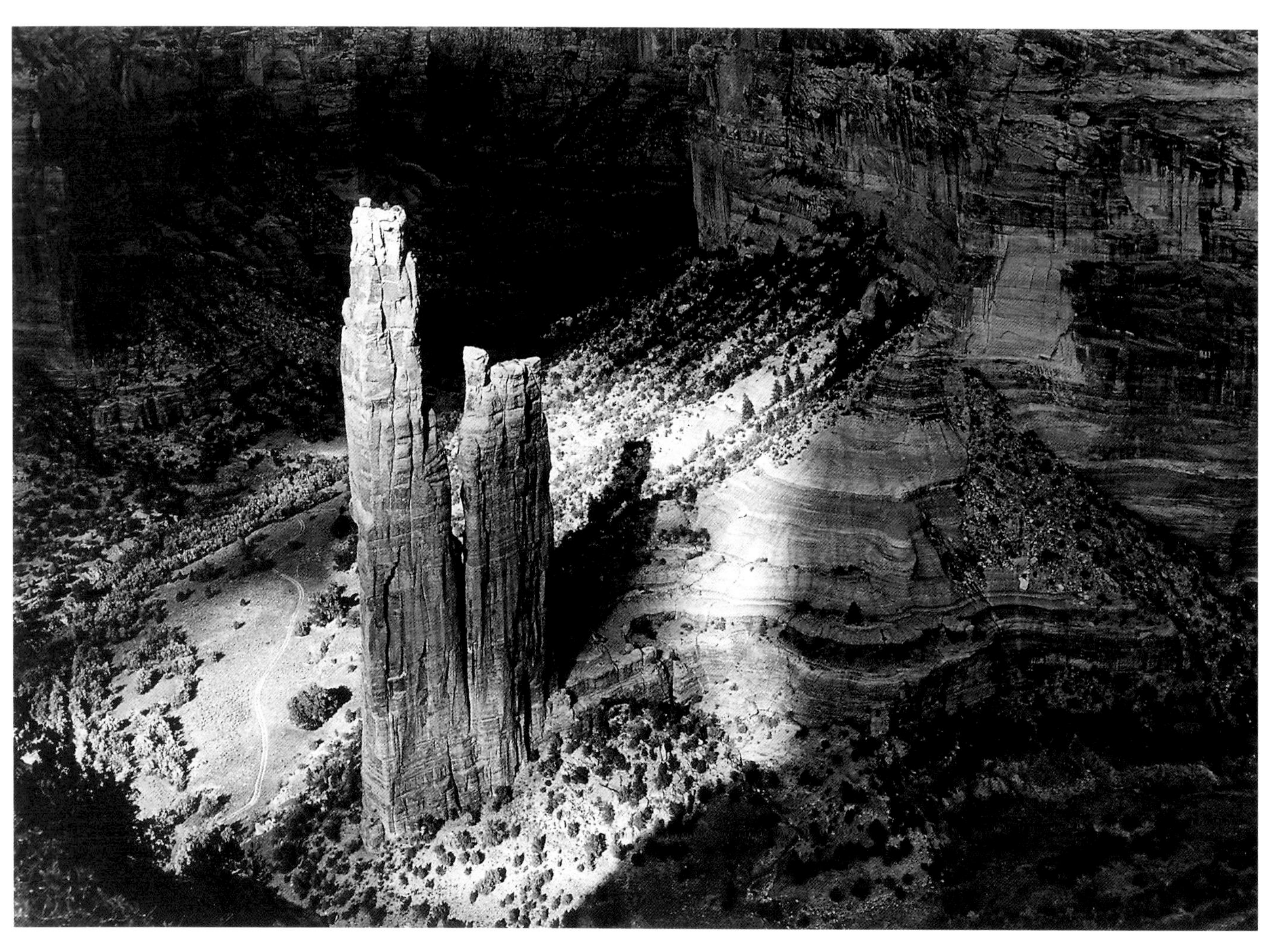

71

Spider Rock, Canyon de Chelley

Peter Clark

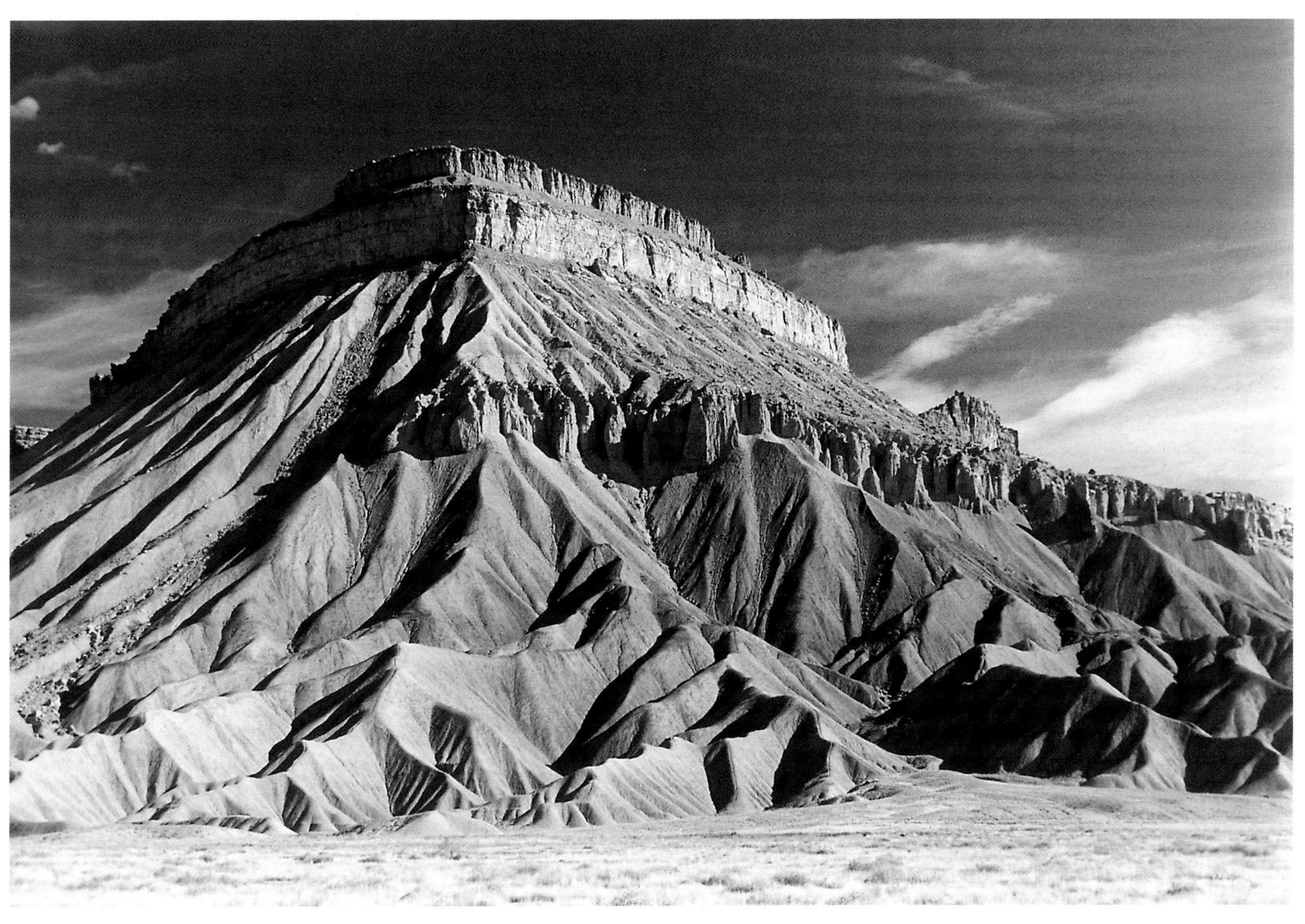

72
Sandcastle
Keith Saunders

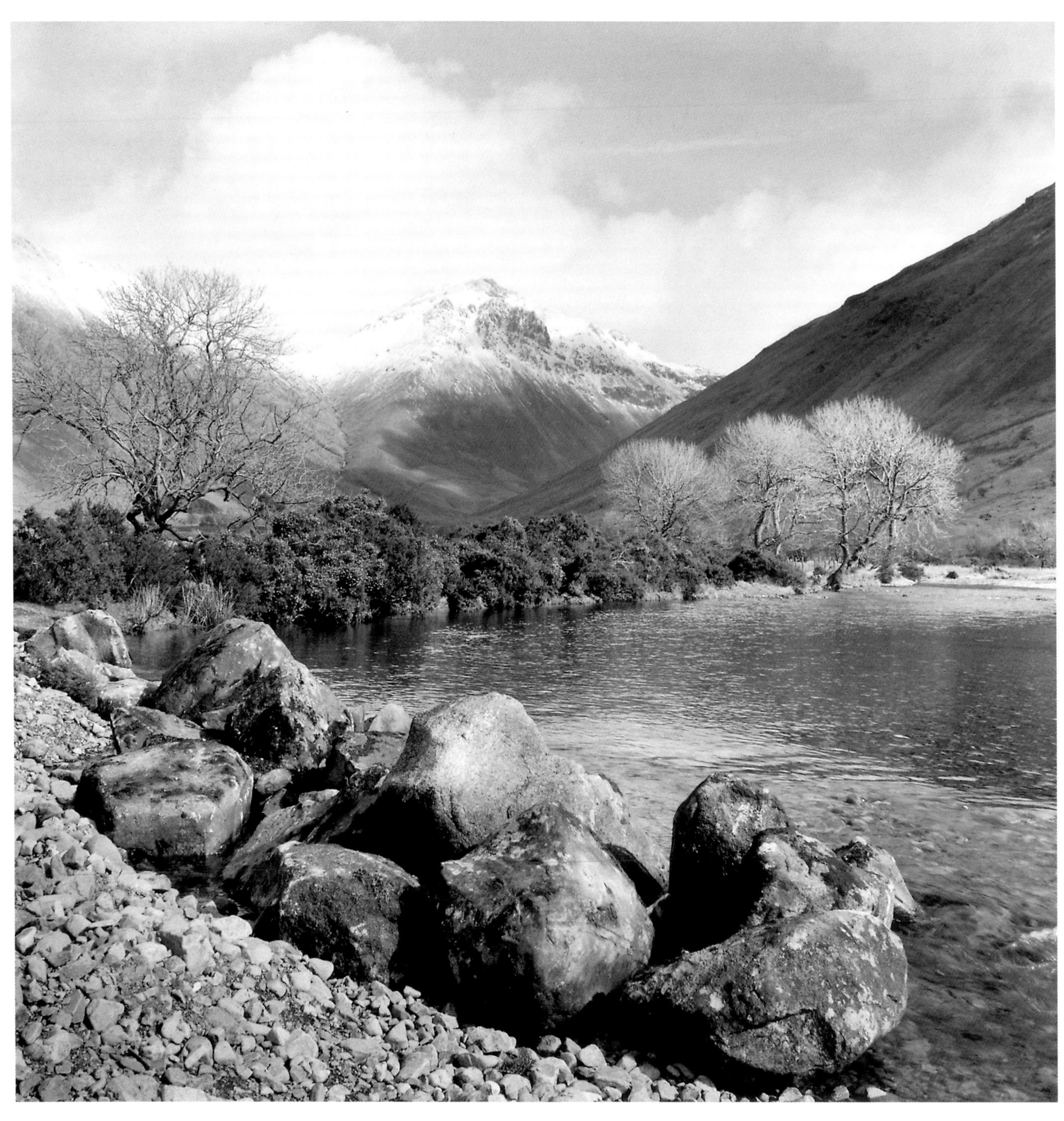

73
Wastwater
Robert Kent

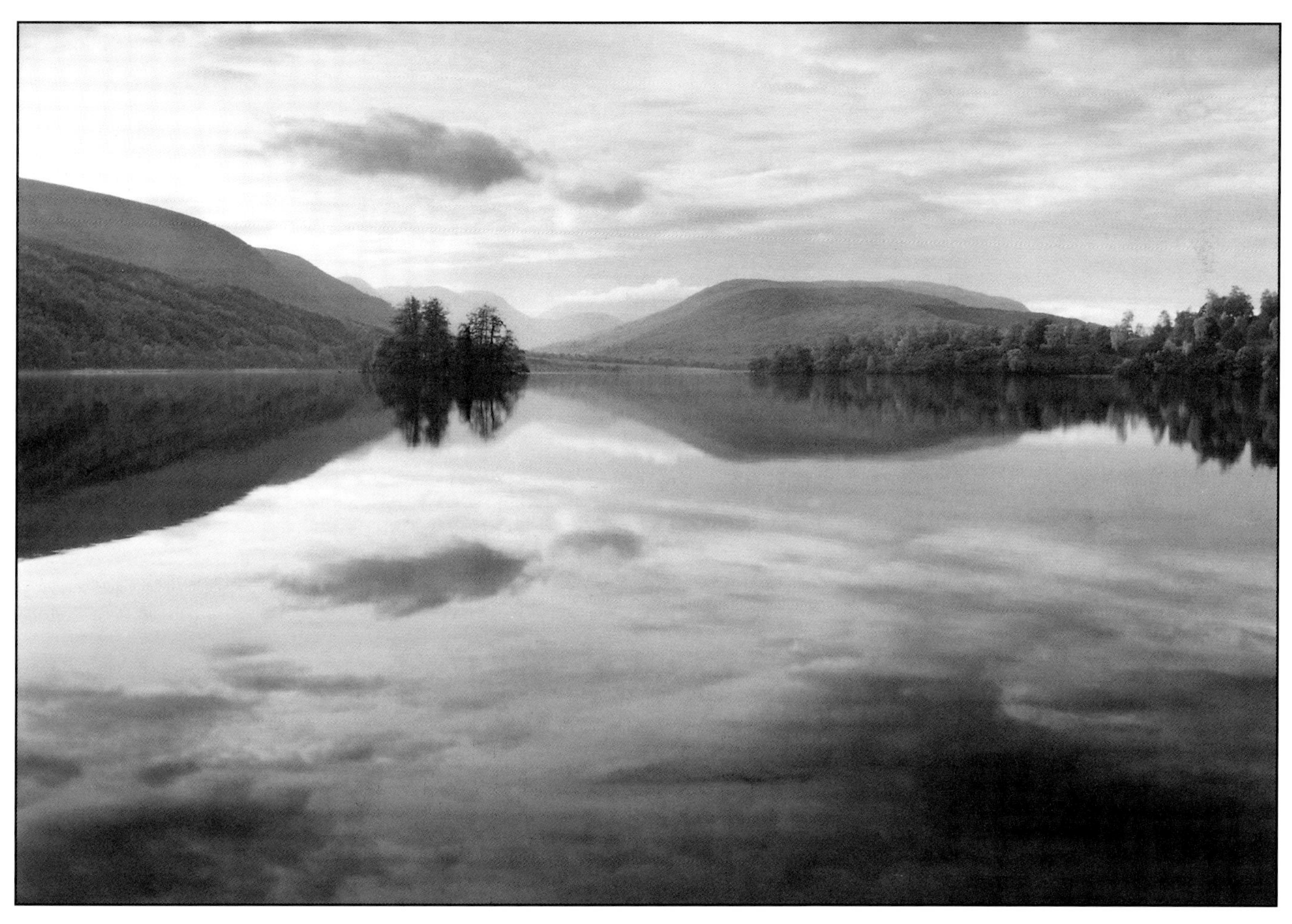

74
Loch Arkaig
Tom Richardson

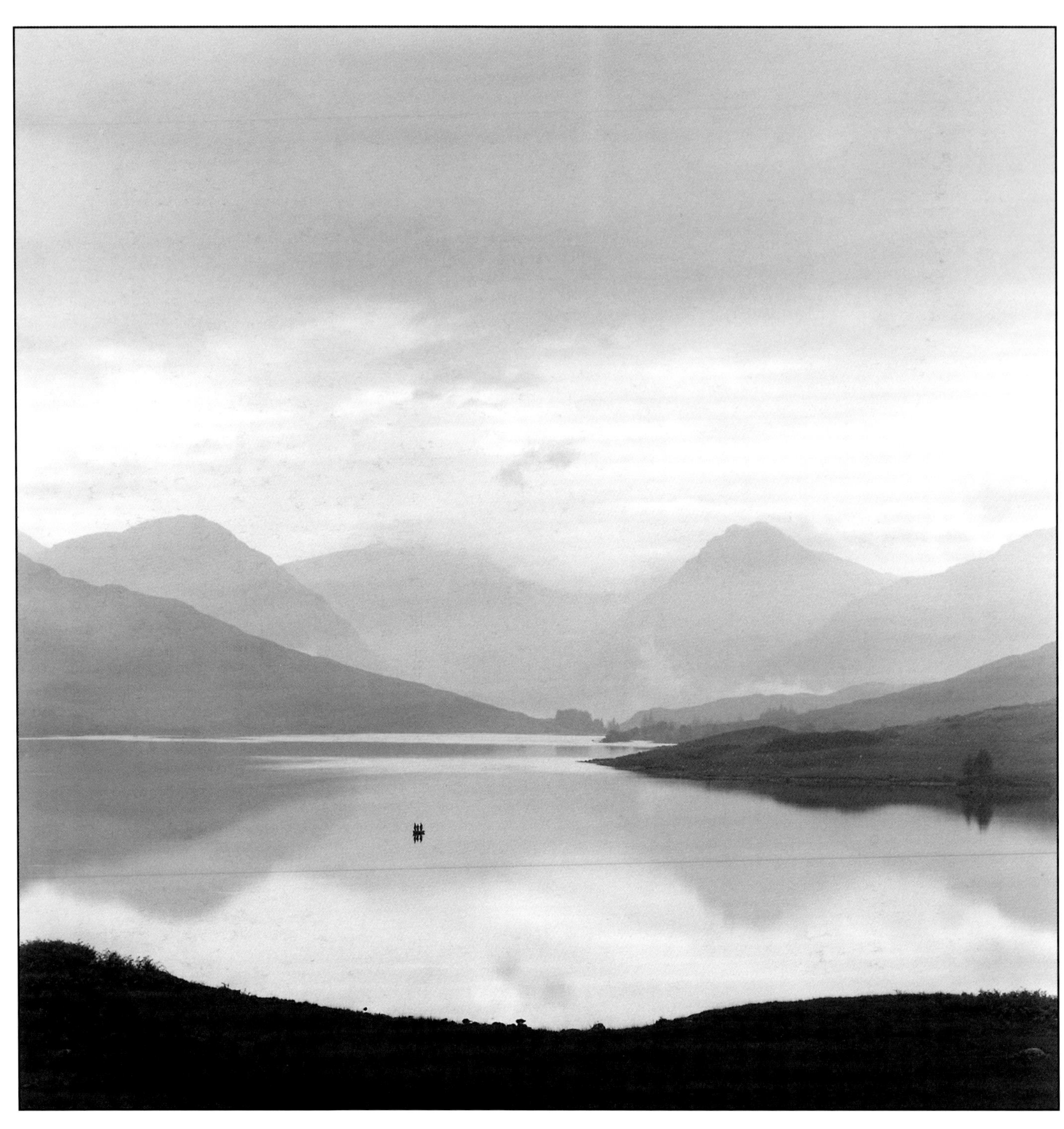

(above) 75 **Three men in a boat**, *Jim Pymer*
(top right) 76 **Tranquillity**, *Jim Shipp*
(bottom right) 77 **Llynau Mymbyr**, *Emma Weal*

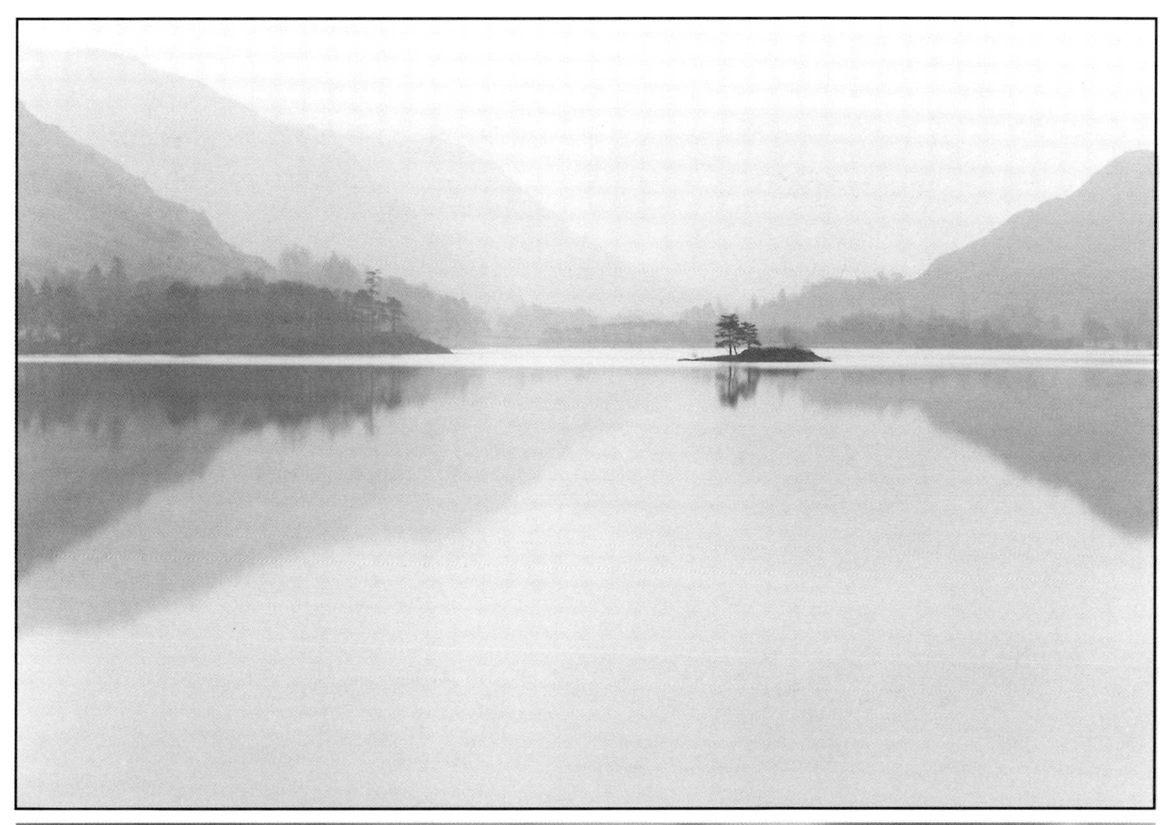

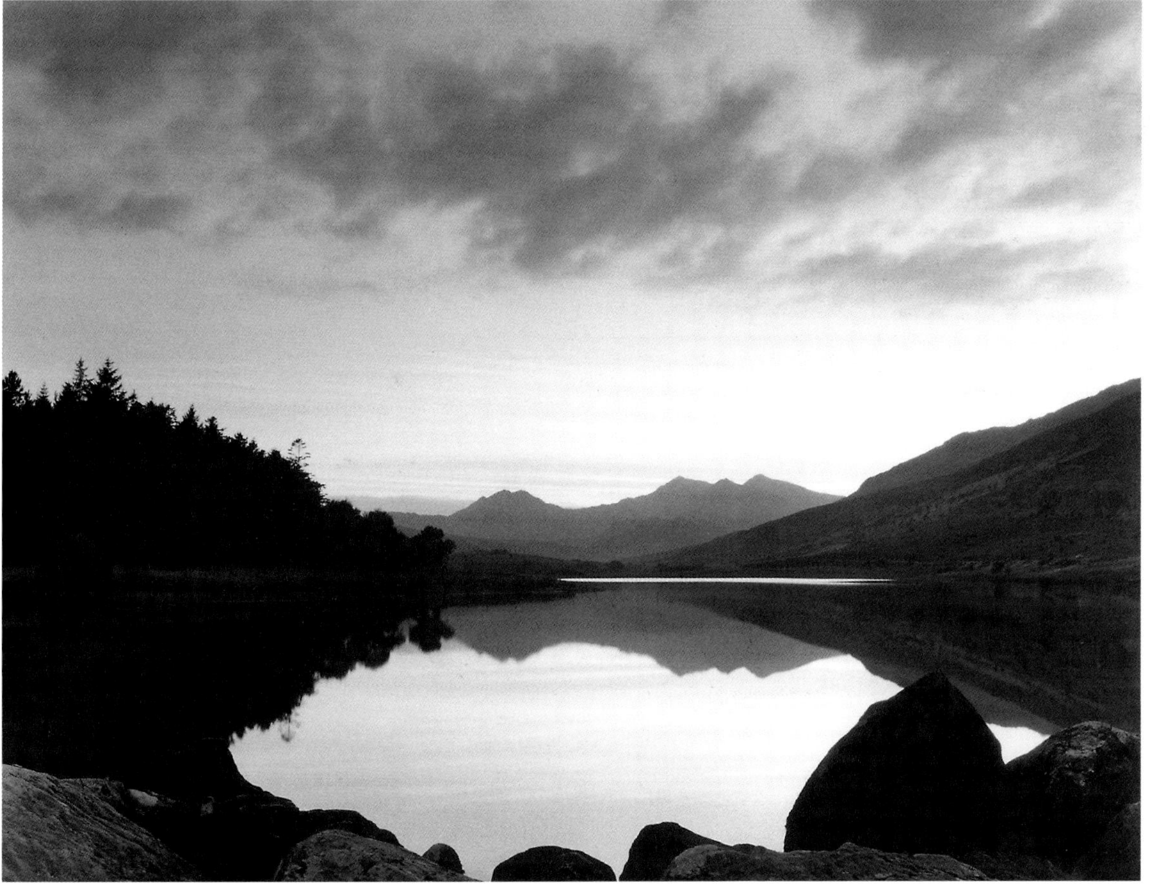

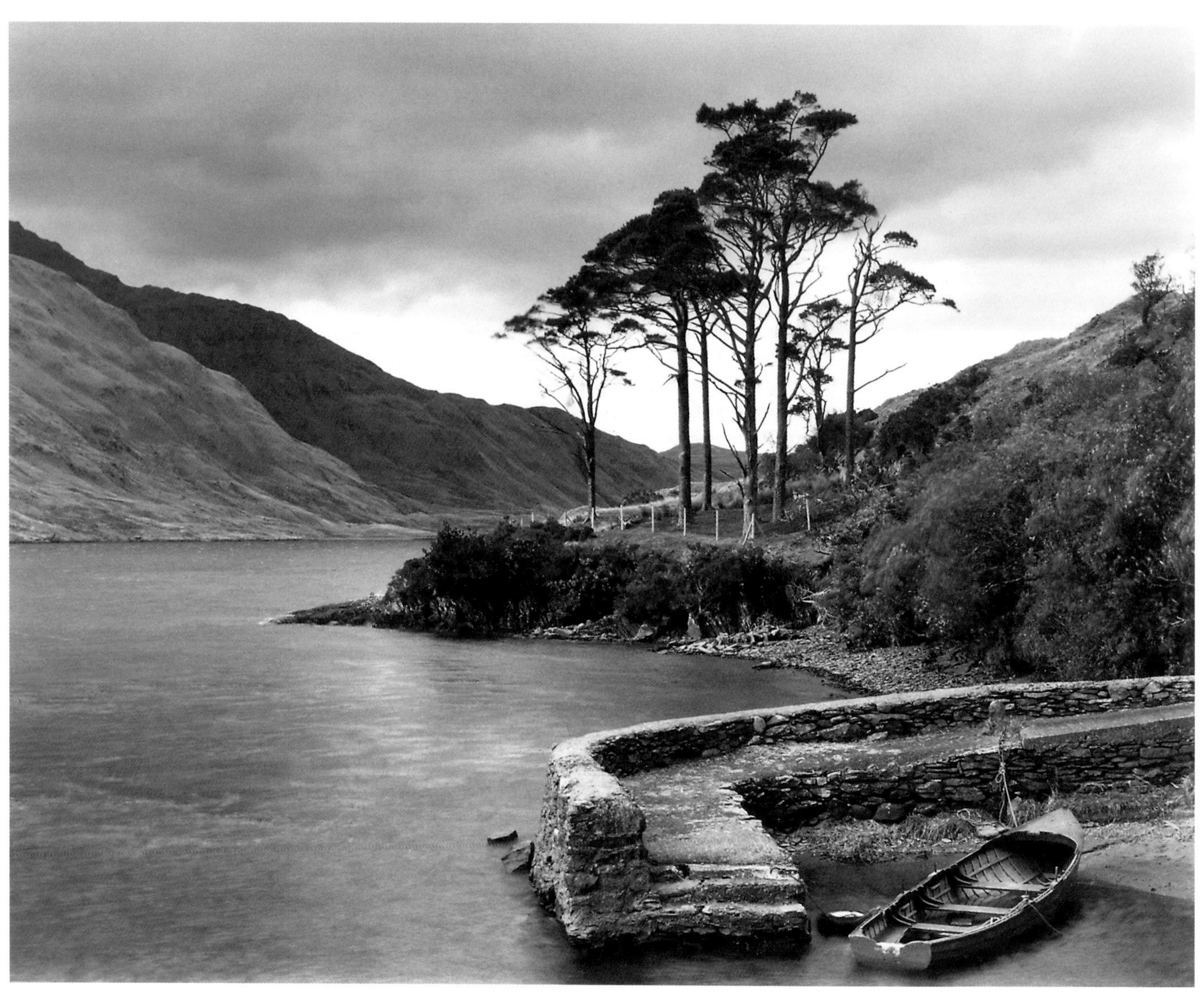

78
Doo Lough, Ireland
Carolyn Bross

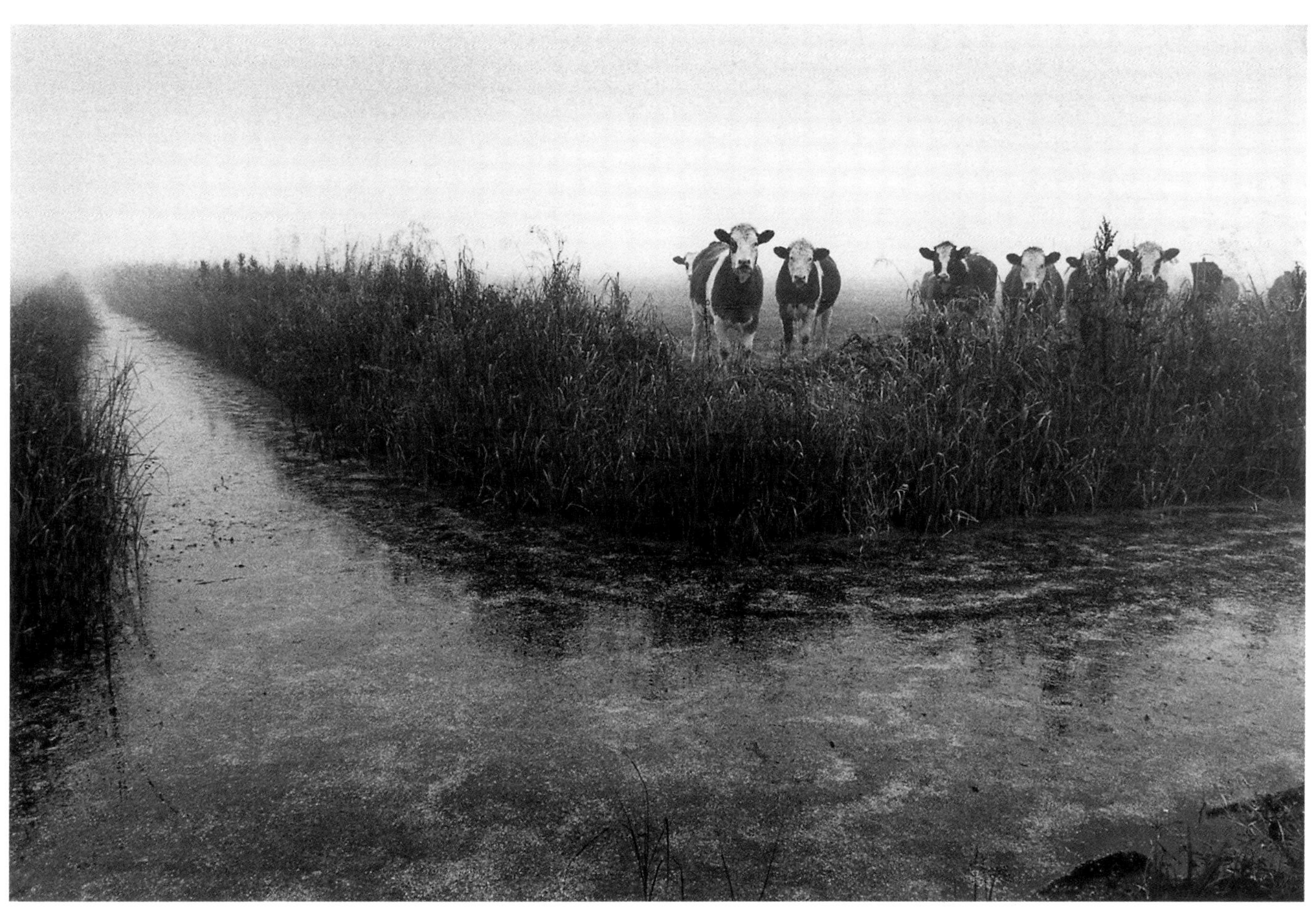

79
Cattle, West Sedgemoor
Richard Bland

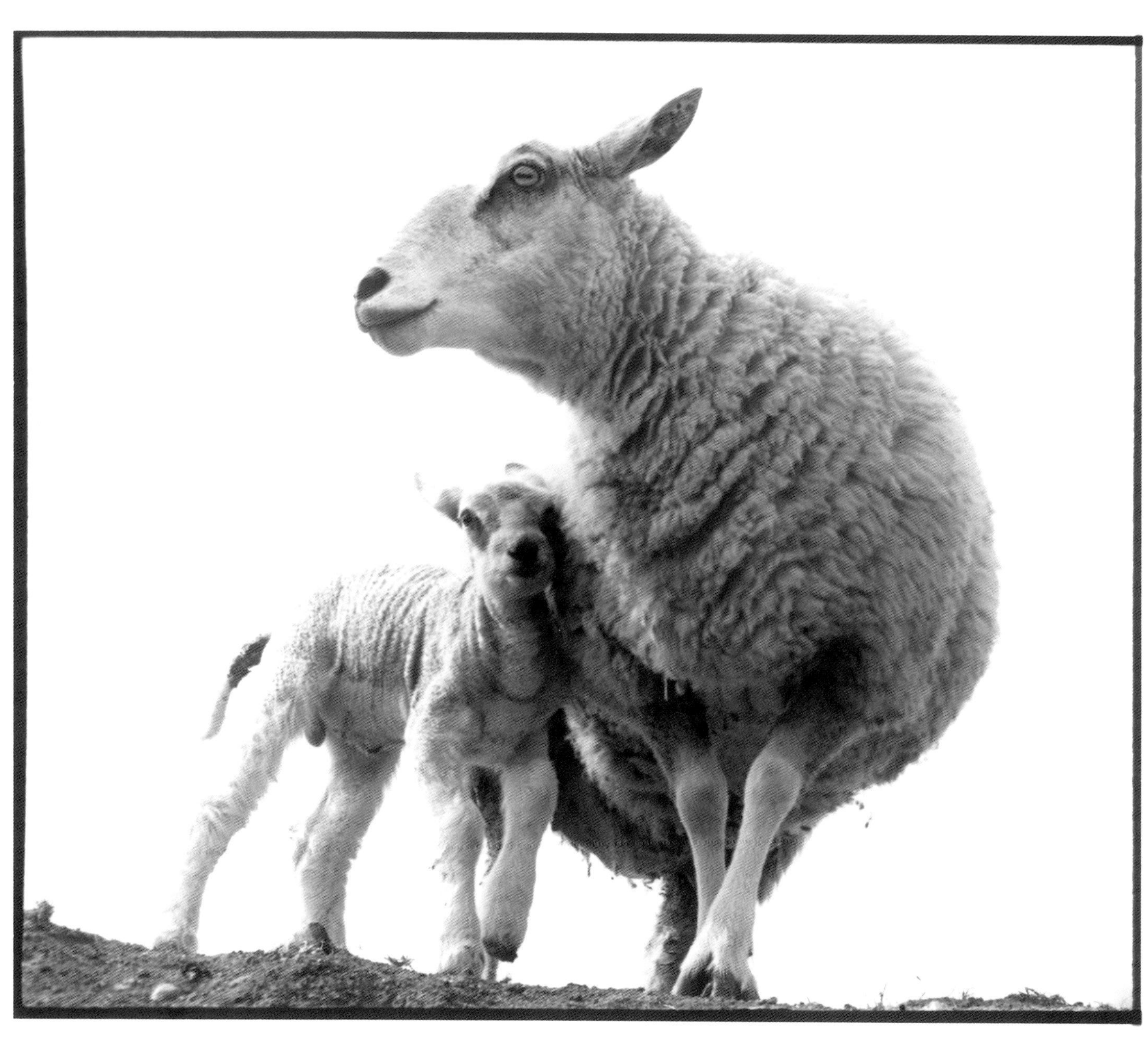

(above) 80 **Mother and child**, *Caroline Hyman*
(top right) 81 **Pookin**, *Susanne Waldock*
(bottom right) 82 **Odd one out**, *Terry Farnell*

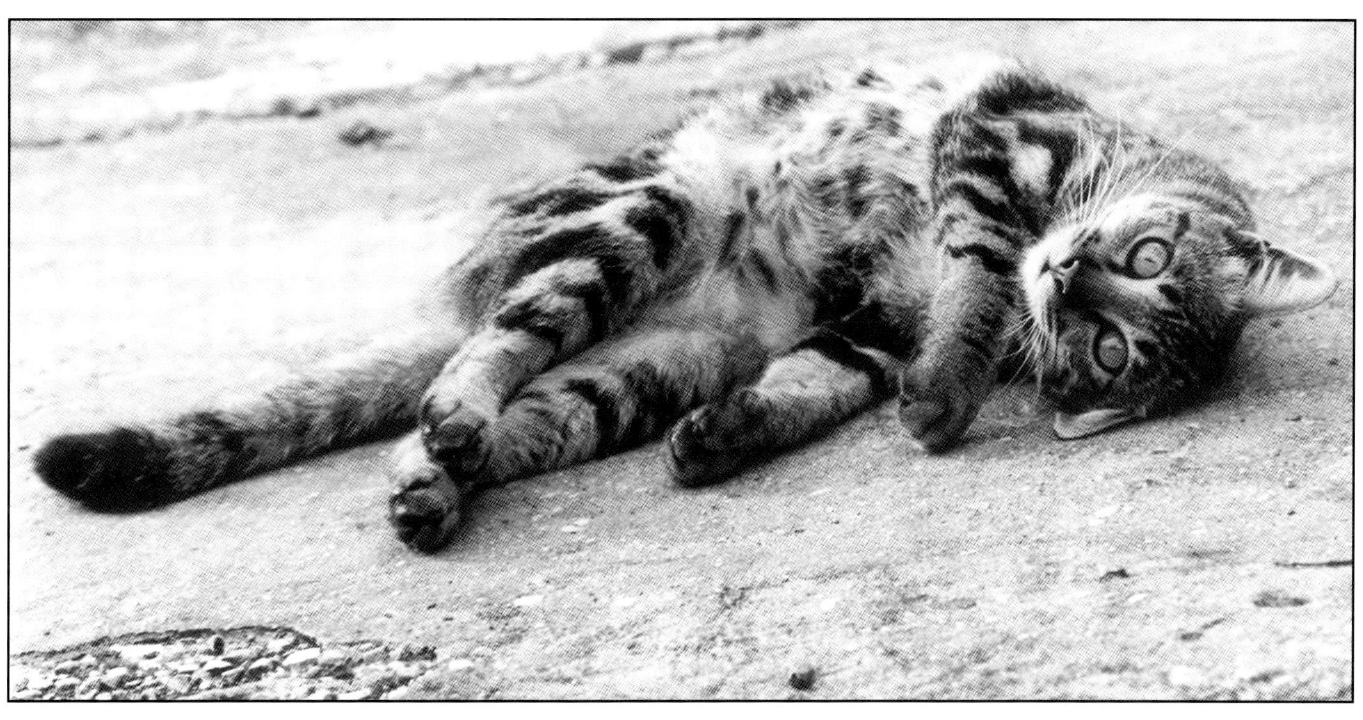

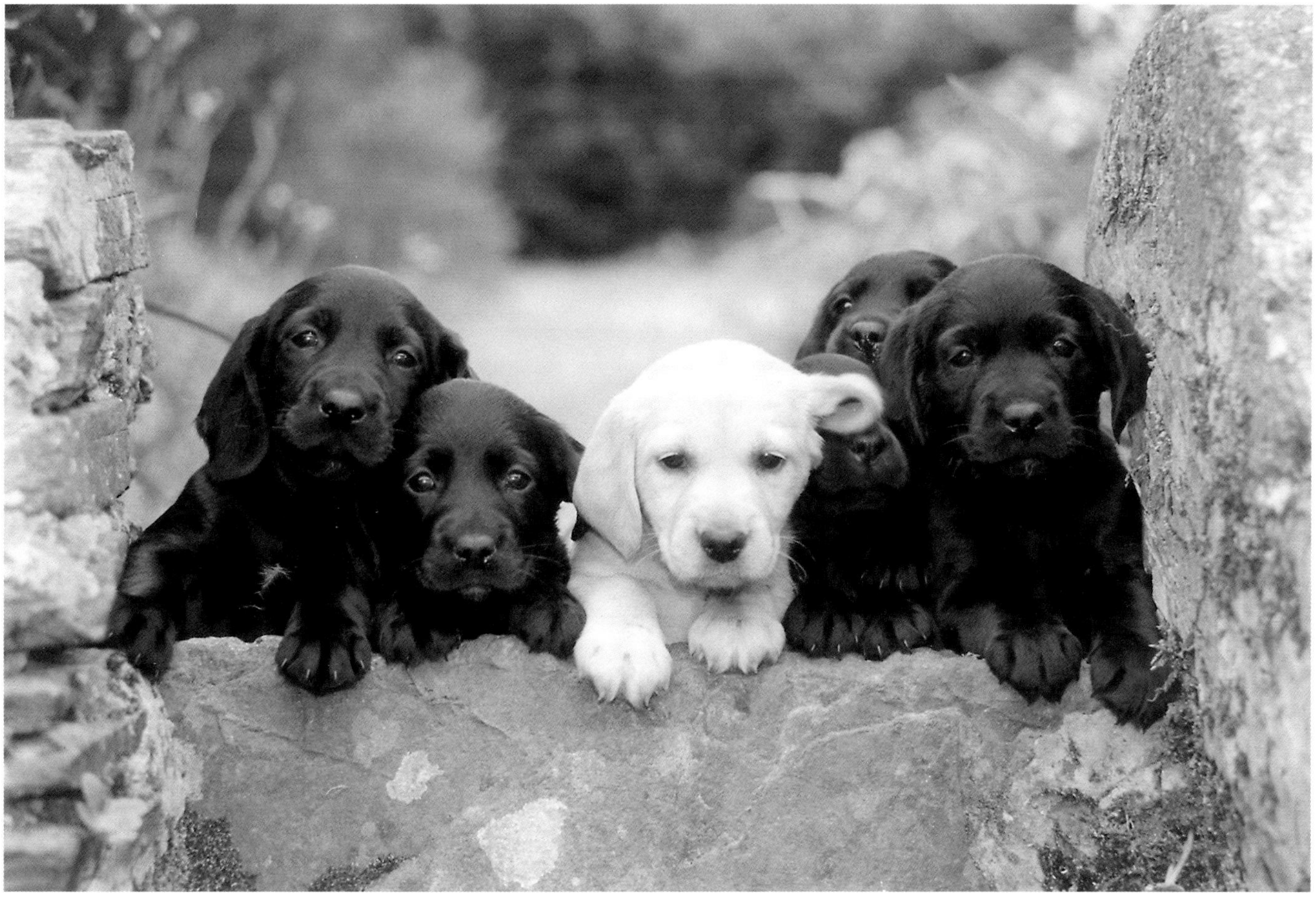

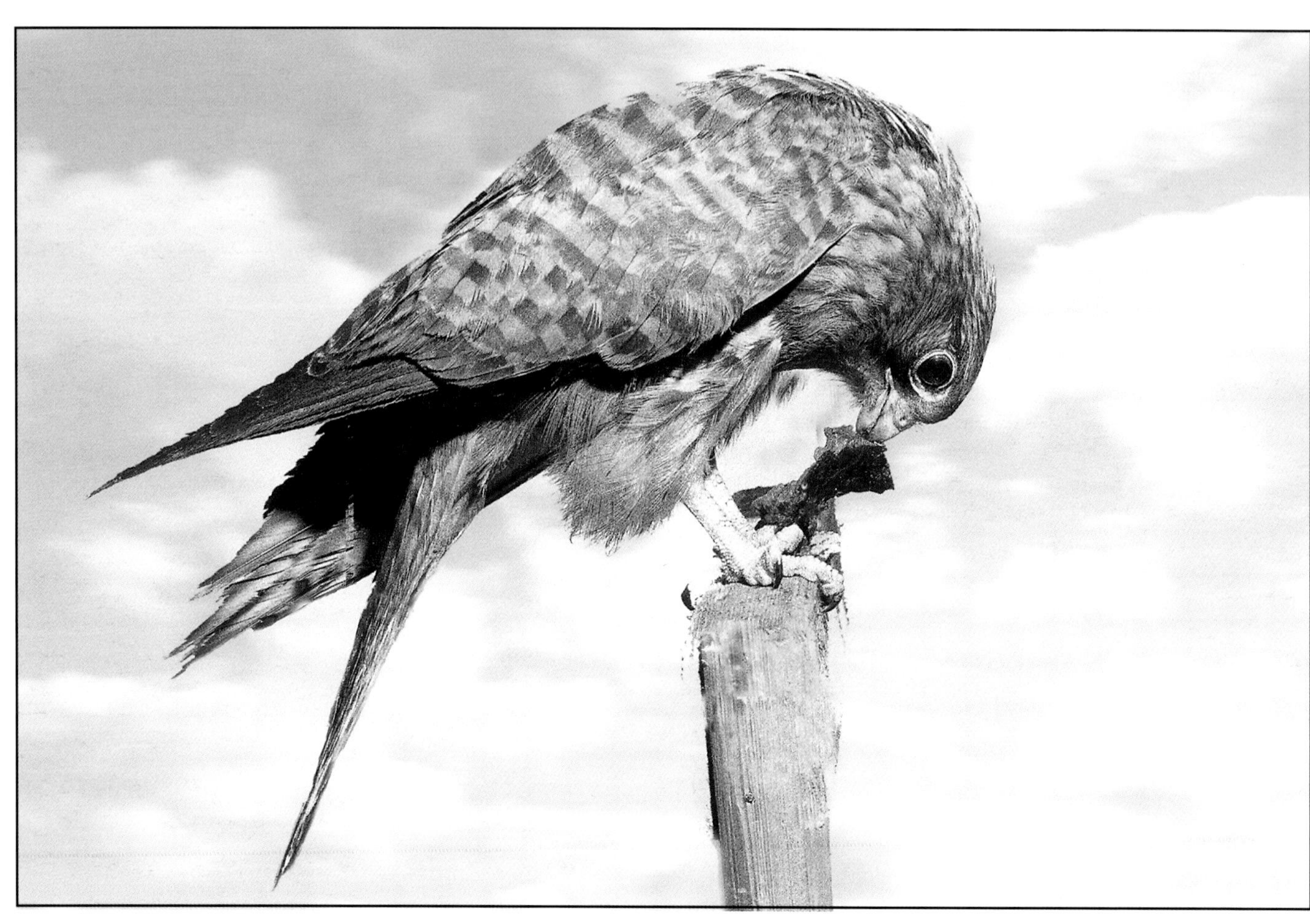

83
Kestrel
Stuart Noble

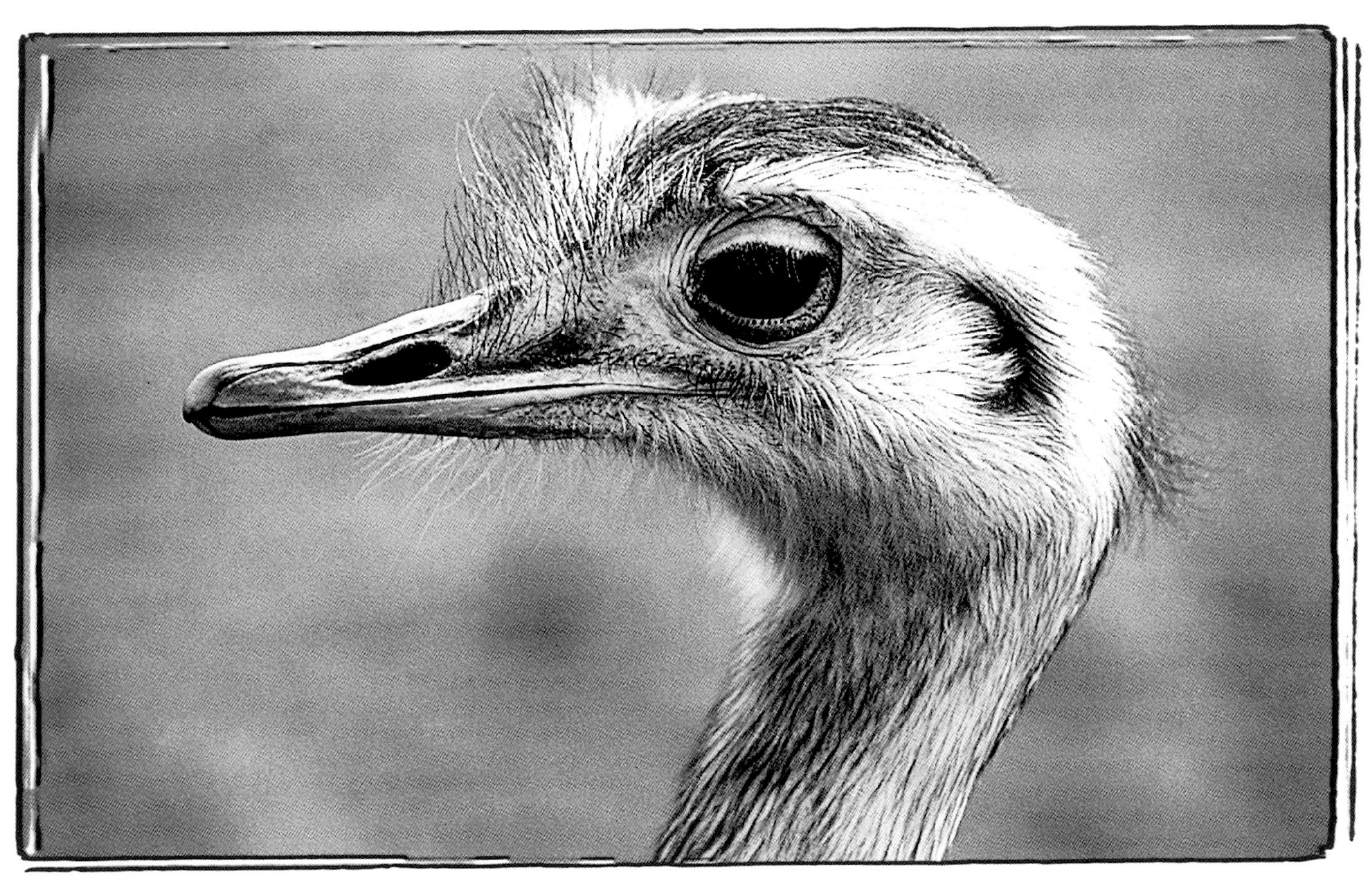

84
Rhea
Trevor Smithers

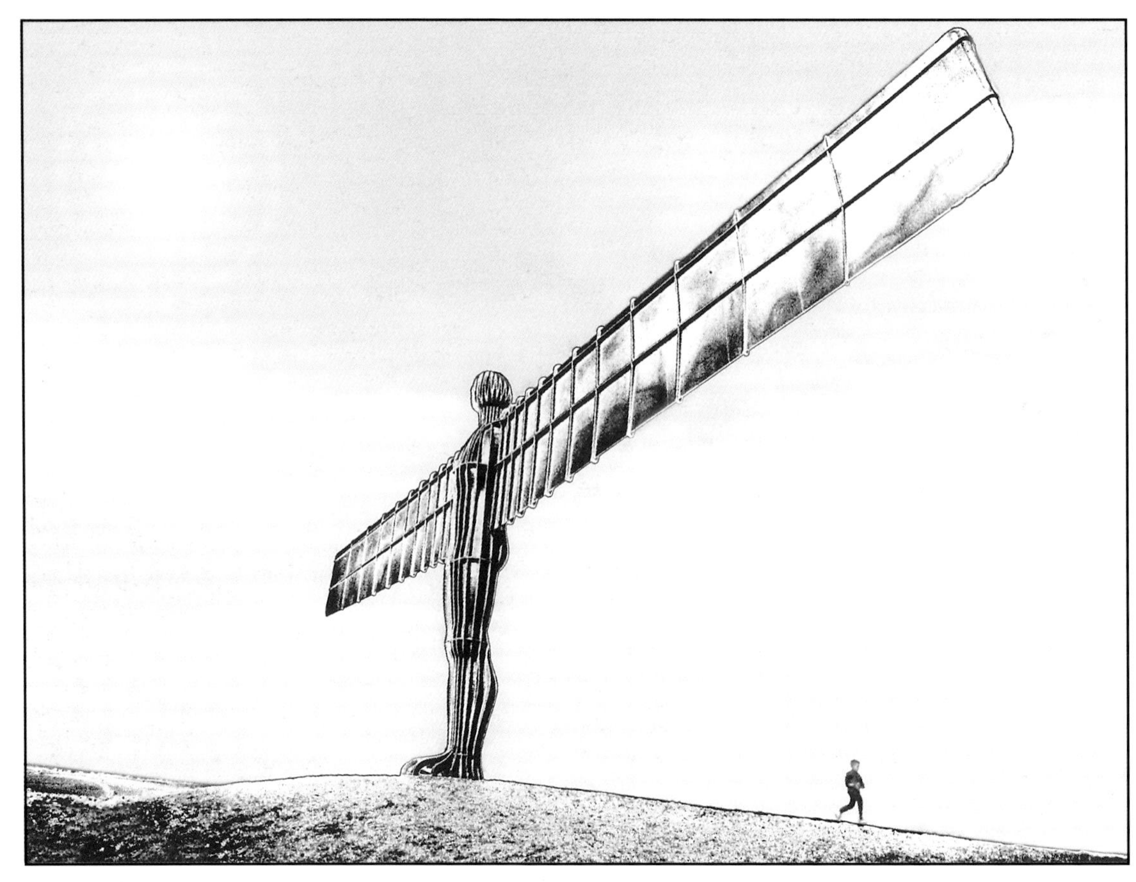

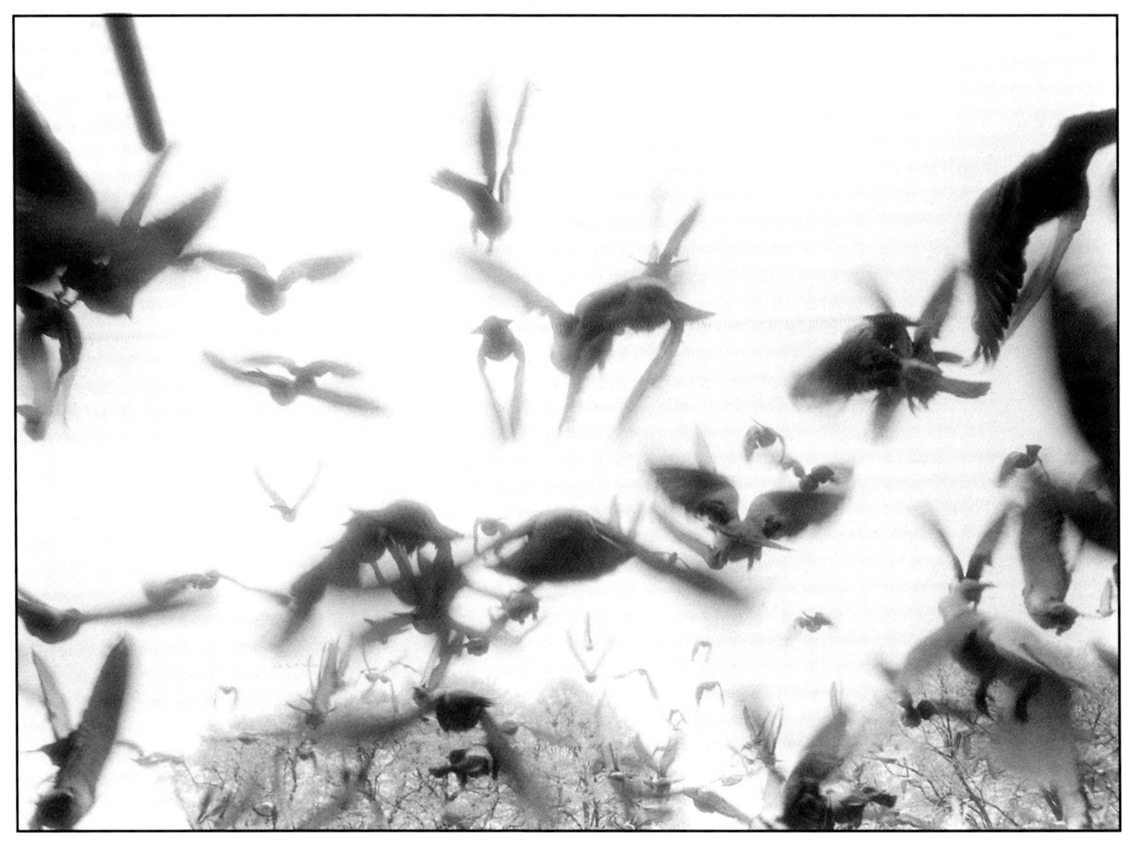

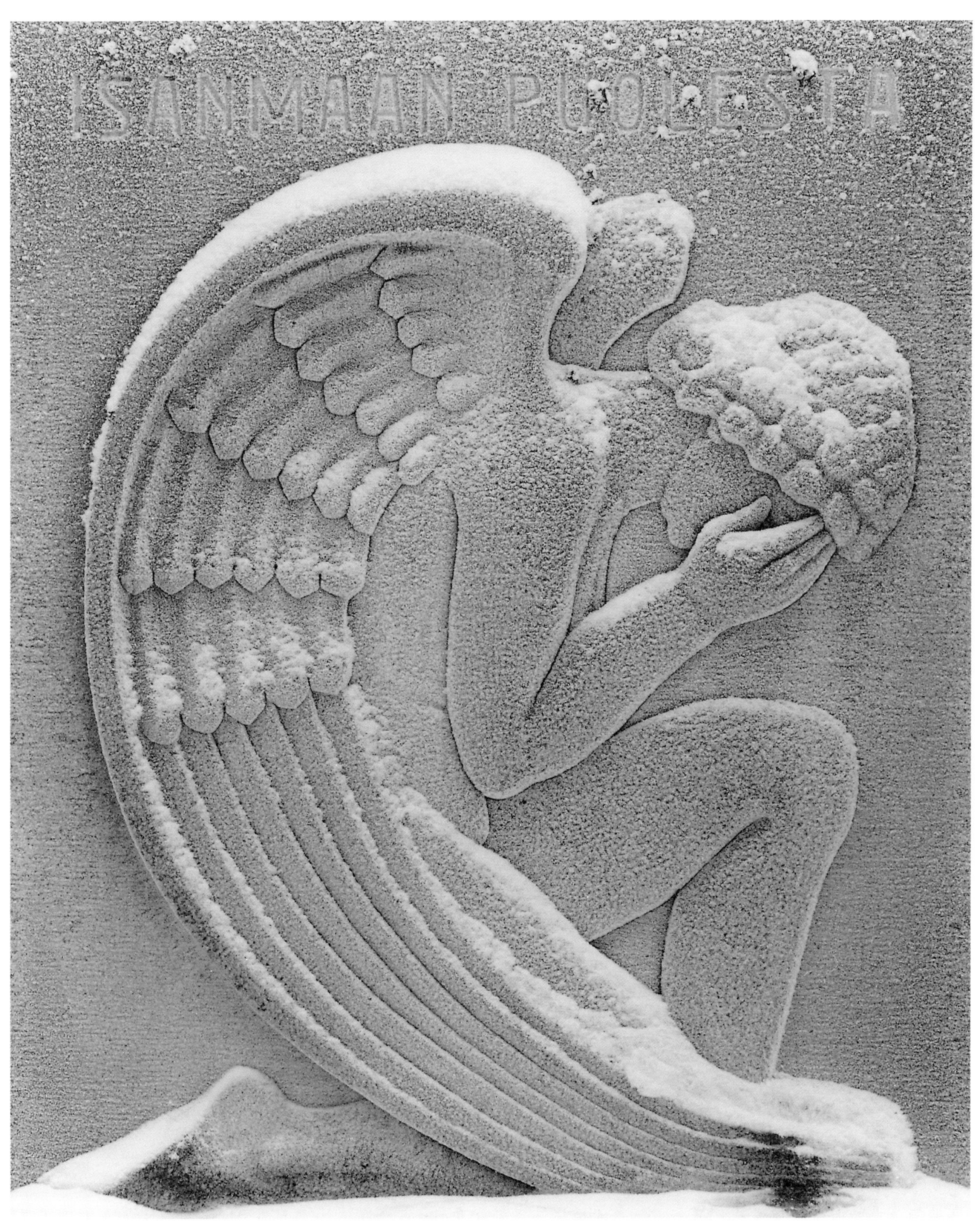

(left) 85 **Angel of the North**, *Sheila Haycox*
(above top) 86 **The release #2**, *Paul Damen*
(bottom) 87 **Frozen angel**, *Juha Taponen*

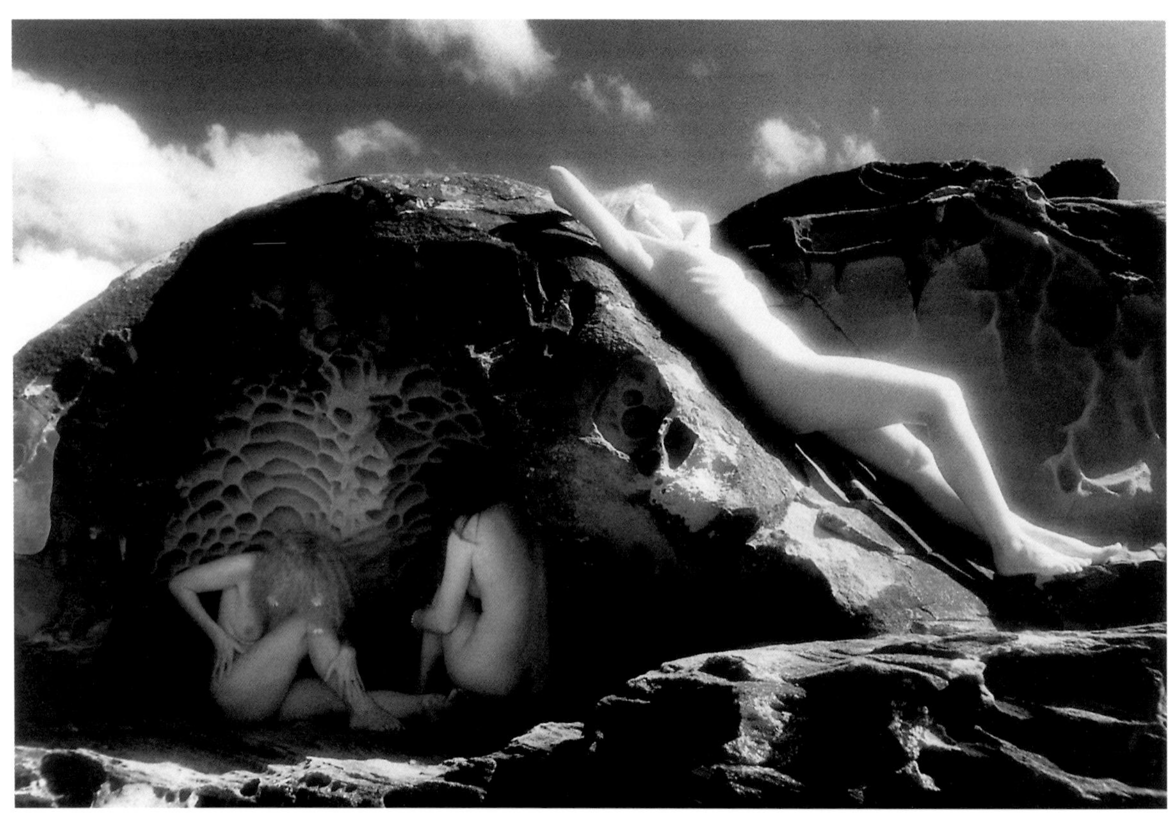

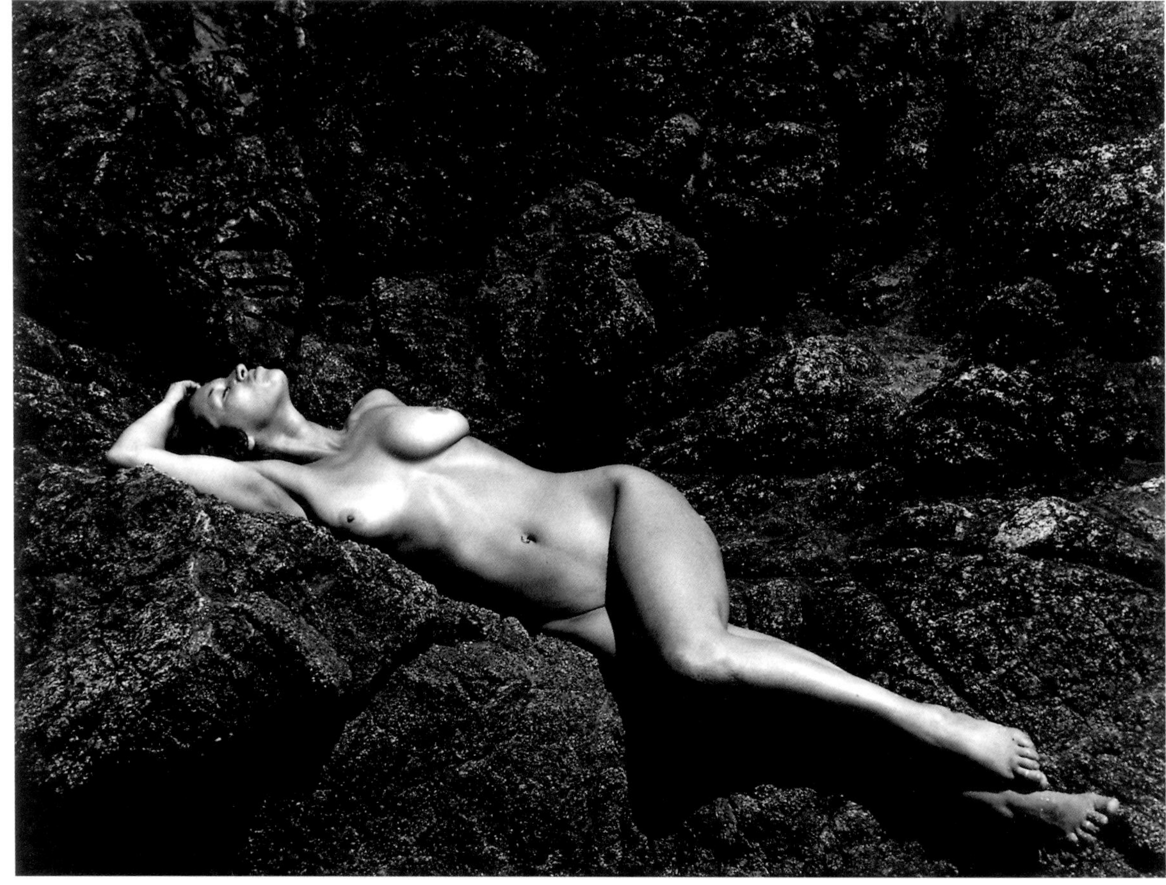

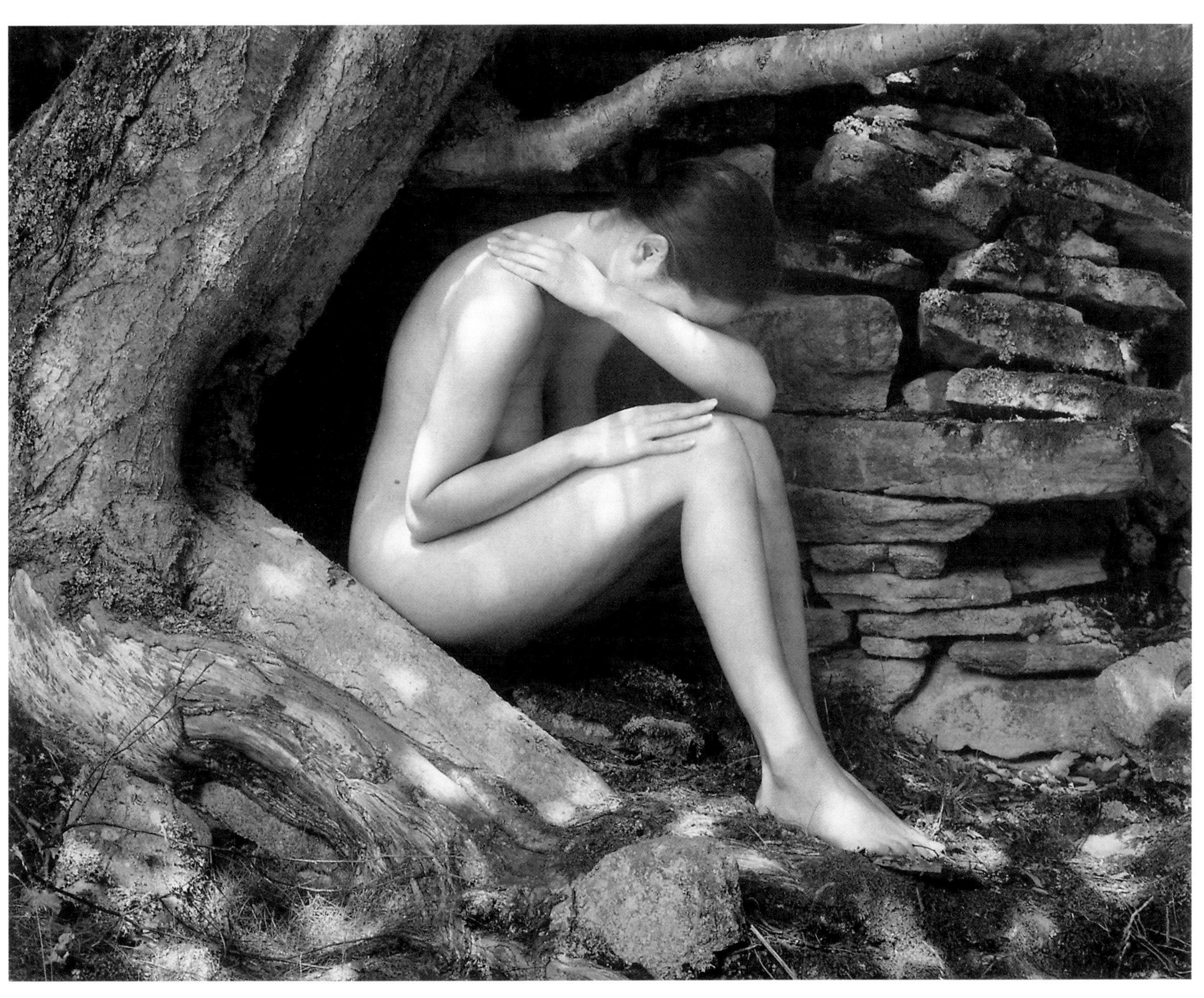

(left) 88 **Genesis**, *Shirlie Phillips*
(above top) 89 **Rosie I**, *Edward Gordon*
(bottom) 90 **Untitled**, *Roy Elwood*

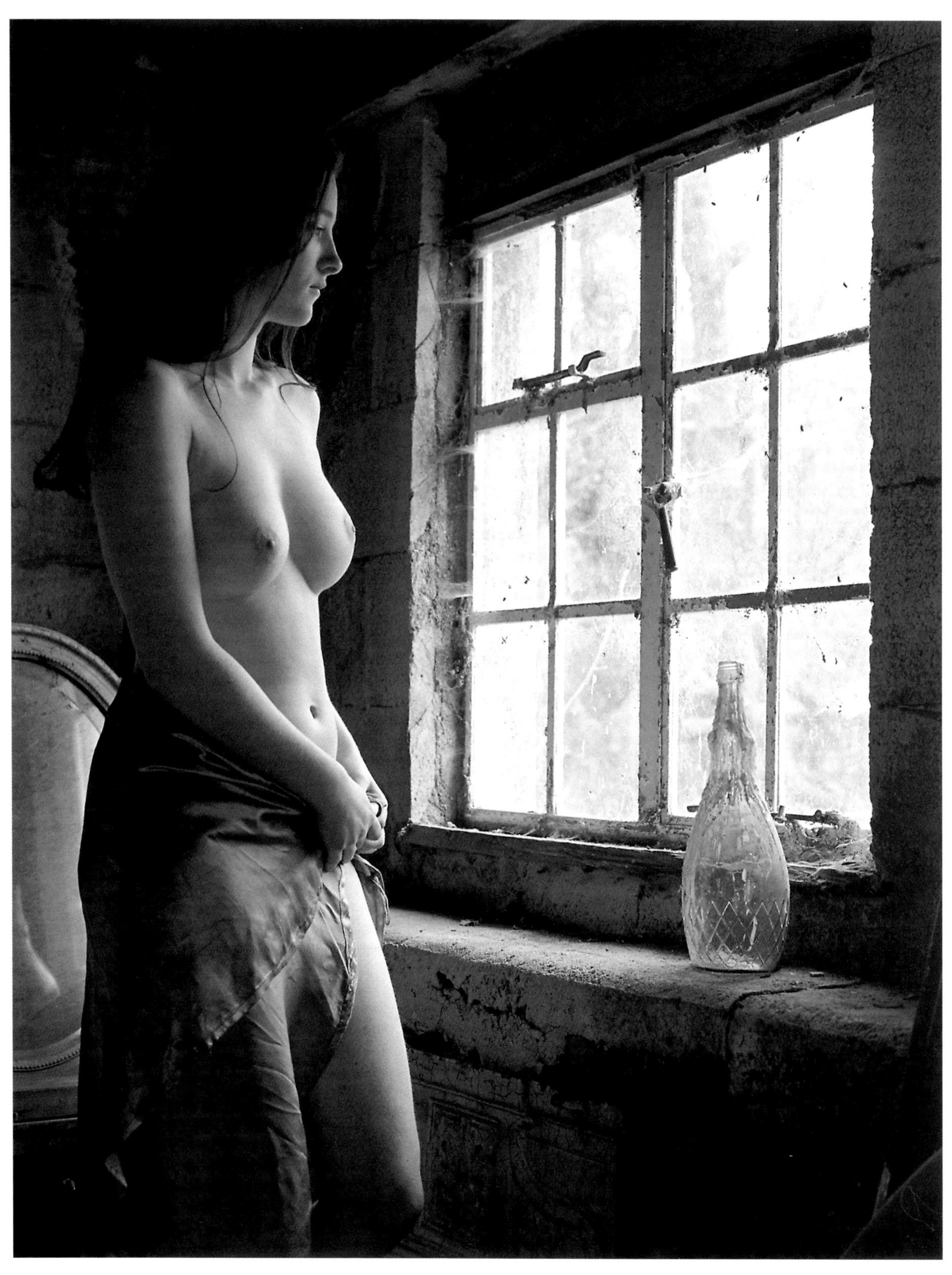

91
Josie wrth y ffenestr
O Tudur Owen

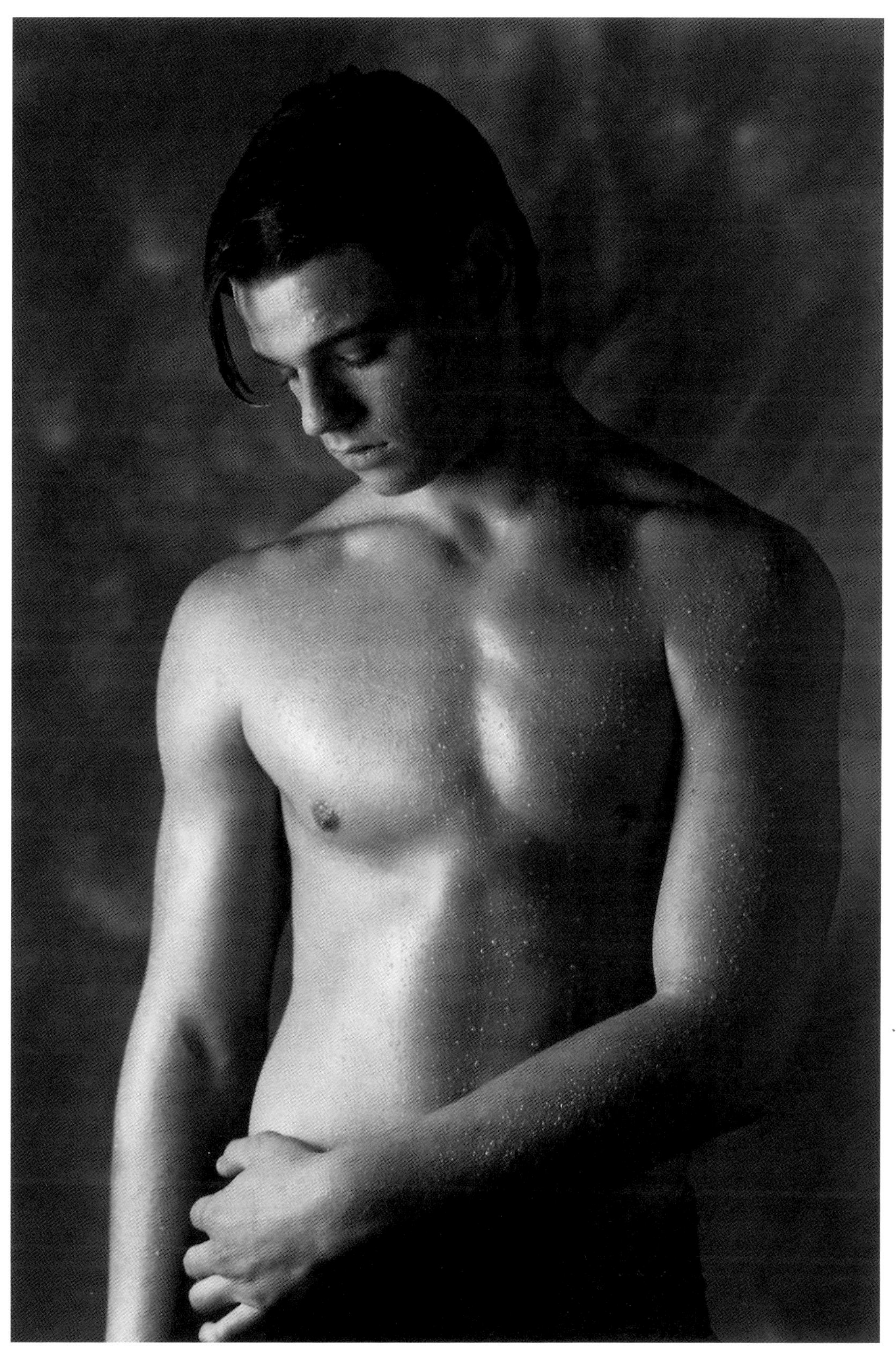

92
Gareth
Mike Kielecher

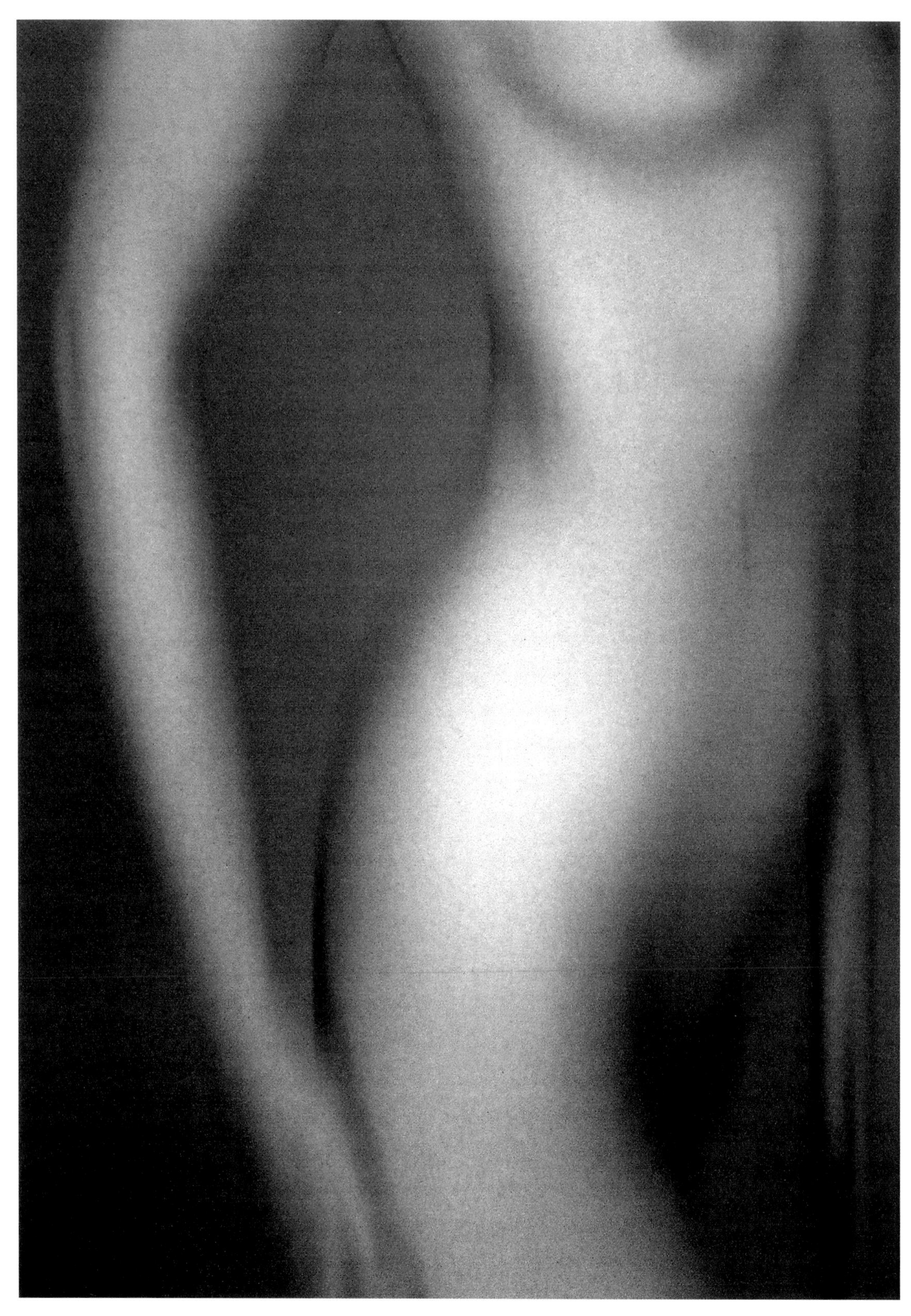

93
Torso
Ian Mellor

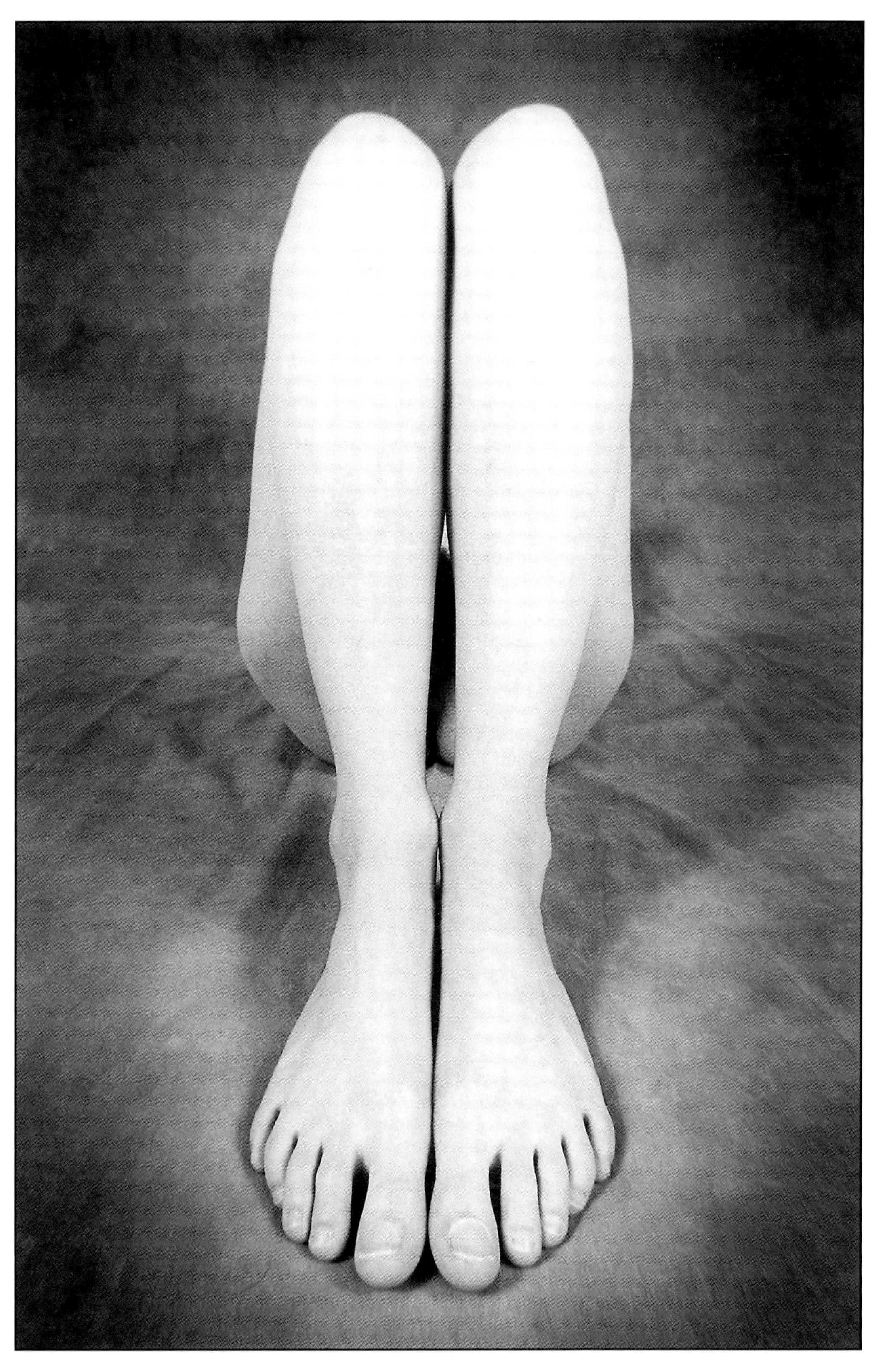

94
Feet
Charles Baynon

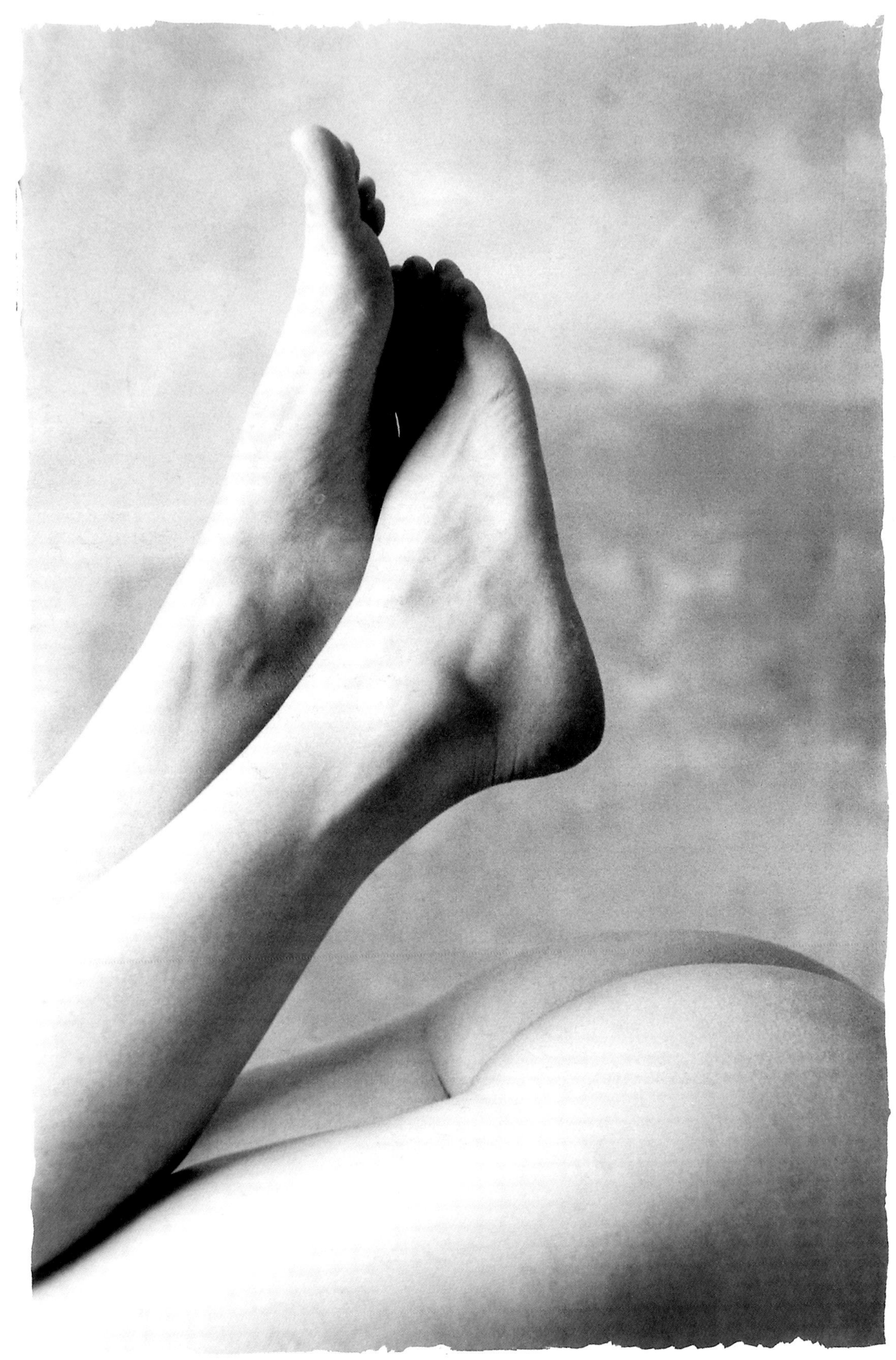

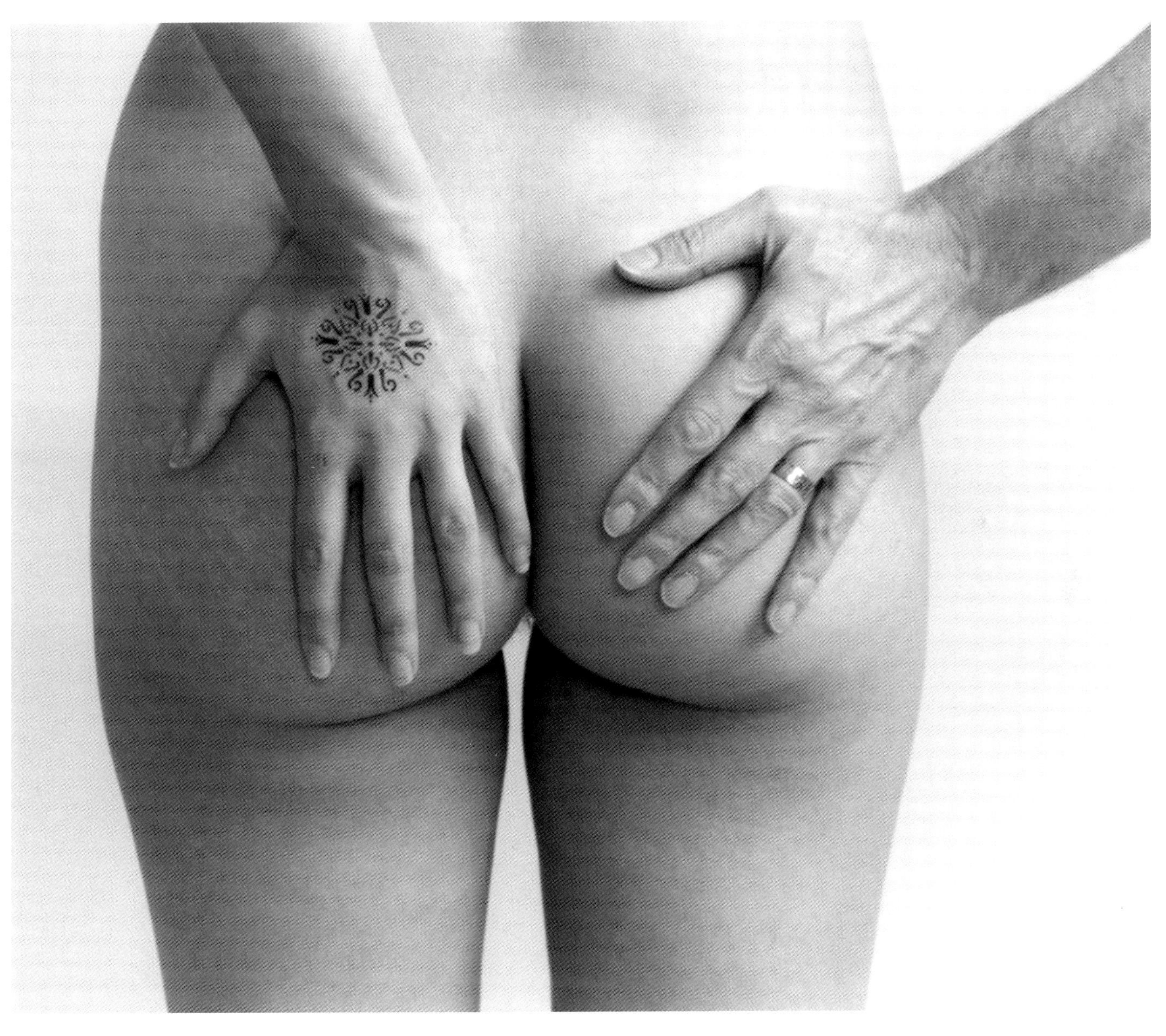

(left) 95 **Feet II**, *Charles Baynon*
(above) 96 **One of hers, one of mine!**, *Glyn Edmunds*

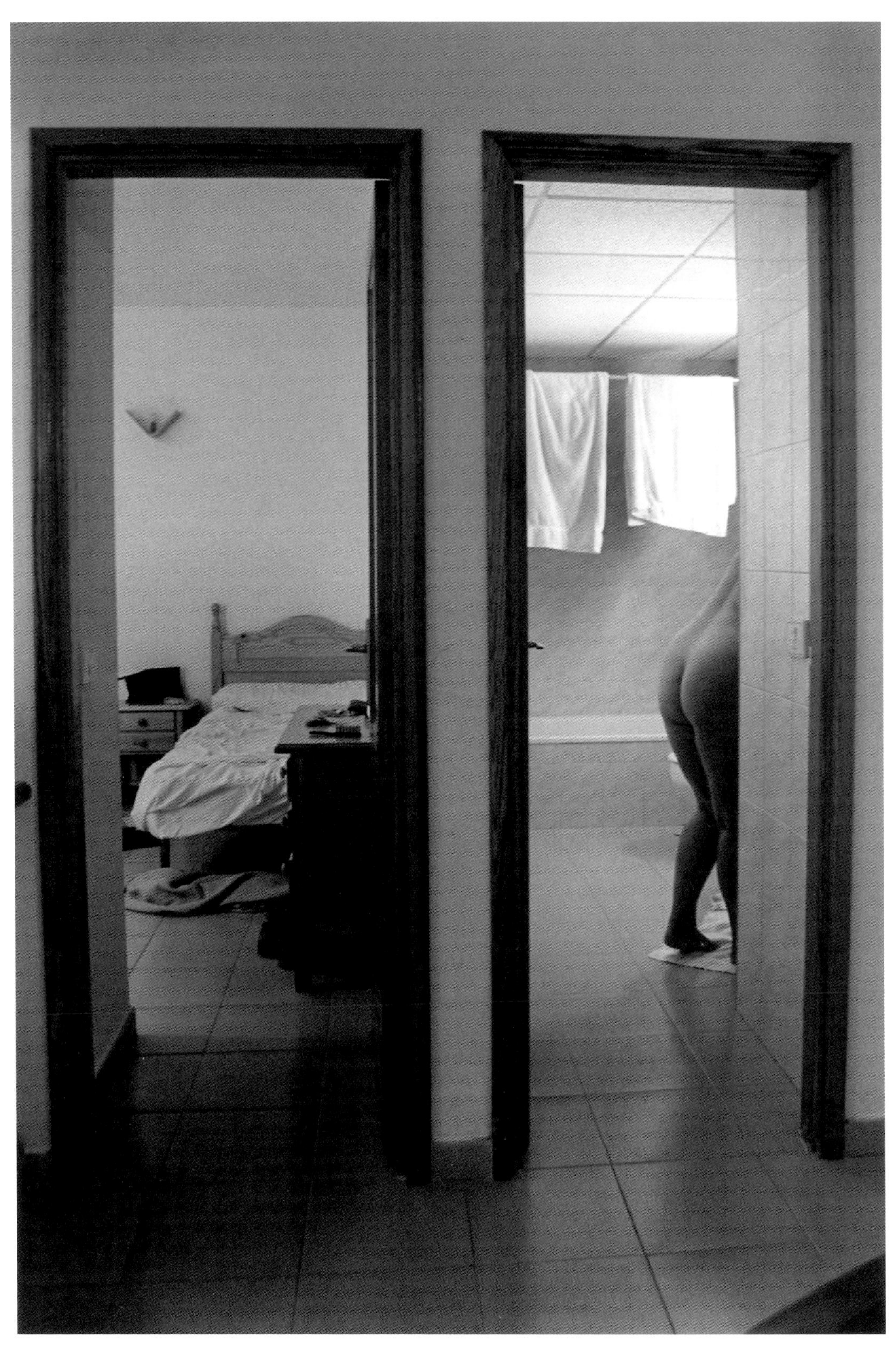

97
Lanzarote morning
Andy Wilson

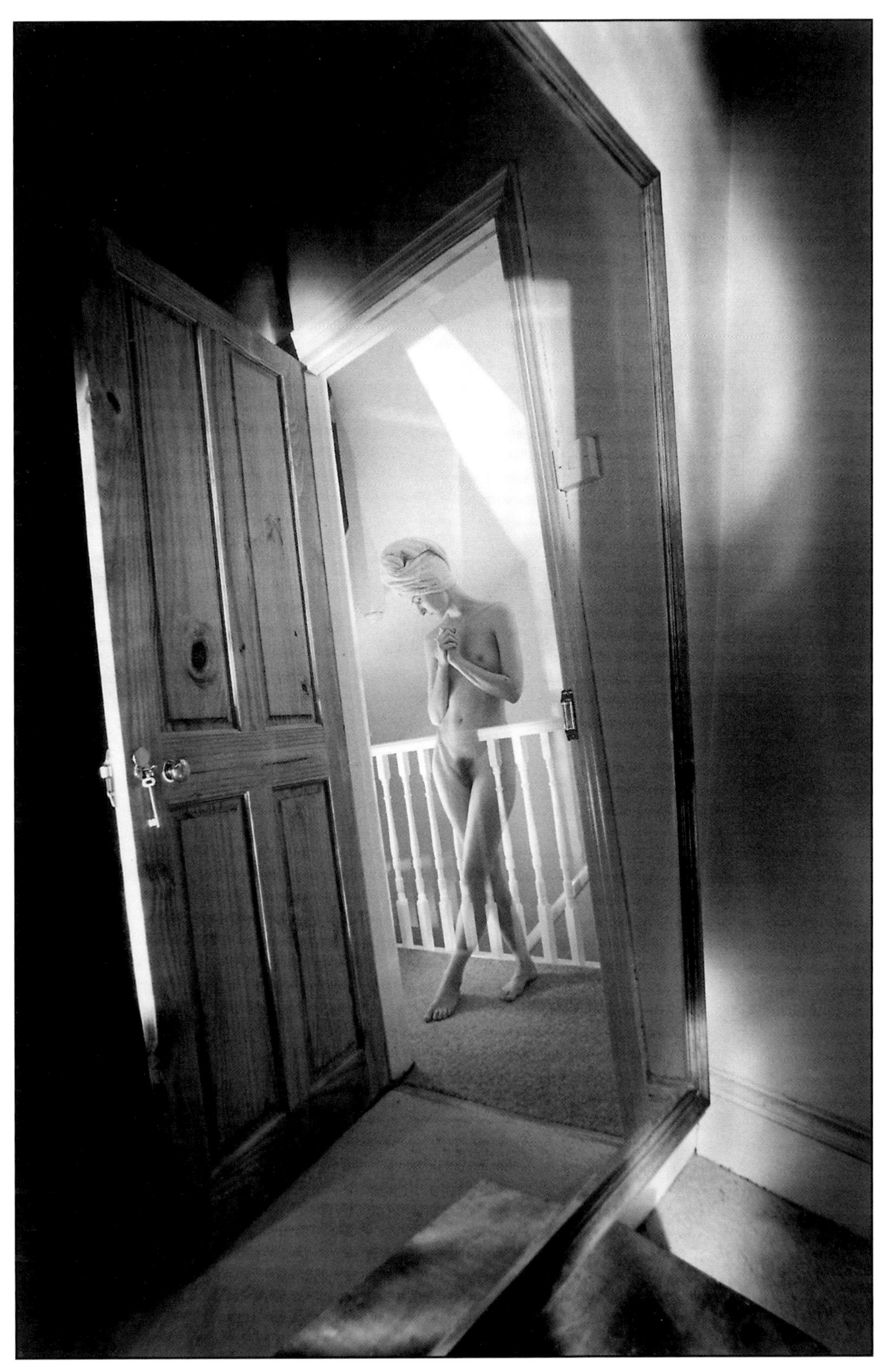

98
Figure in a doorway
Charles Baynon

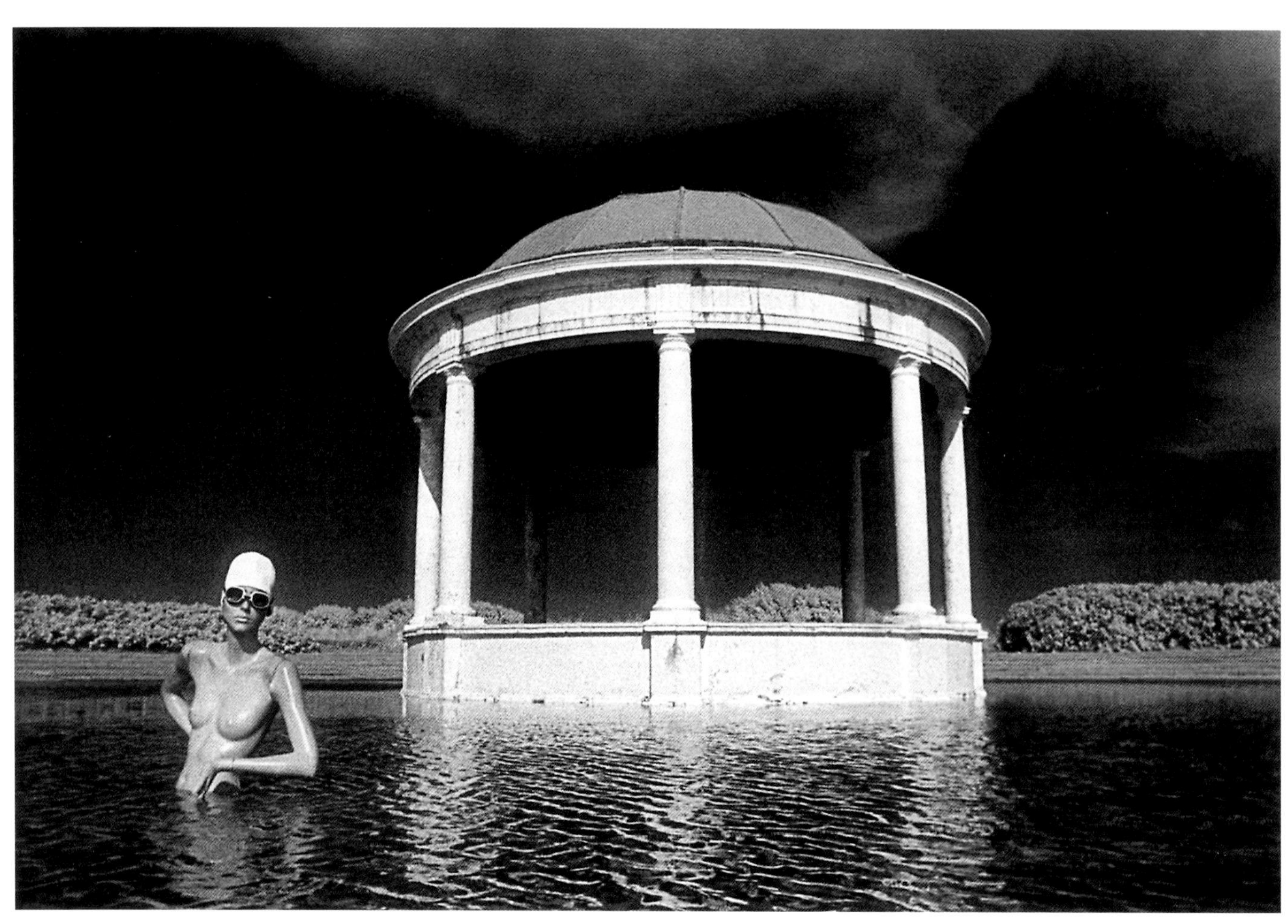

99
In at the deep end
Arthur Smith

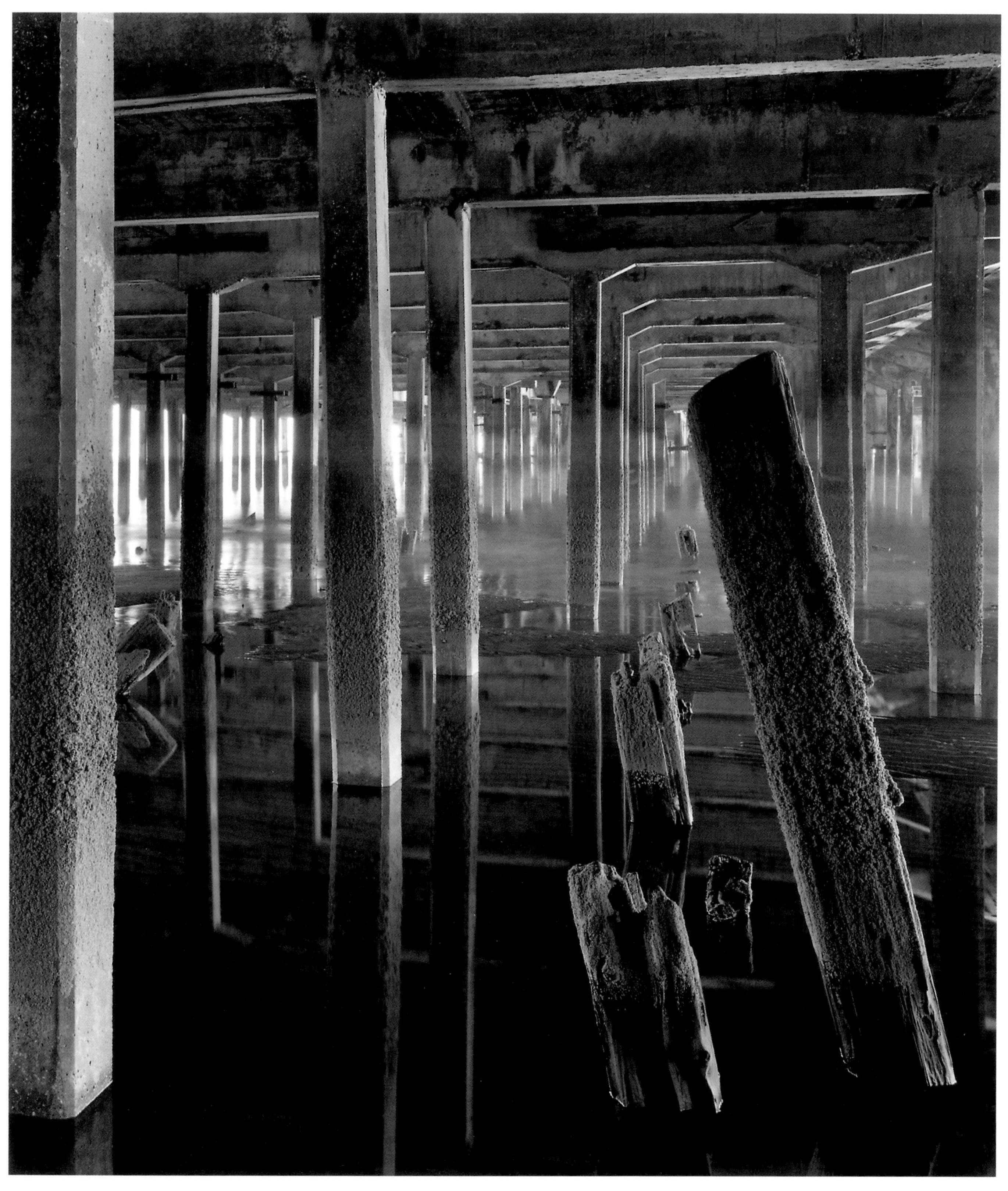

100
Walton Pier
Trevor Crone

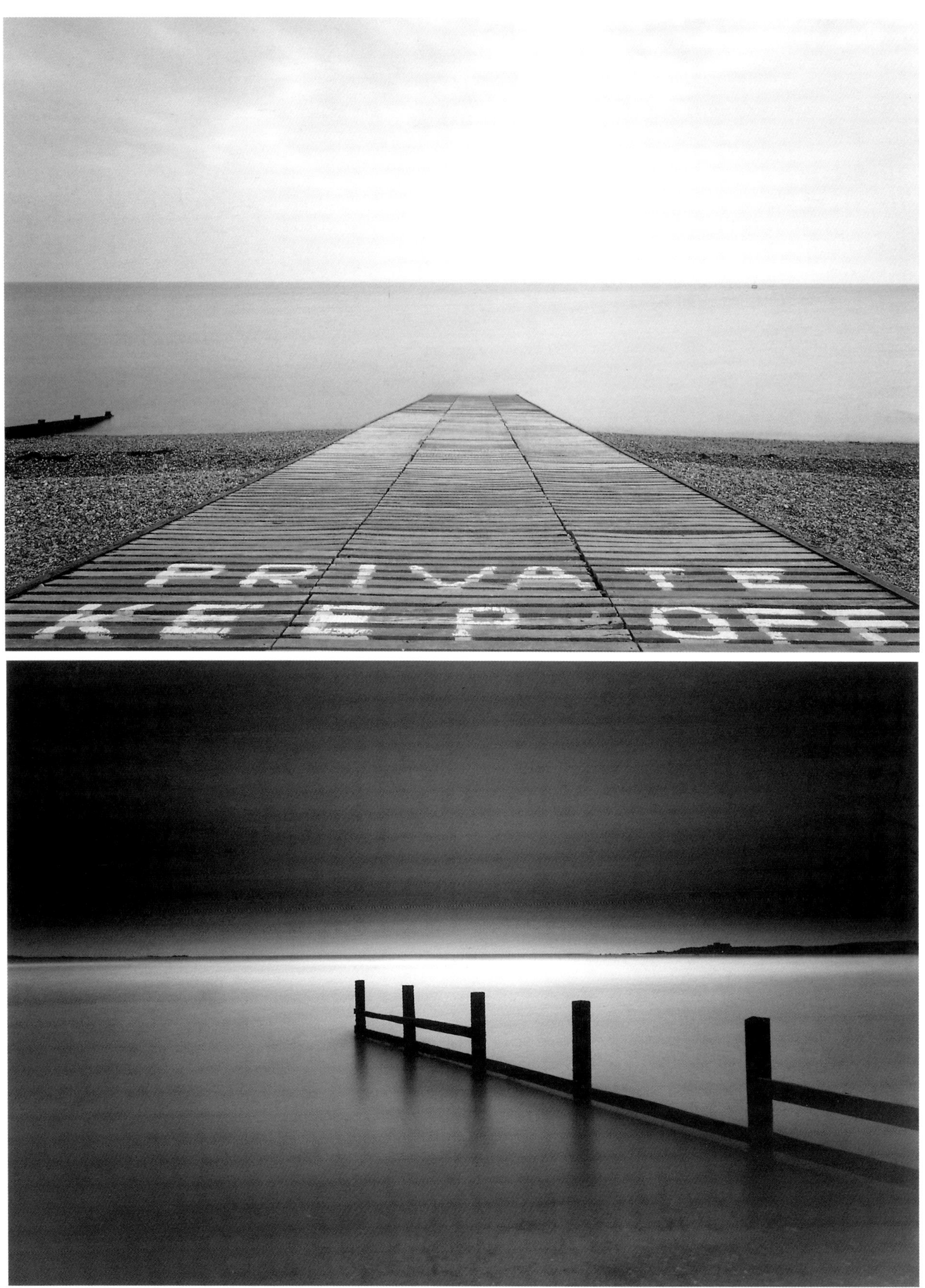
PRIVATE
KEEP OFF

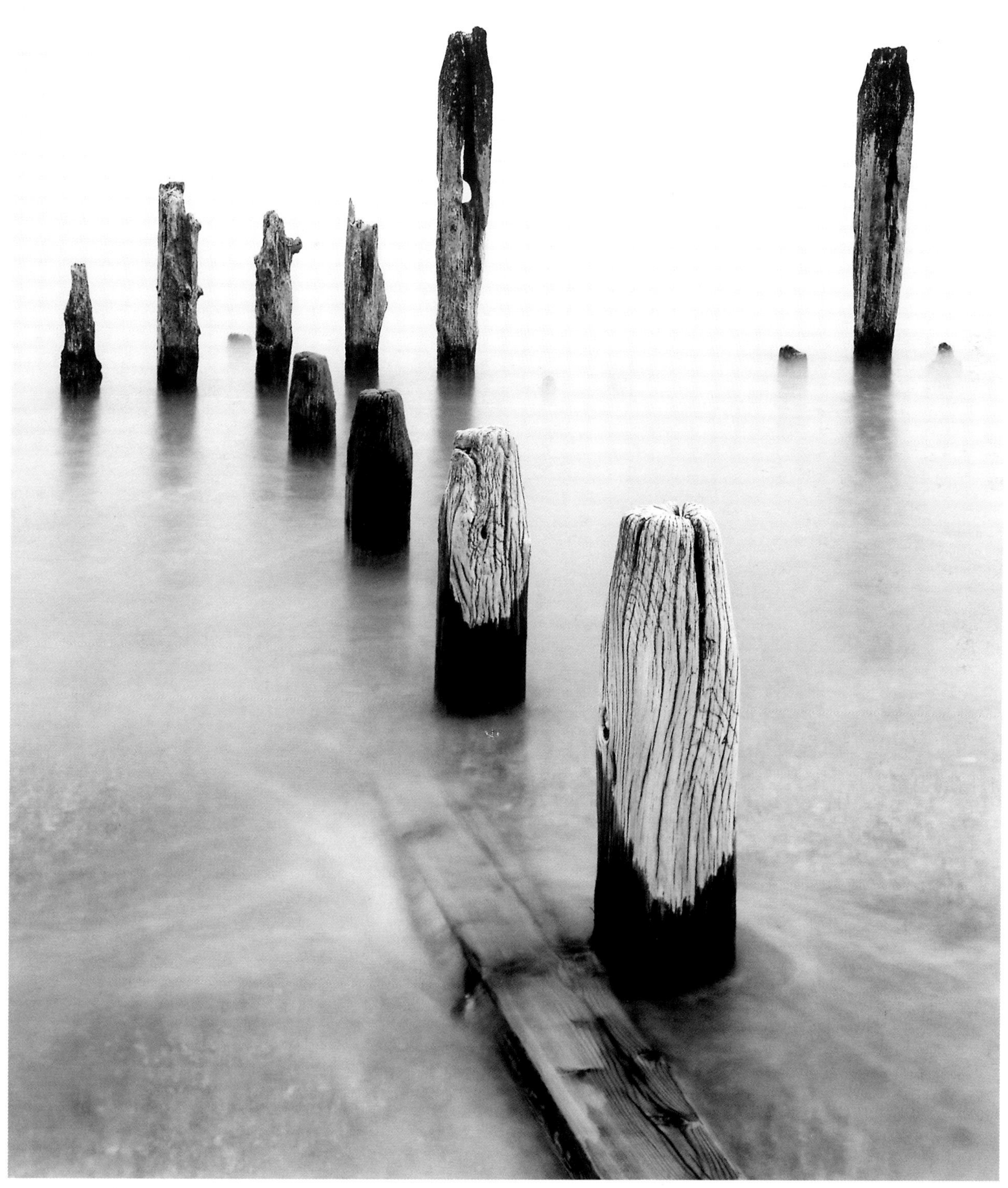

(top left) 101 **Slipway, Herne Bay**, *Trevor Crone*
(bottom left) 102 **Groynes #5**, *Nick Després*
(above) 103 **Weathered groynes**, *Chris Shore*

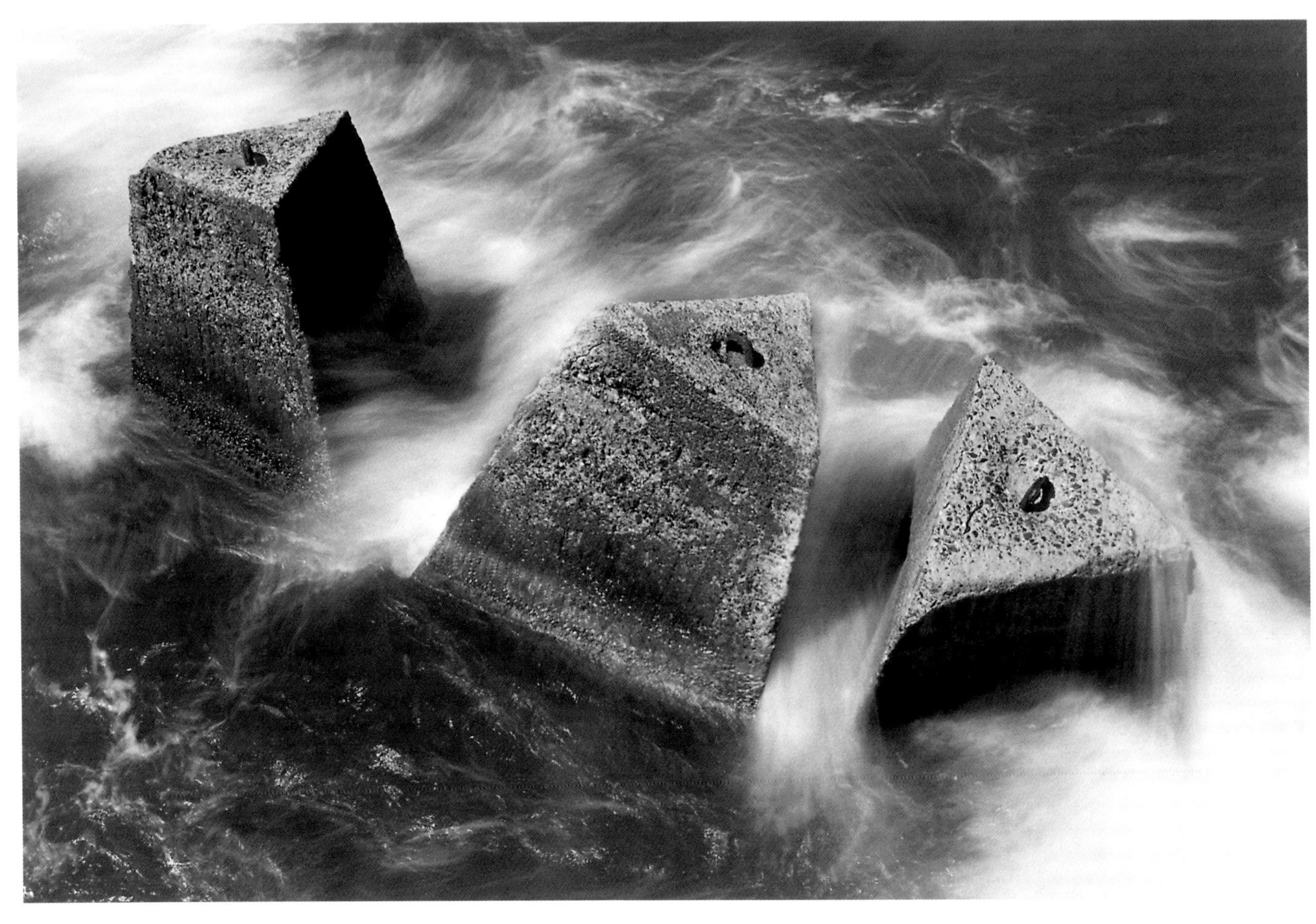

104
Coastal defences, Andros
Simon Denison

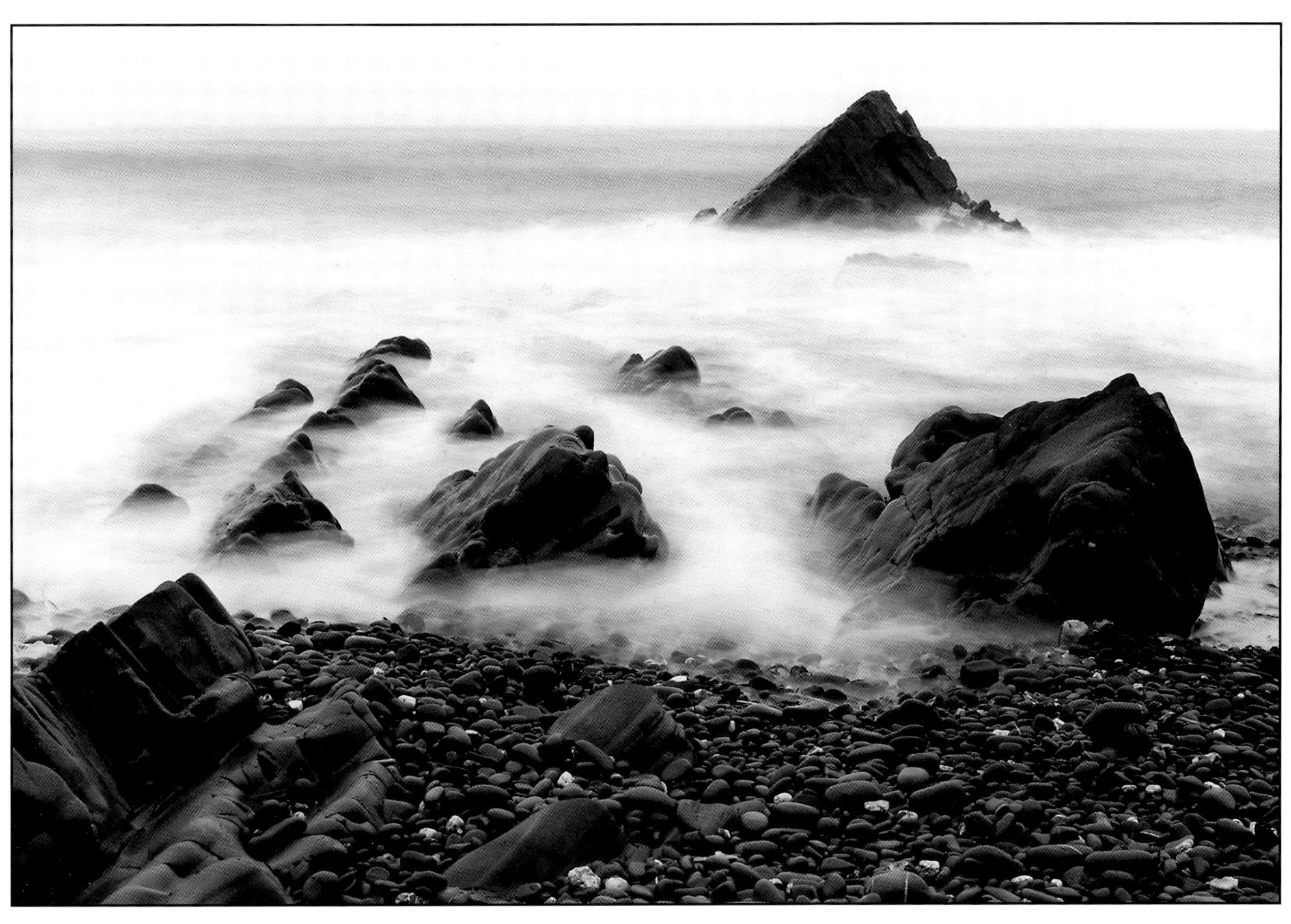

105
Incoming tide
Kathleen Harcom

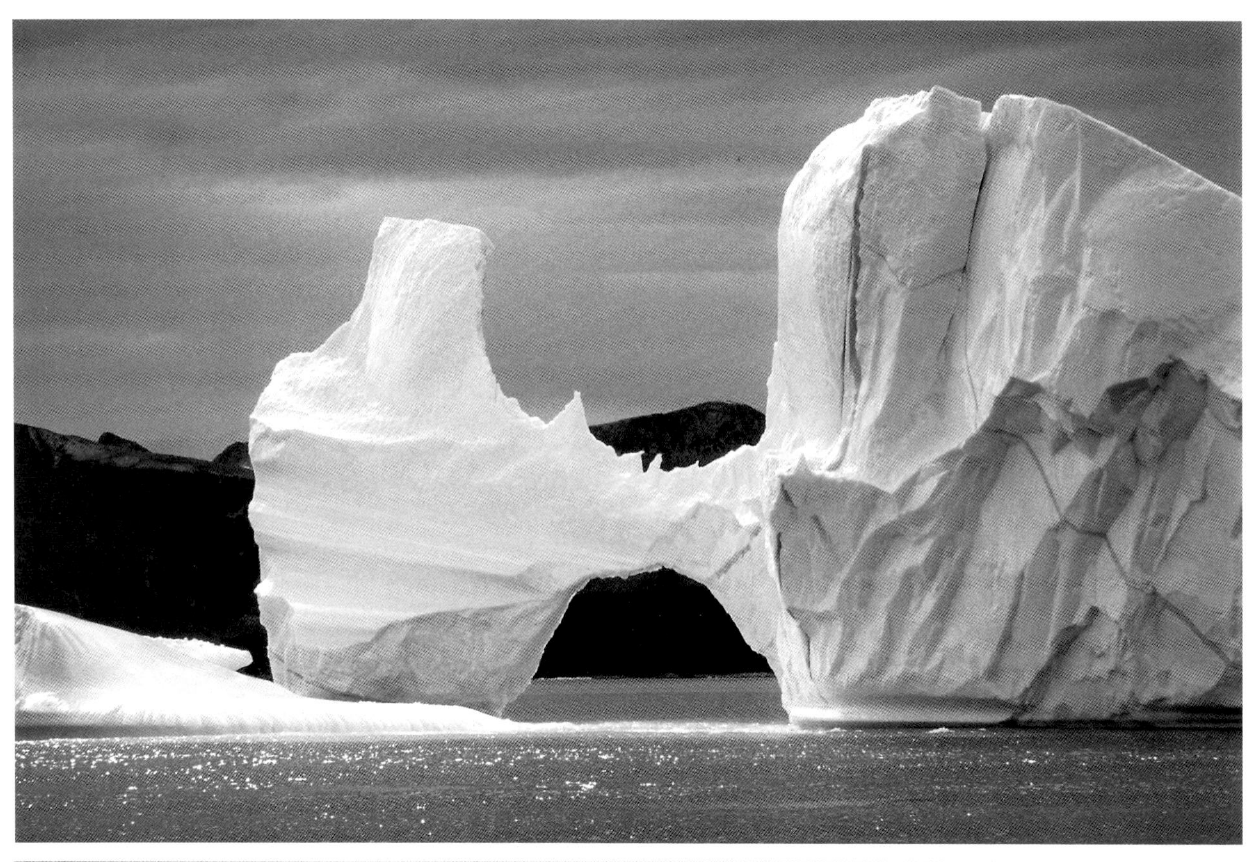

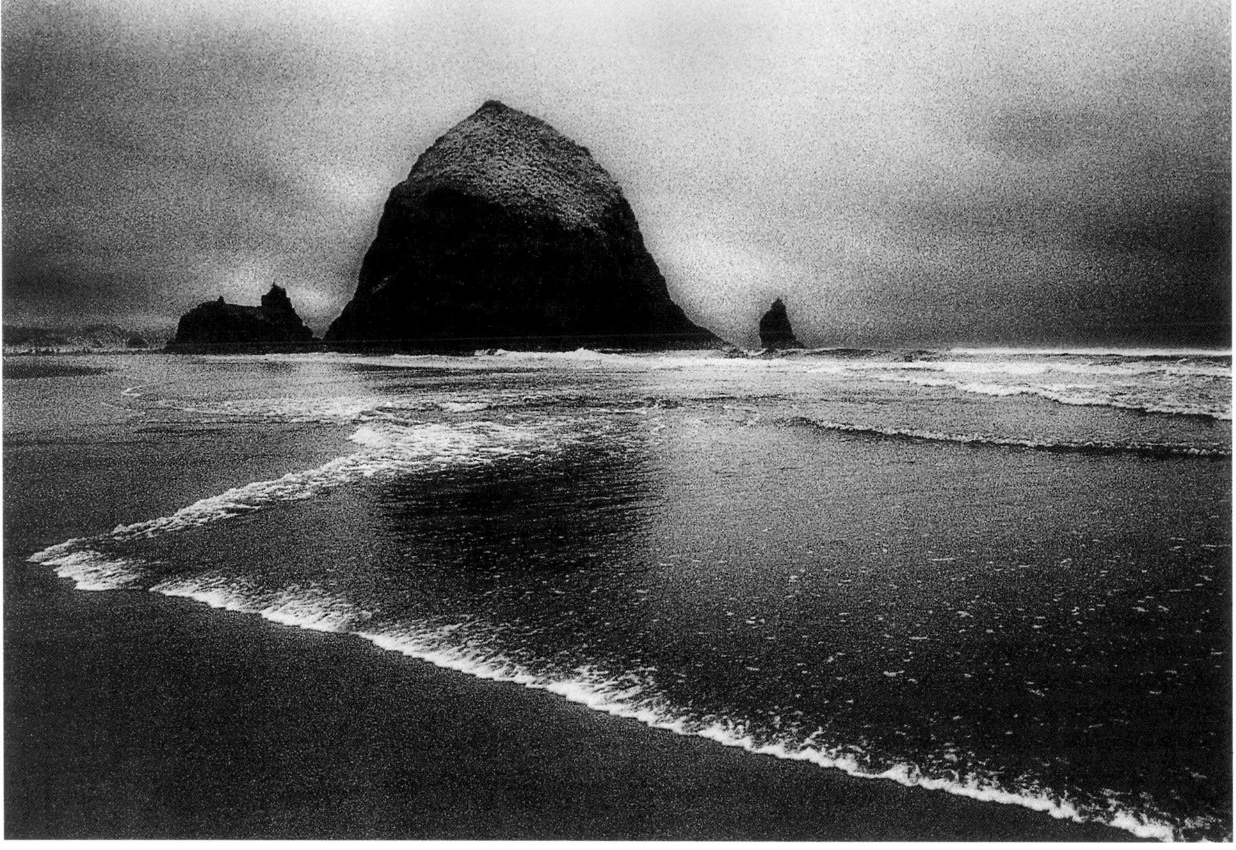

(top left) 106 **Arctic light**, *Mike Chambers*
(bottom left) 107 **Haystack**, *Alastair Rucklidge*
(above) 108 **Staffin Bay**, *Paul Booth*

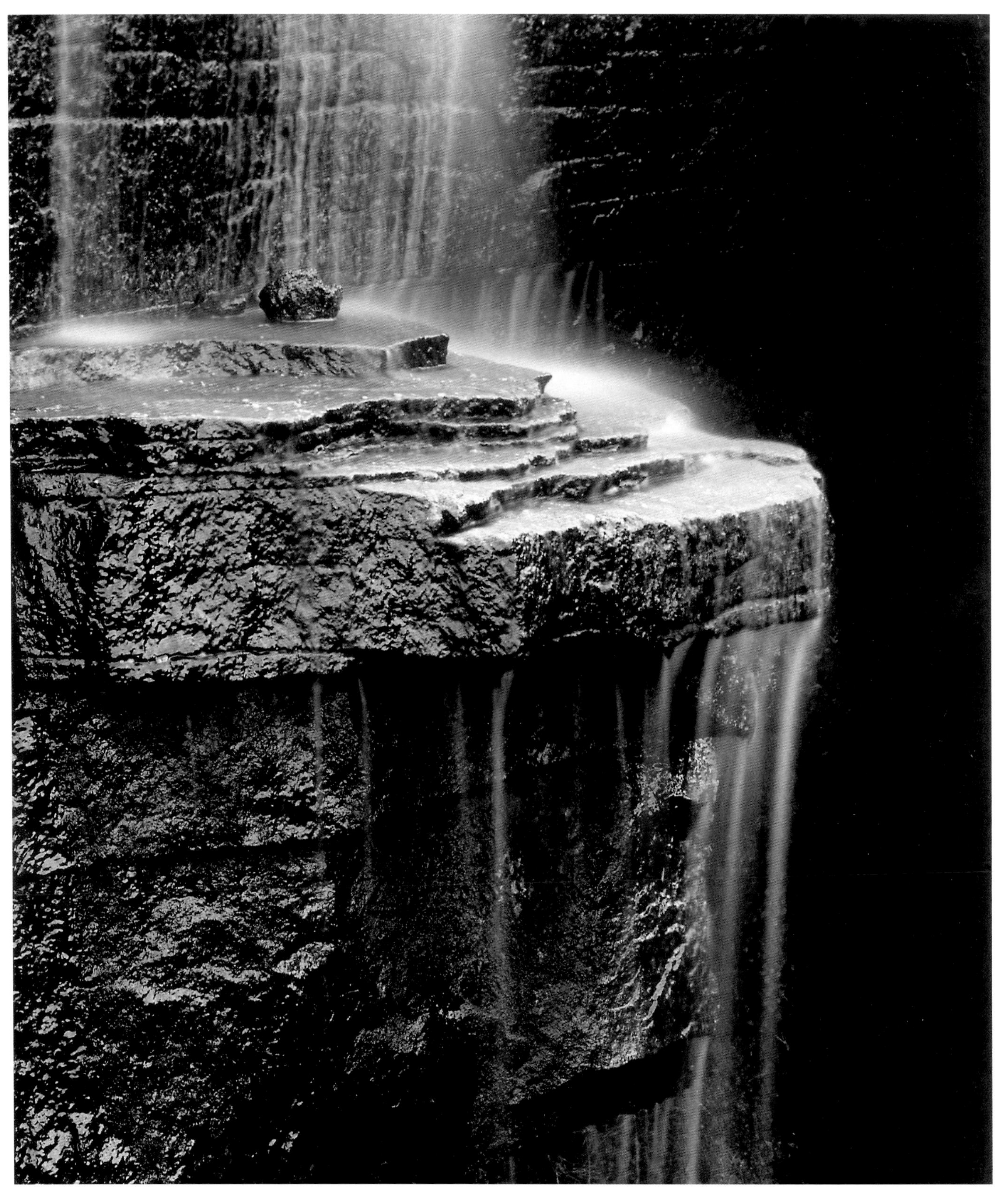

109
Timeless II
David Cobley

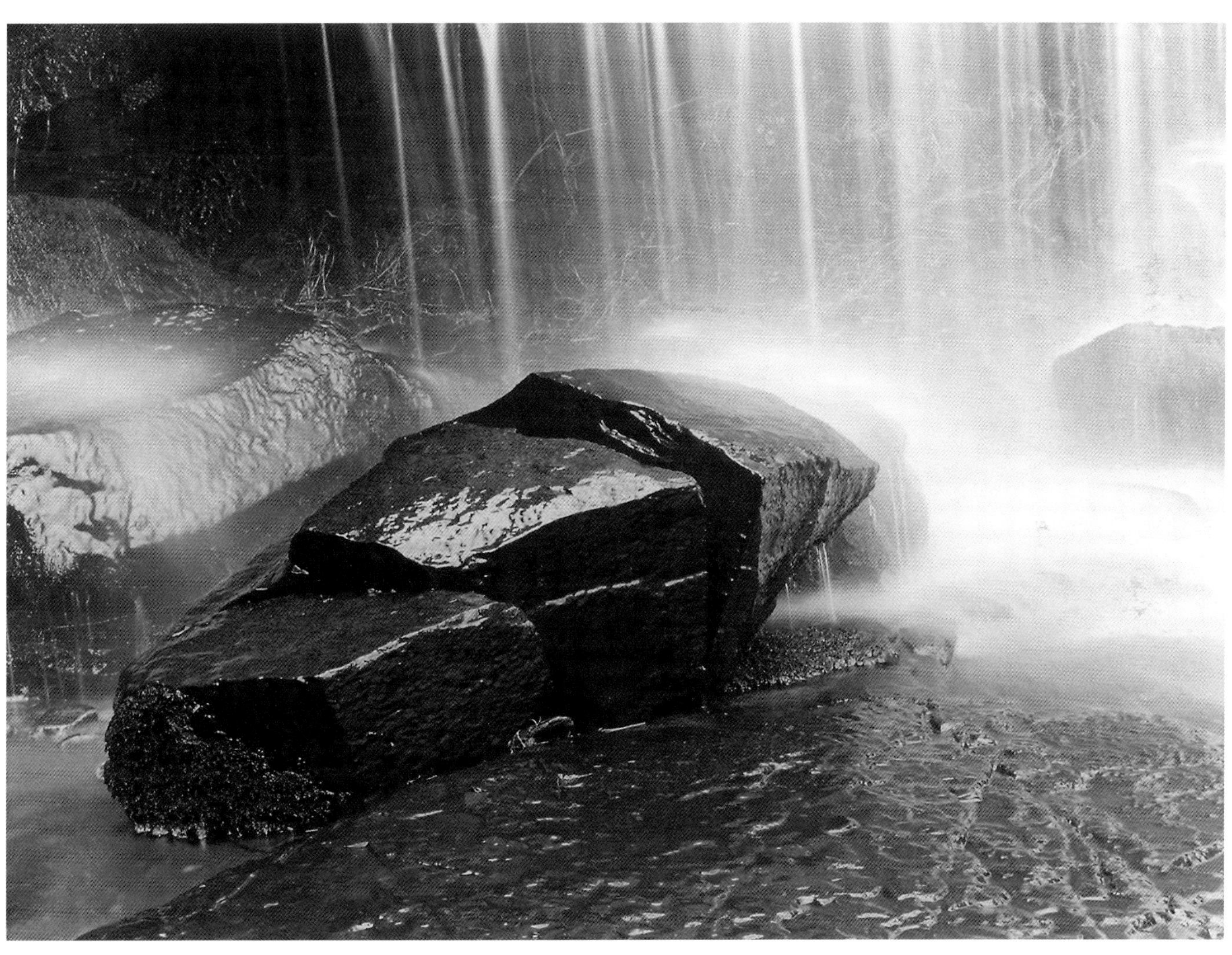

110
Fall's edge
Neil Souch

(above) 111 **No title**, *Clive Vincent*
(top right) 112 **The Corran Narrows, Loch Linnhe**, *Malcolm Hawkins*
(bottom right) 113 **La Prevoté from La Corbière**, *Nick Després*

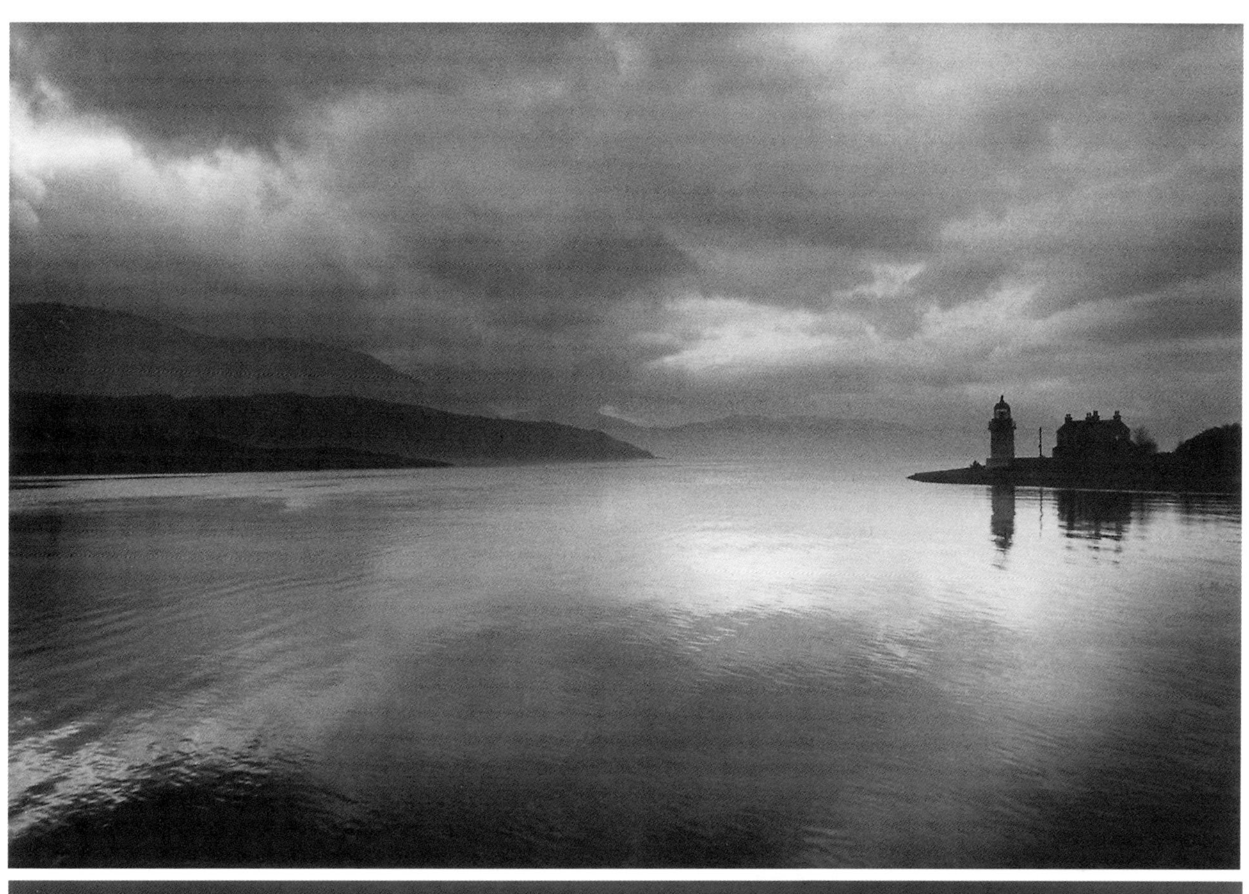

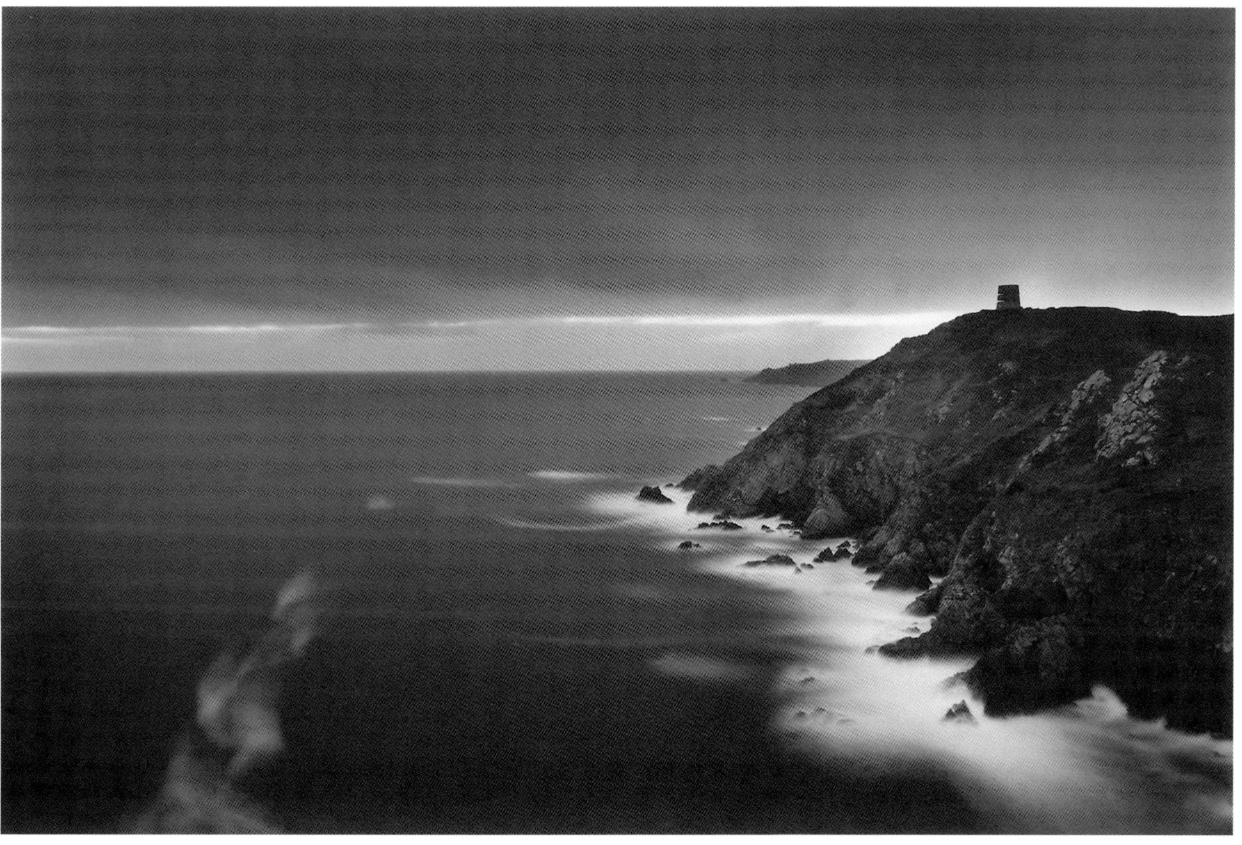

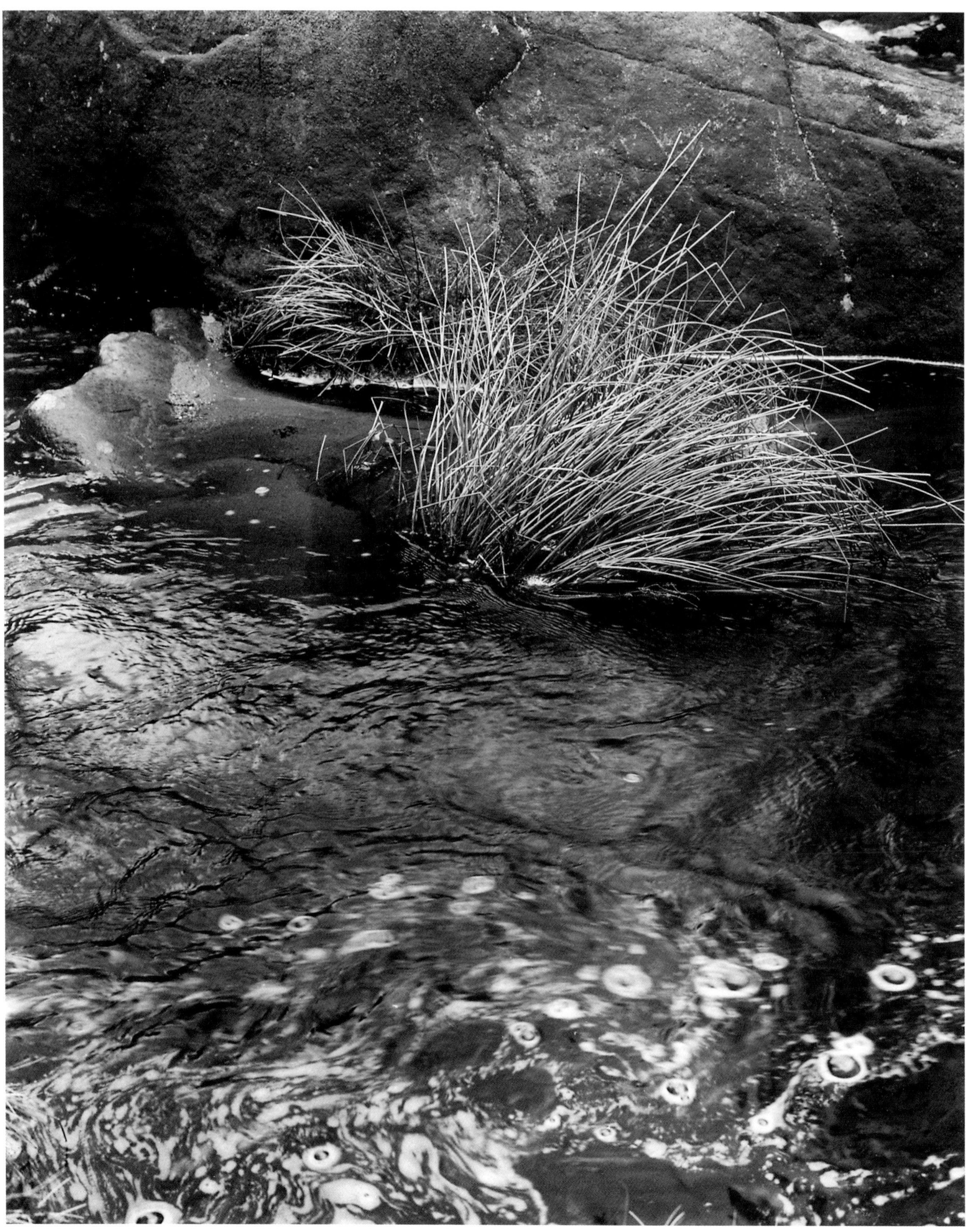

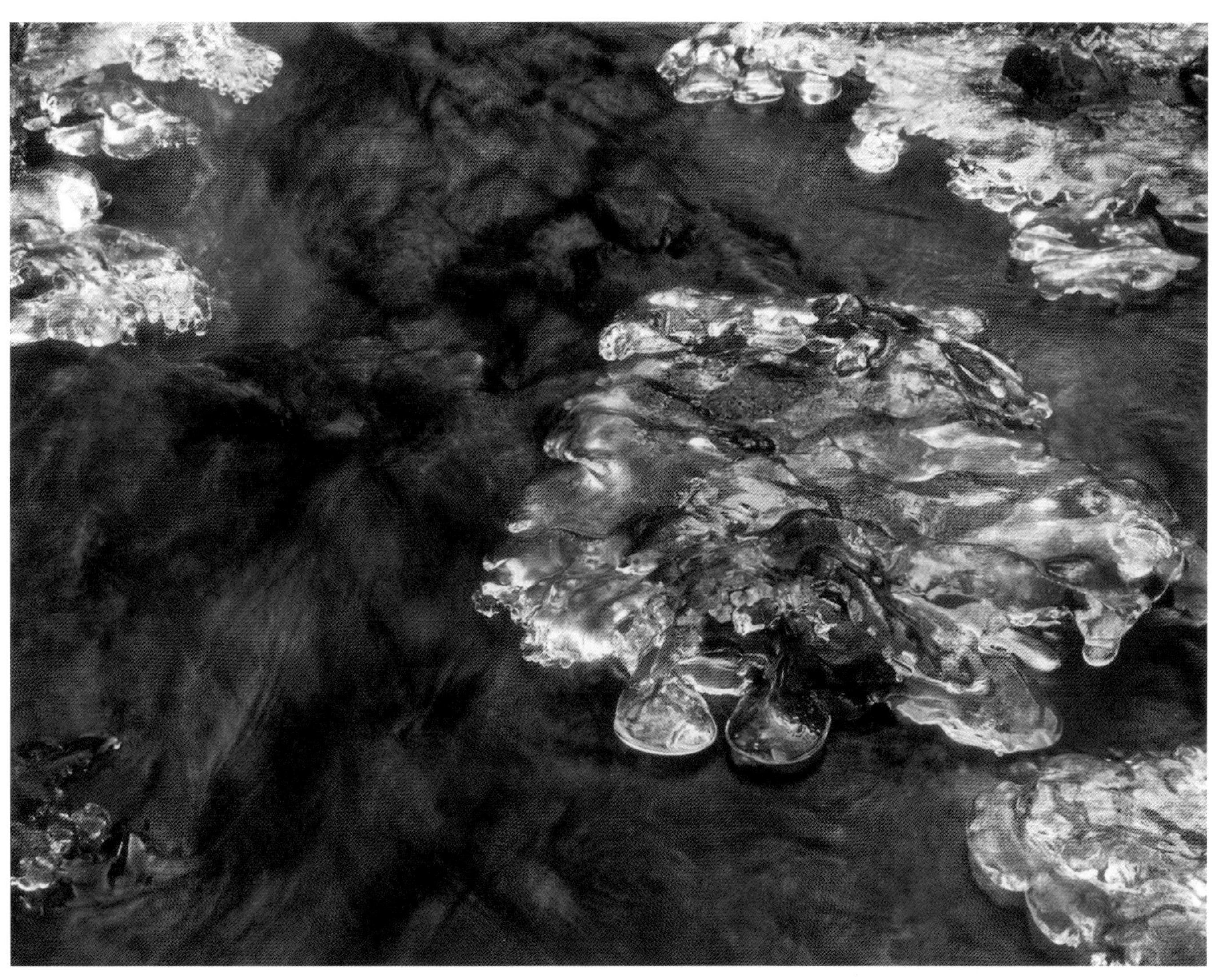

(left) 114 **Timeless I**, *David Cobley*
(above) 115 **Ice in stream**, *Jerry Daniel*

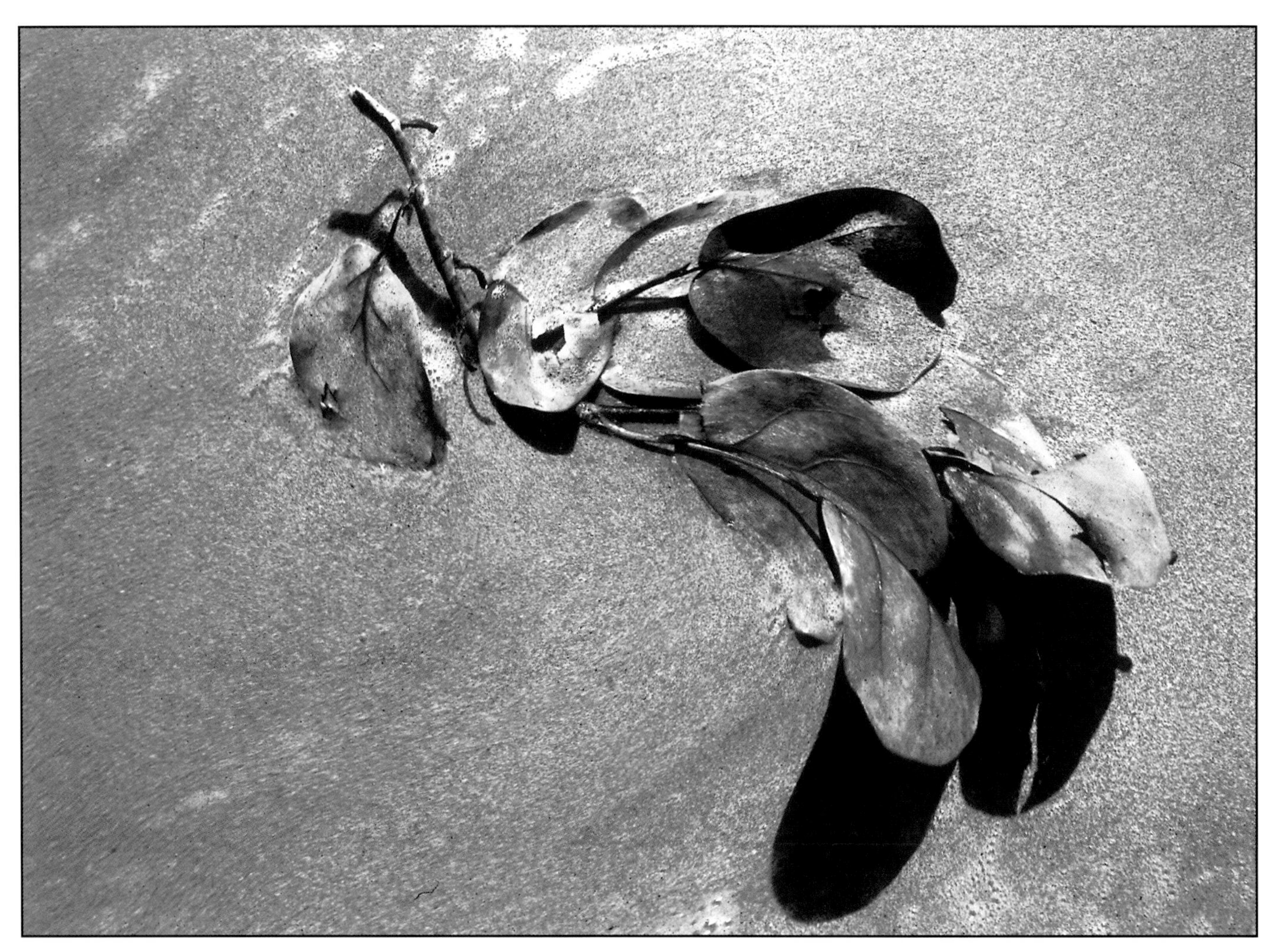

116
Barbados jetsam
Rex Bamber

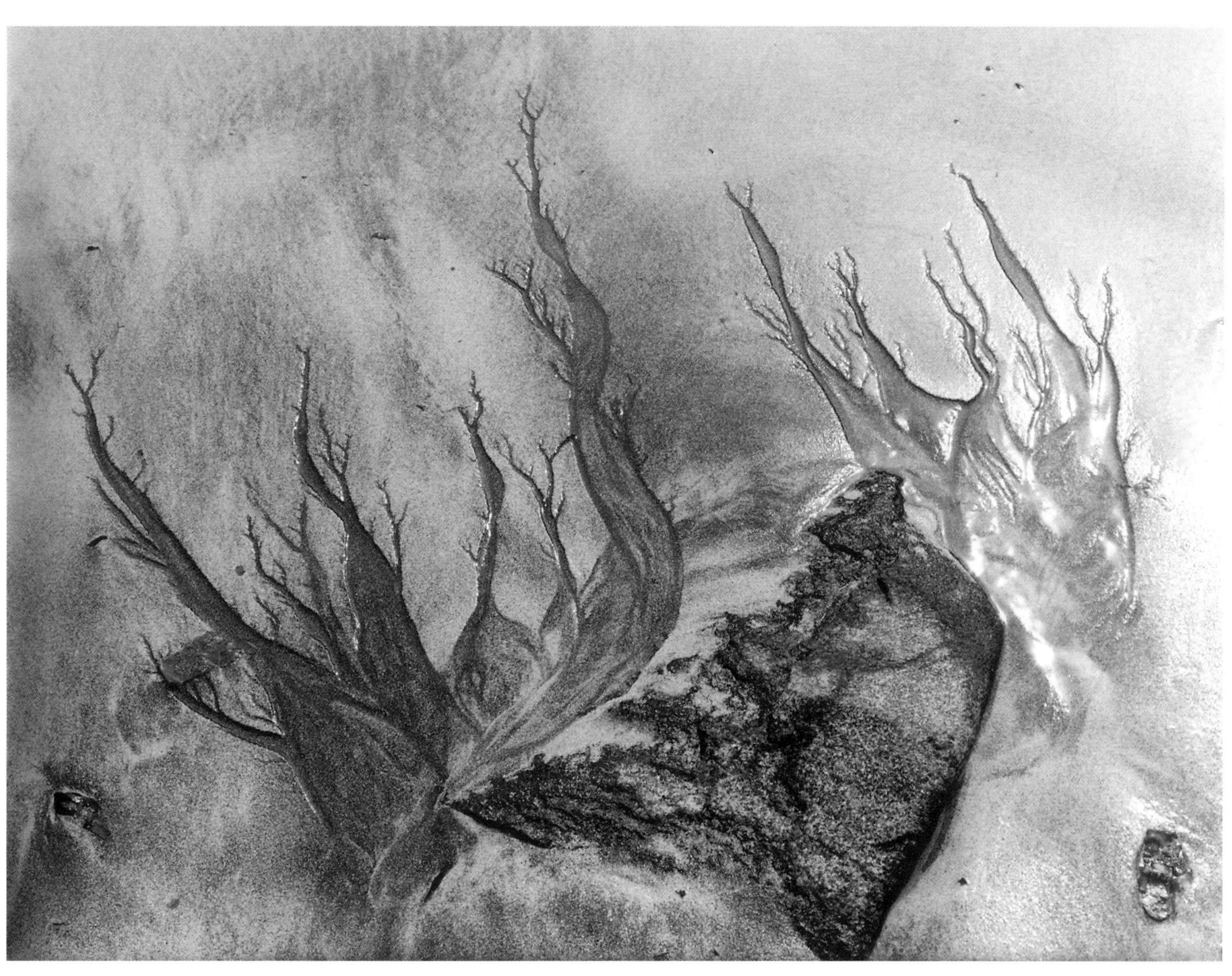

117
Sand pattern, Staffin Bay
Anne Marieke Booij

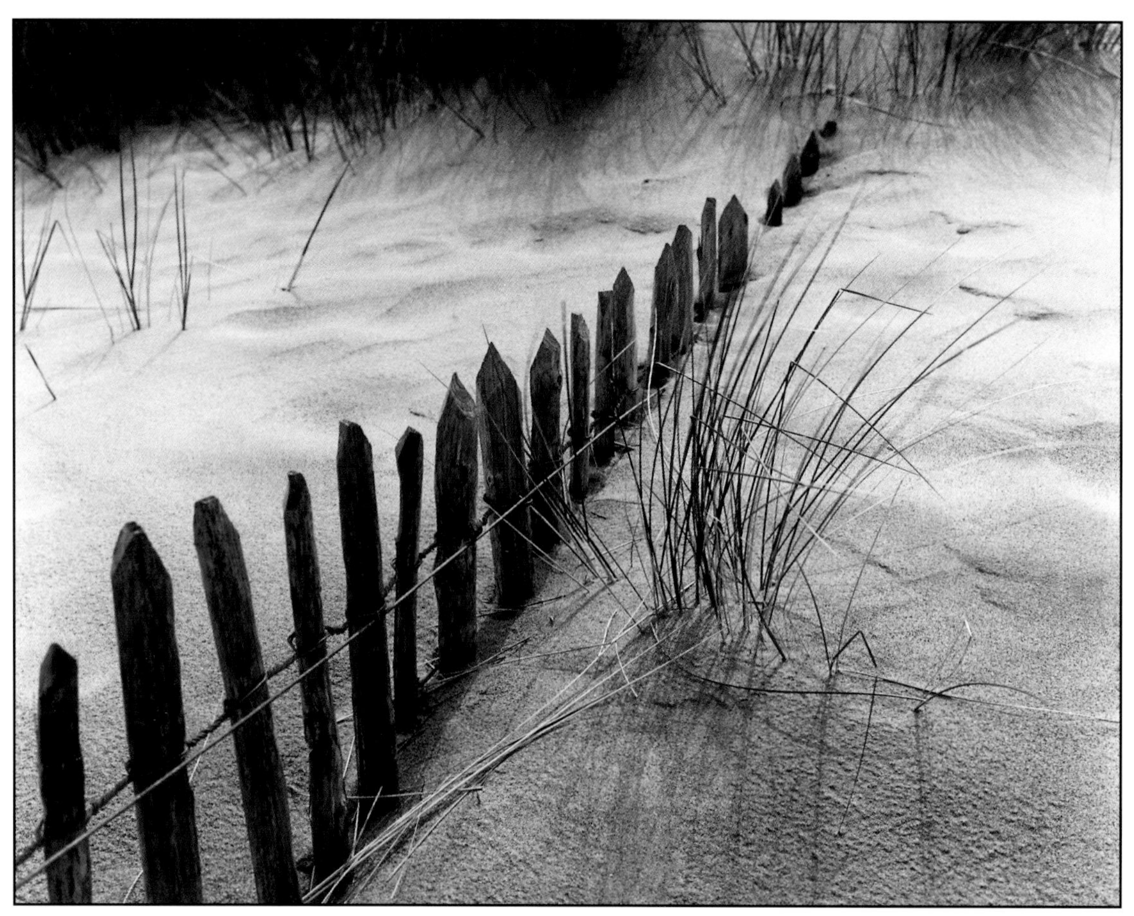

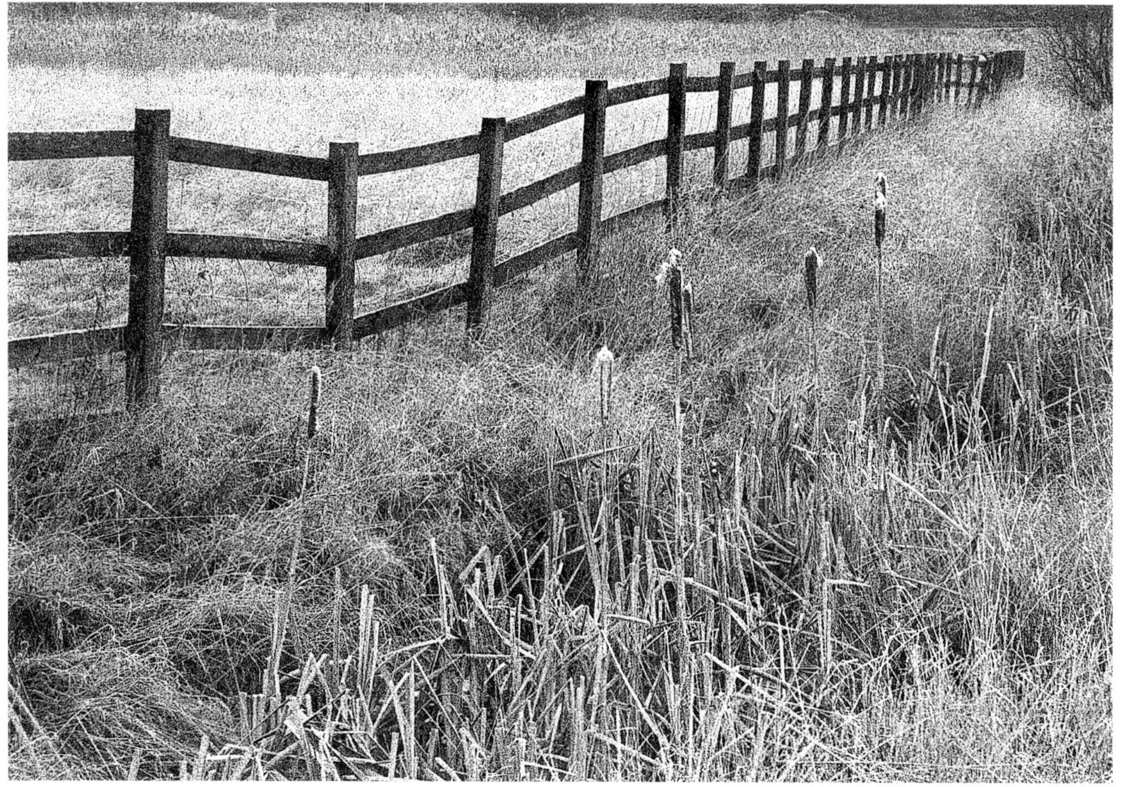

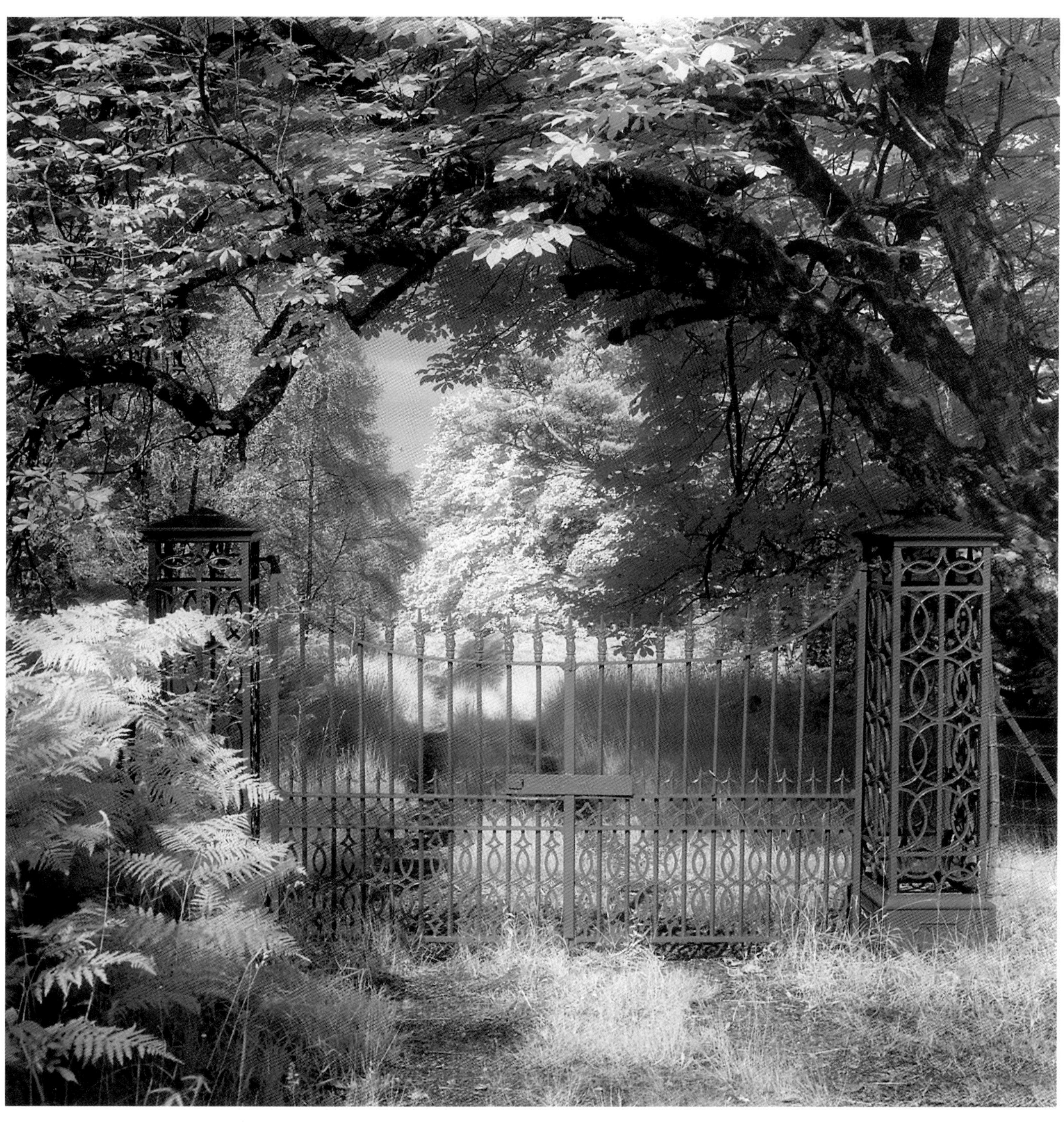

(top left) 118 **Disappearing fence**, *Colin Ivison*
(bottom left) 119 **Frosted reeds**, *Barbie Lindsay*
(above) 120 **Gate**, *Paul Booth*

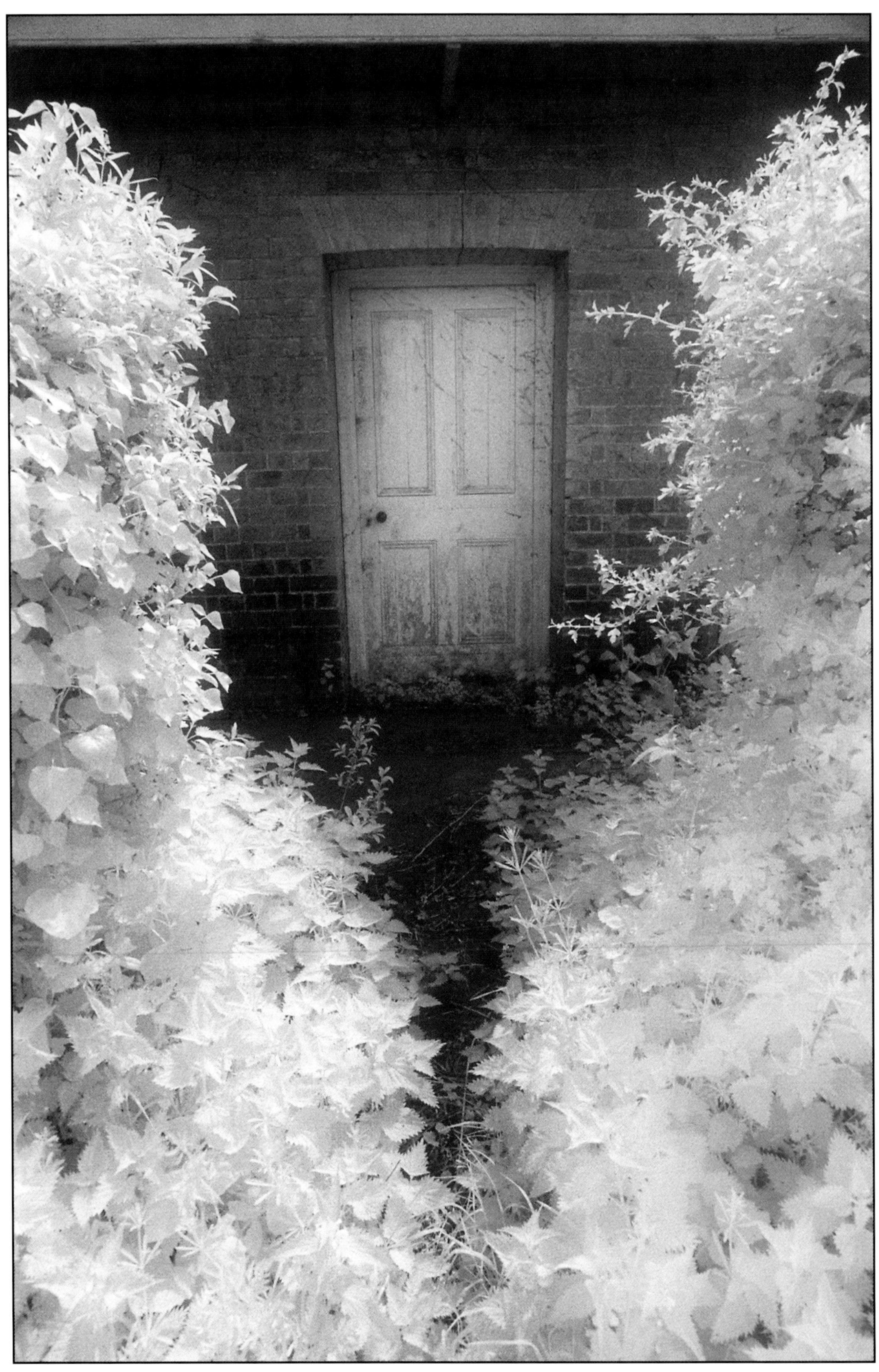

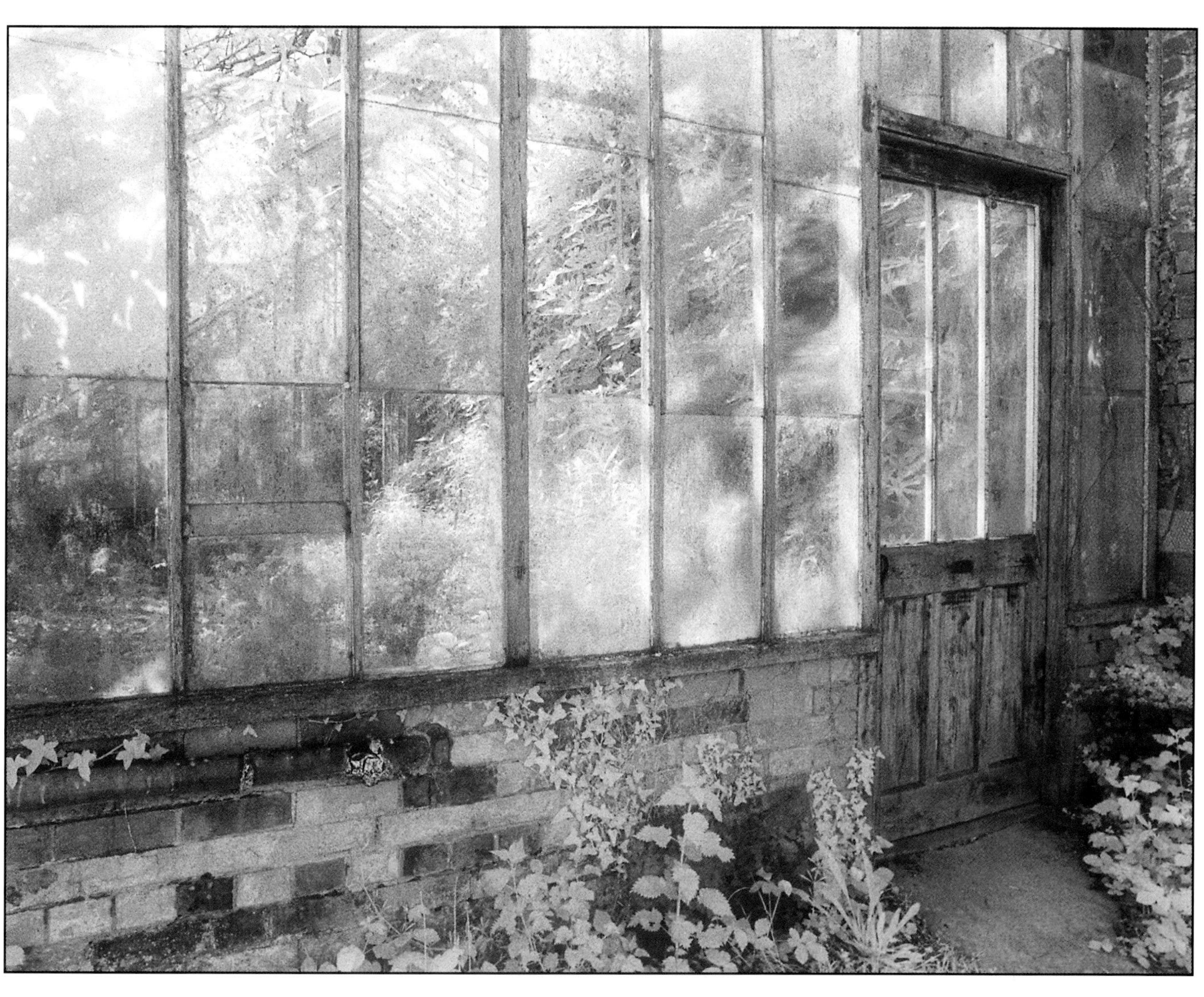

(left) 121 **Doorway**, *Kathleen Harcom*
(above) 122 **The old greenhouse**, *Kathleen Harcom*

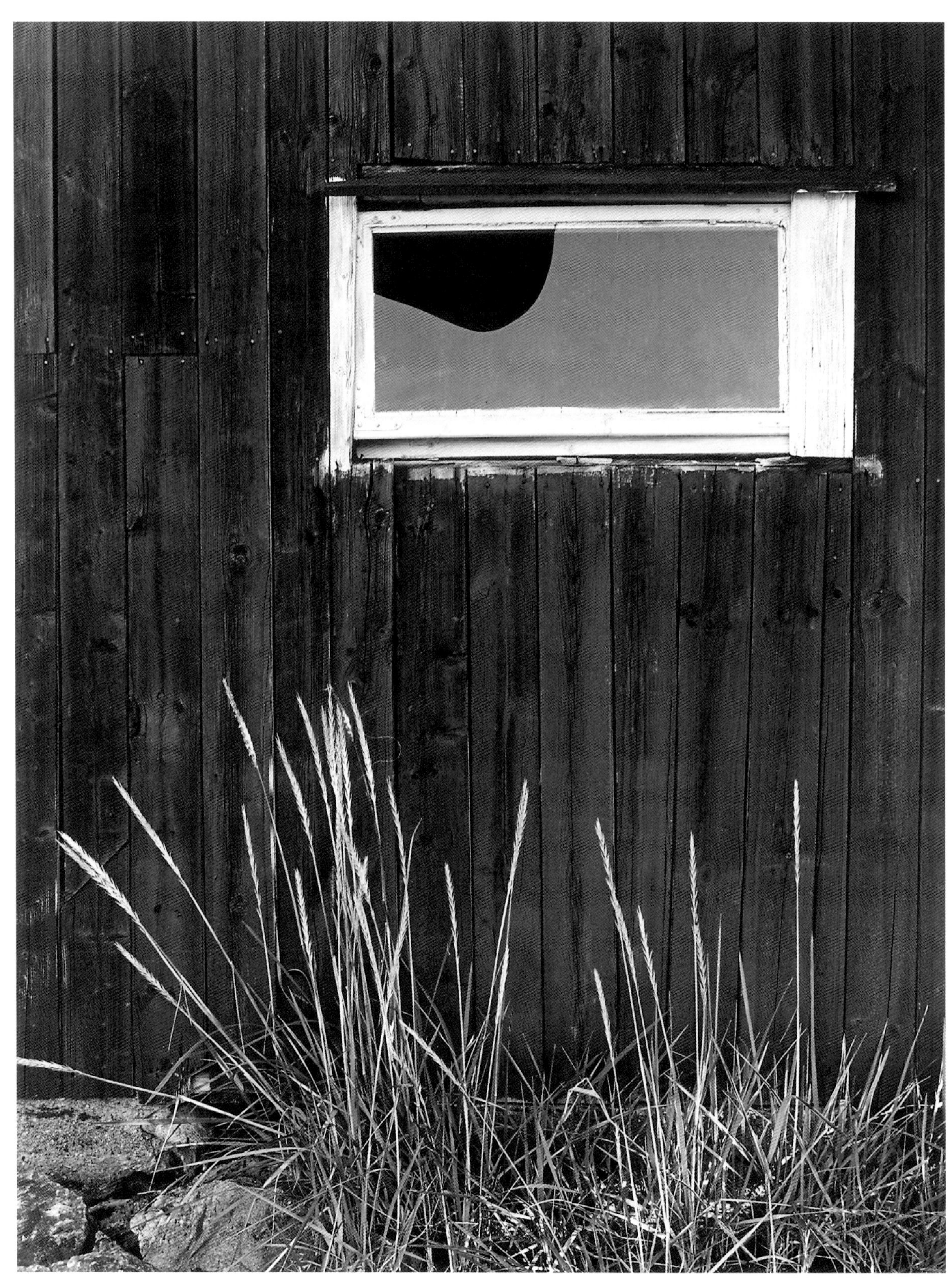

123
Broken window
Len Perkis

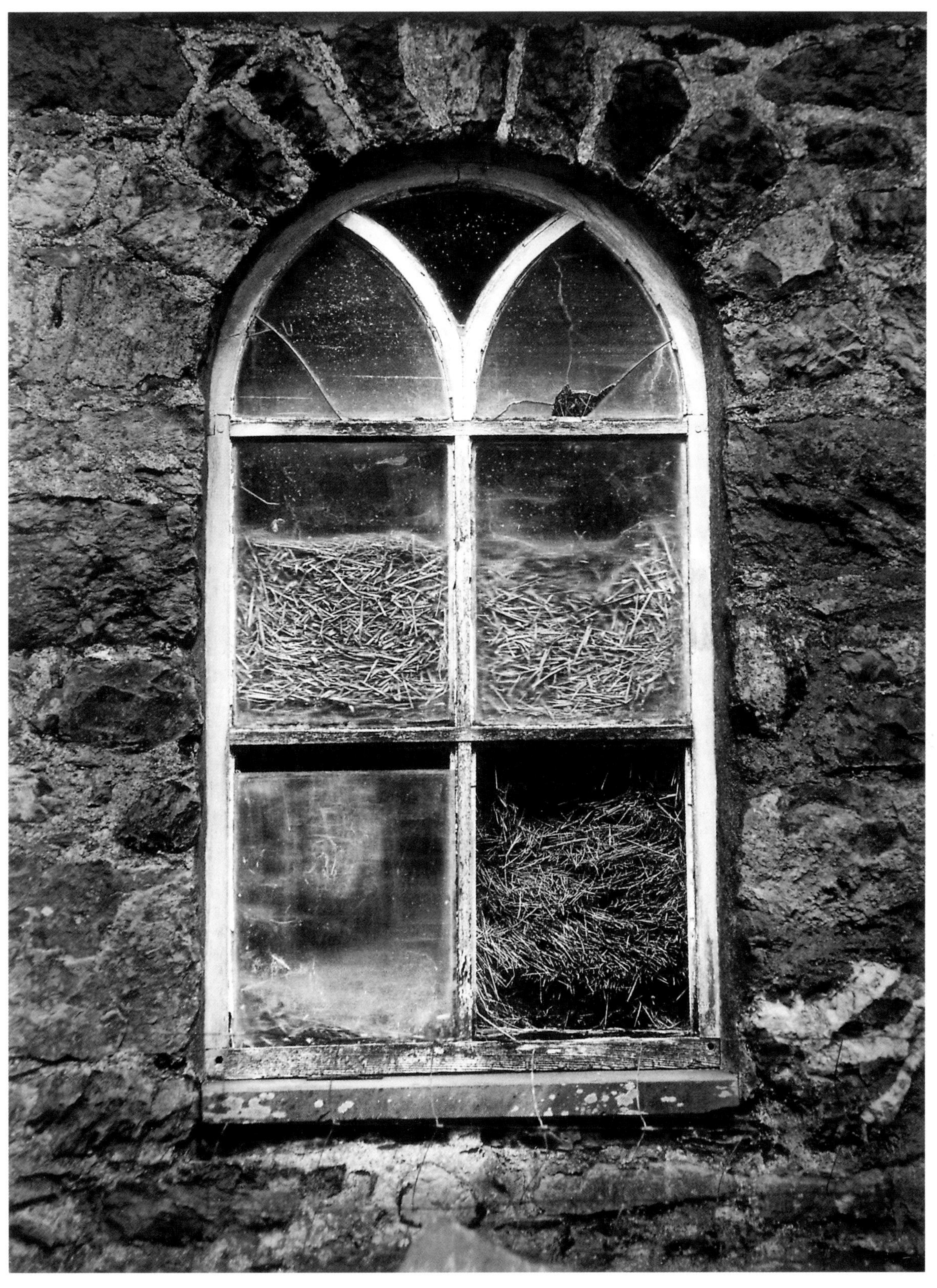

124
Diolchgarwch
O Tudur Owen

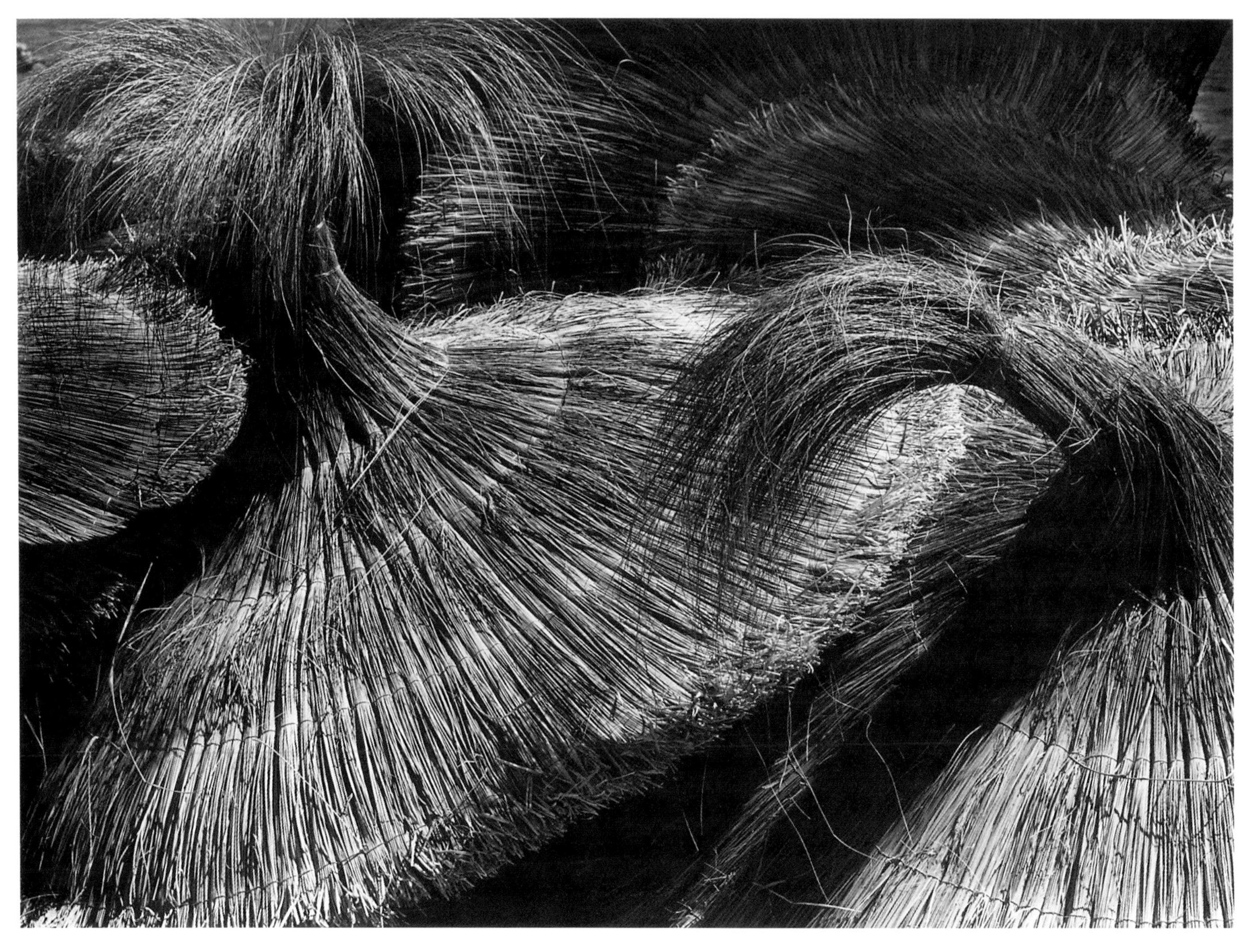

(above) 125 **Sunshades**, *Hazel Sanderson*
(top right) 126 **Pine cones and needles**, *James Austin*
(bottom right) 127 **Roscoff seaweed**, *Shay Nichol*

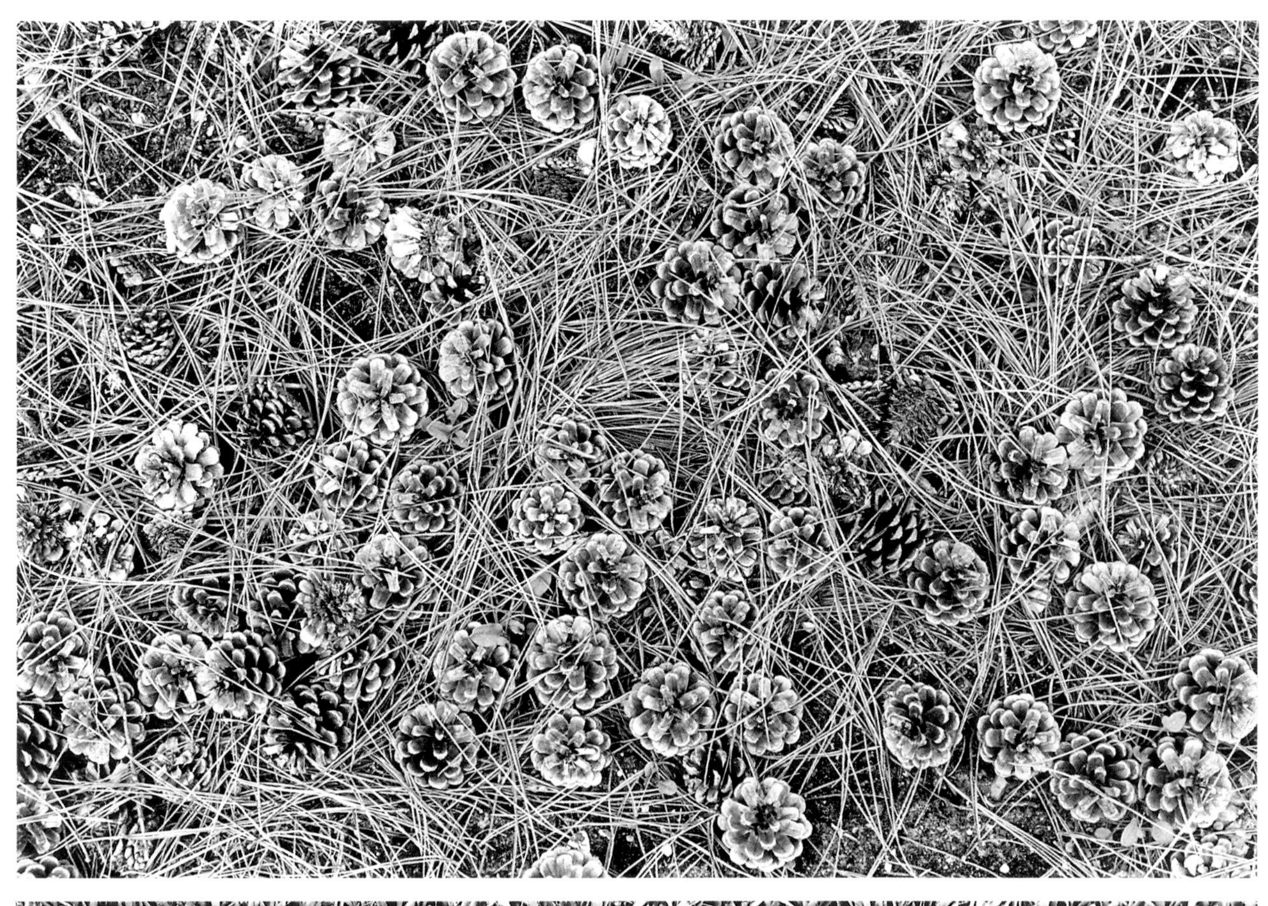

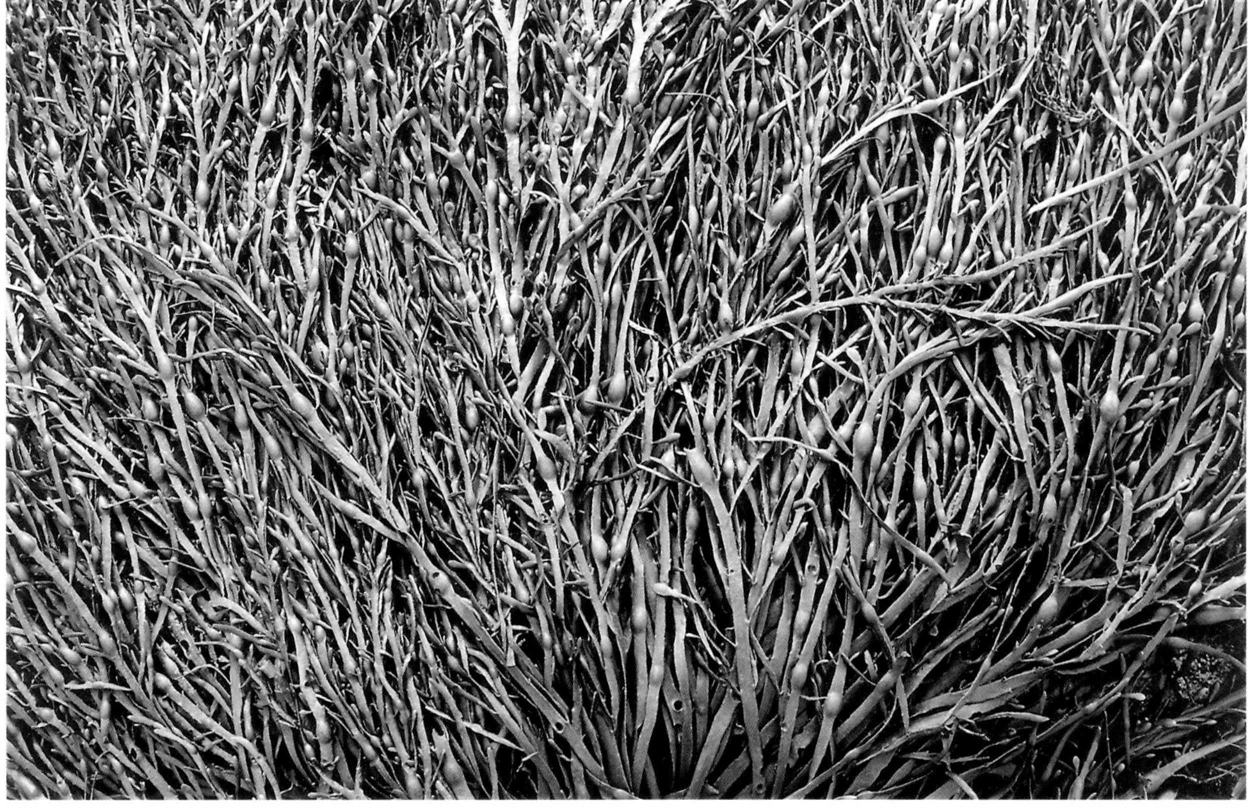

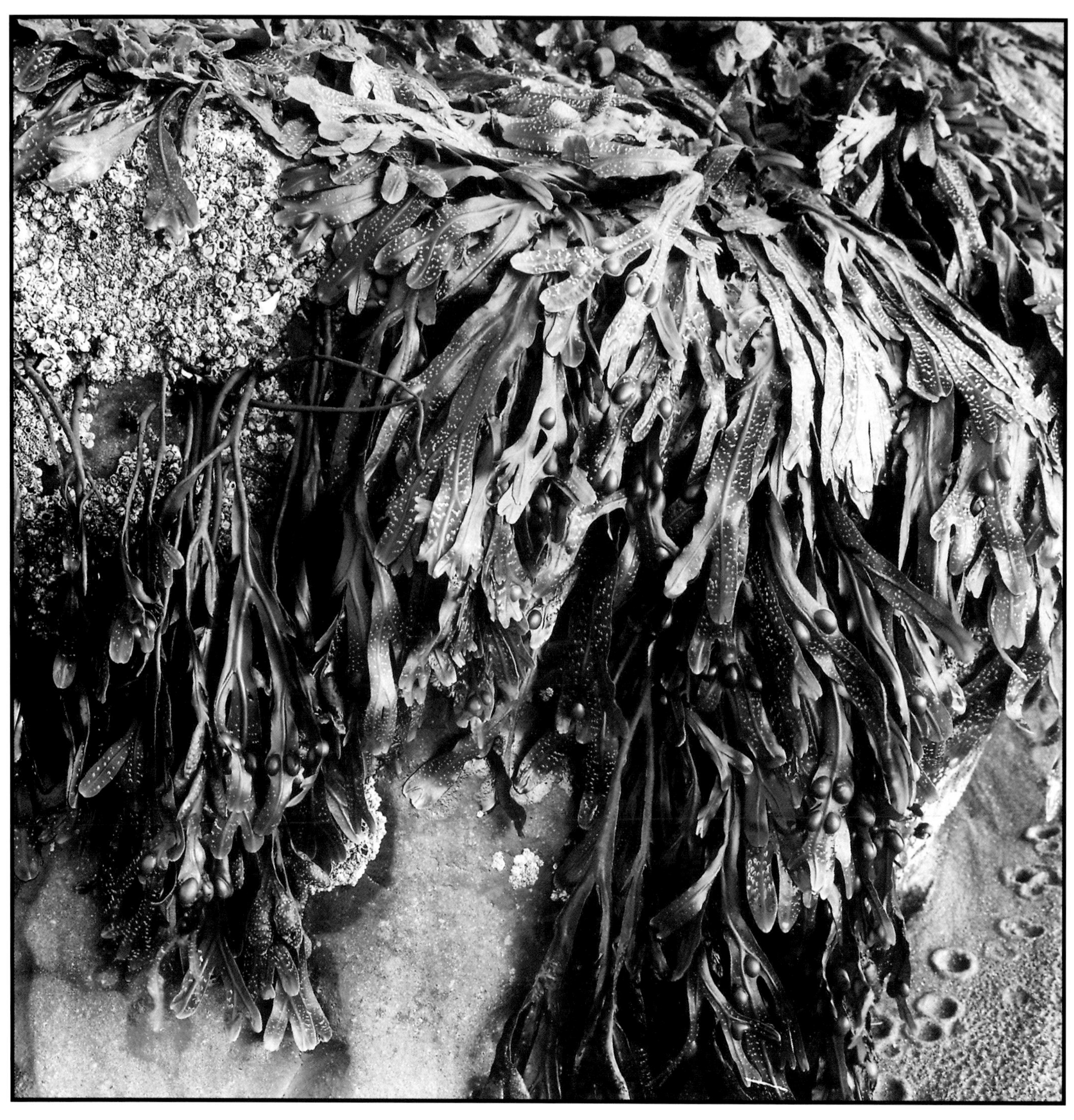

(above) 128 **No title**, *Paul Schofield*
(right) 129 **Connemara stream**, *John Day*

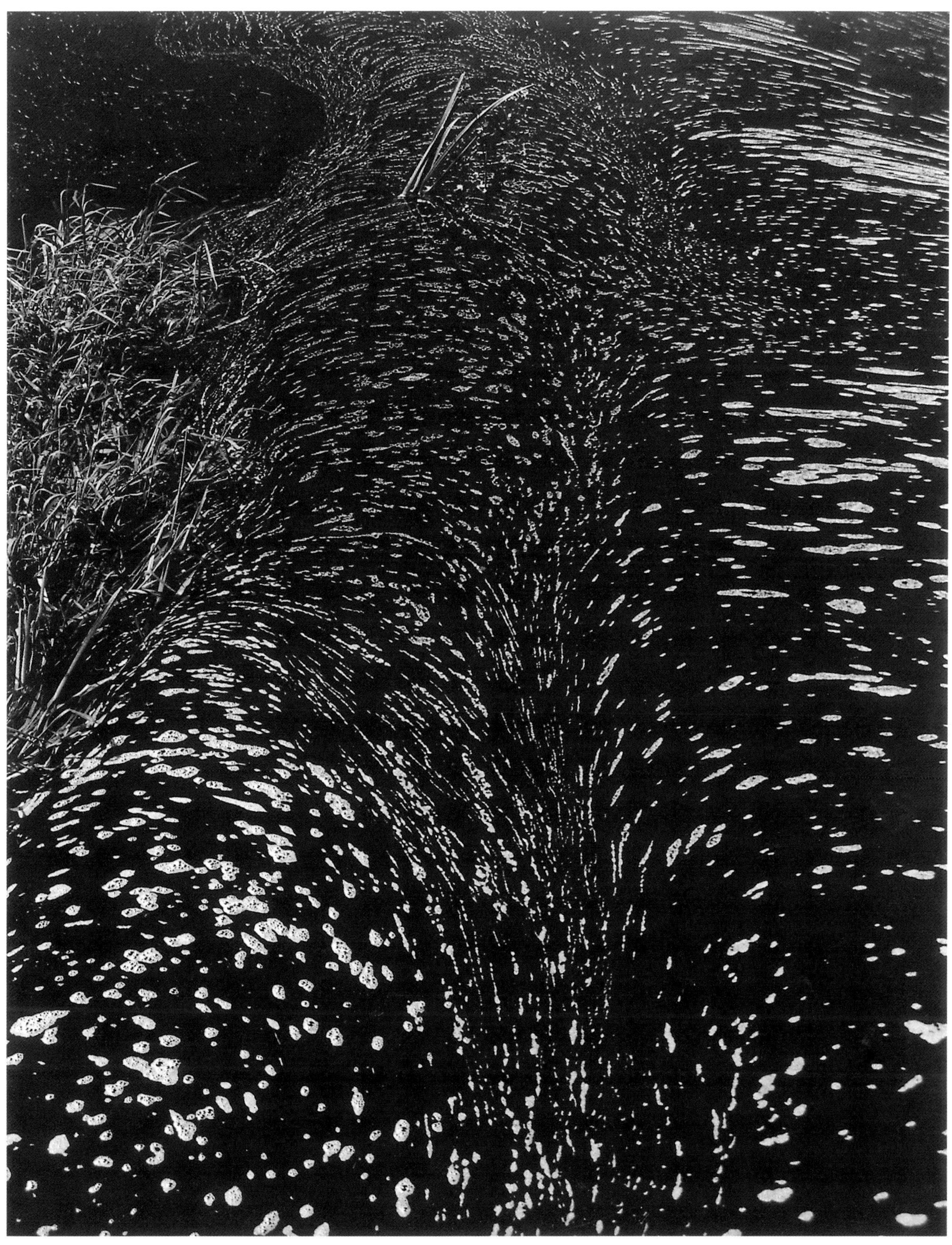

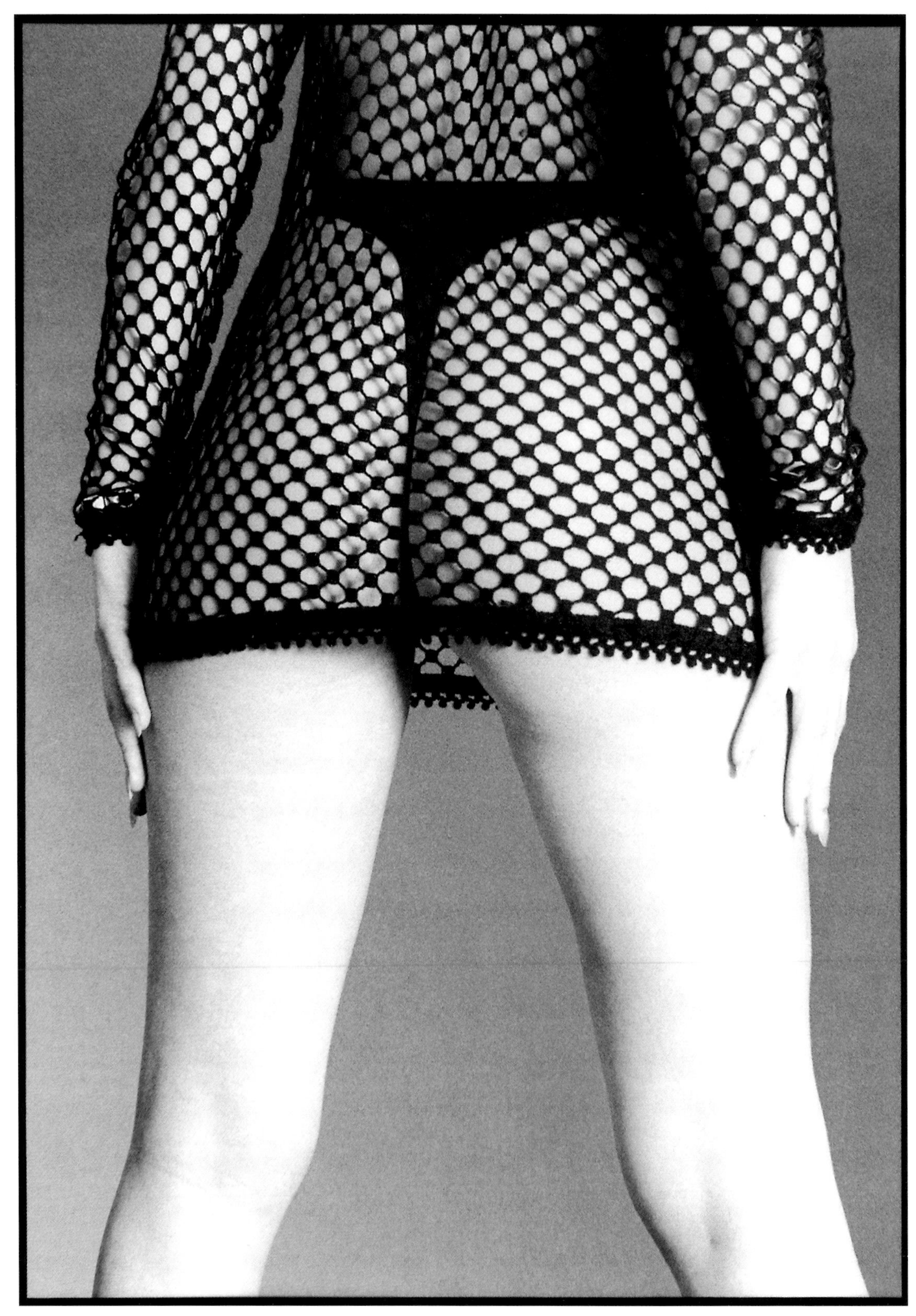

130
The stance
Cliff Street

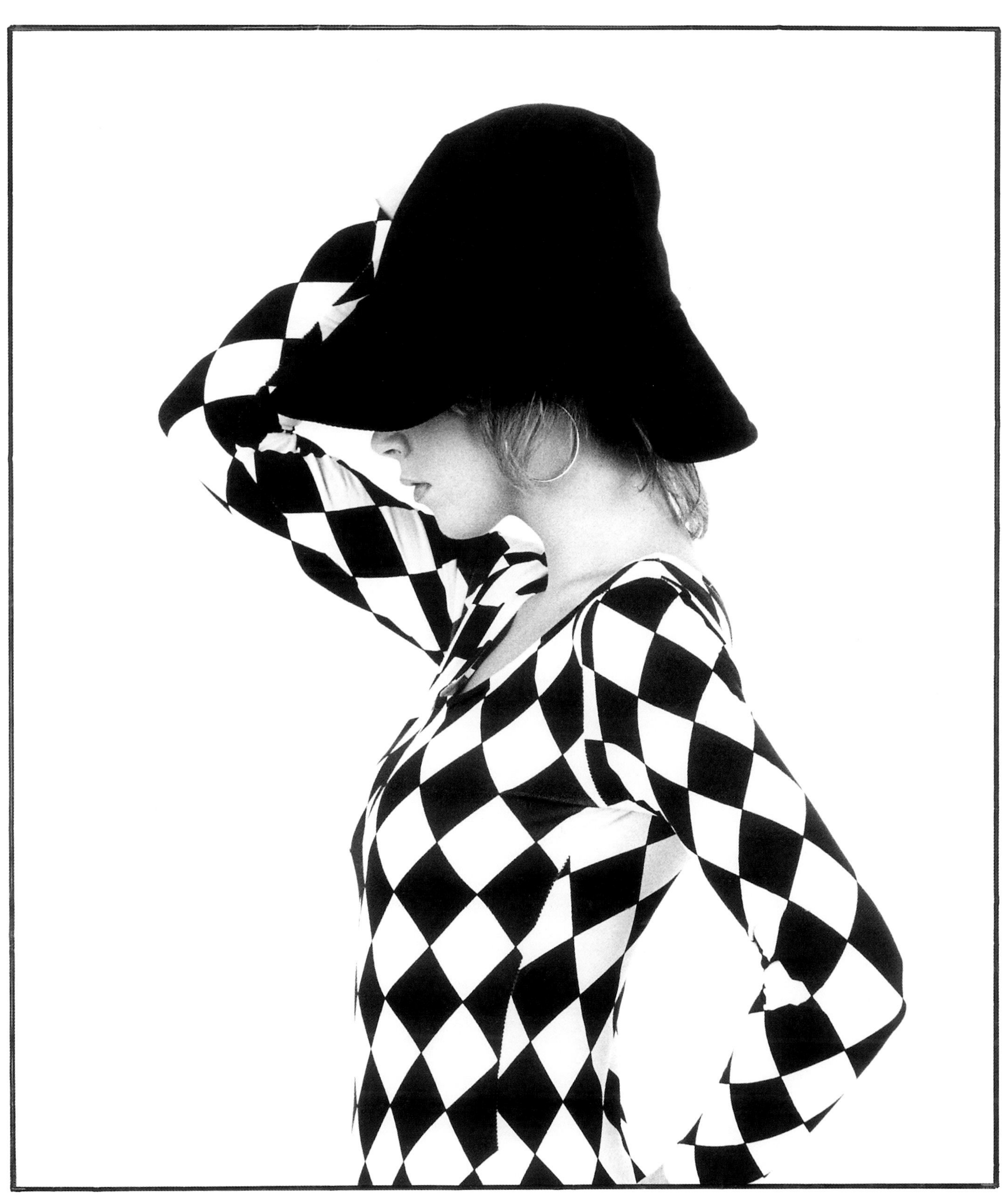

131
Chequers
Ray Anderson

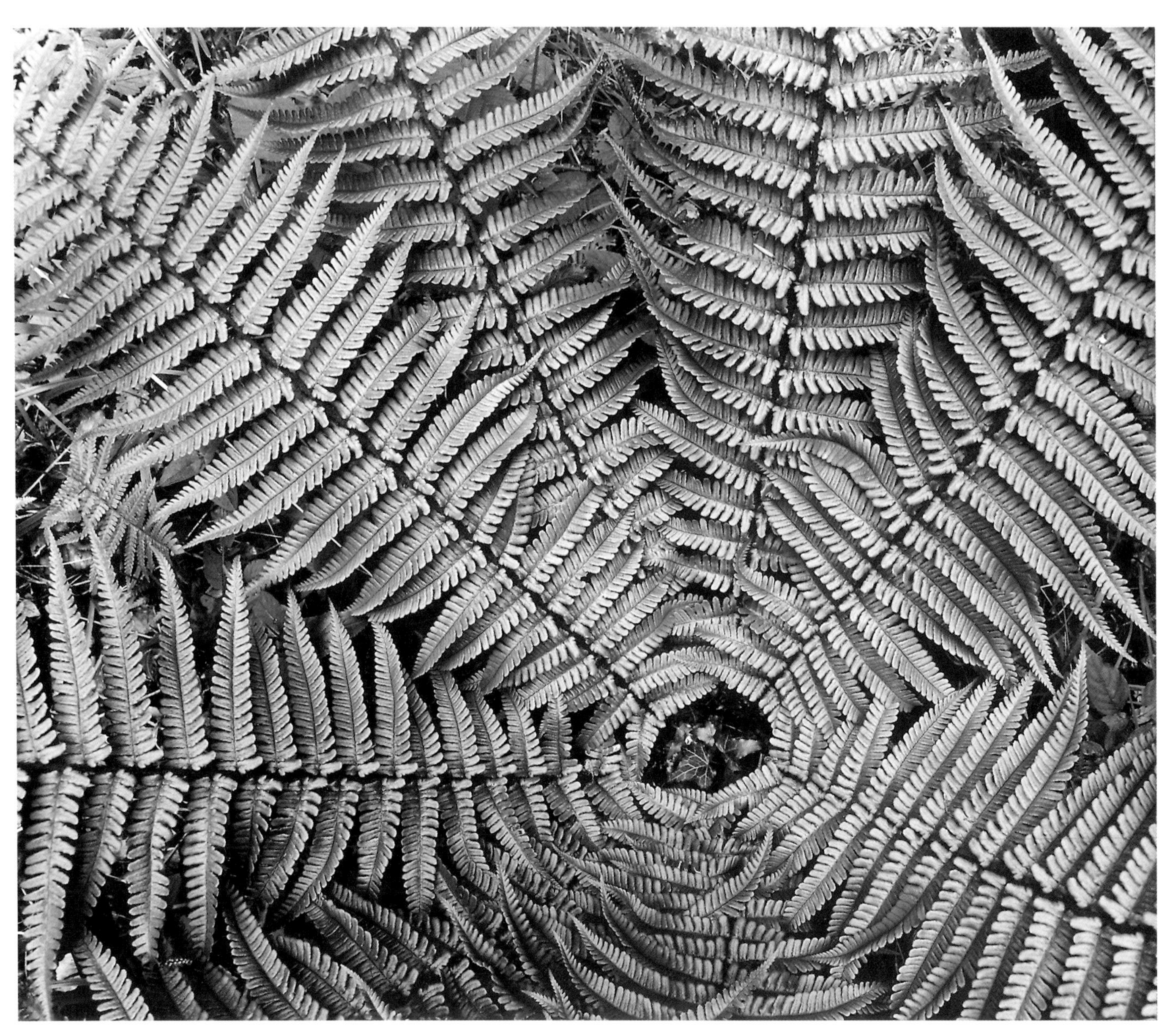

(above) 132 **Radiation**, *Terrick Meakin*
(top right) 133 **Wheel bearing**, *Geoff Hodgson*
(bottom right) 134 **Cartwheel**, *Geoff Hodgson*

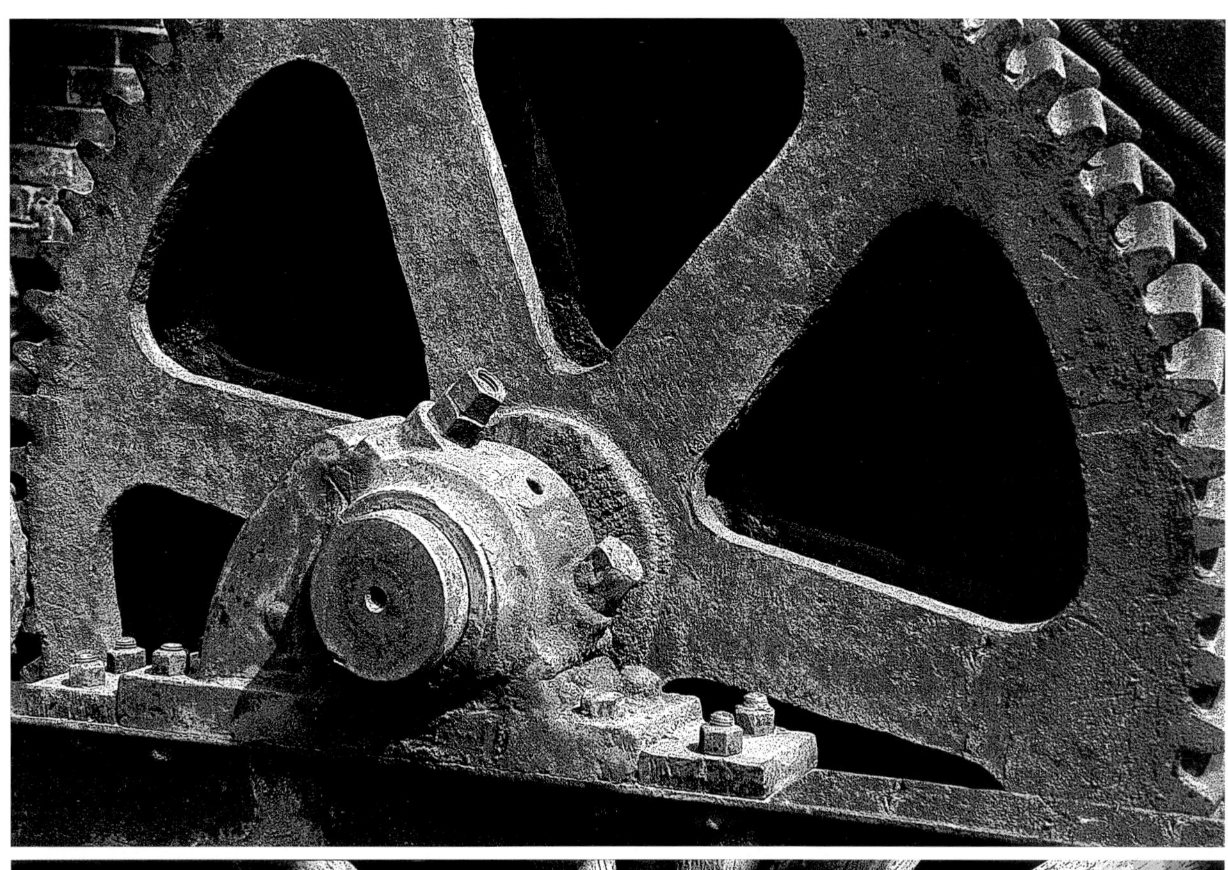

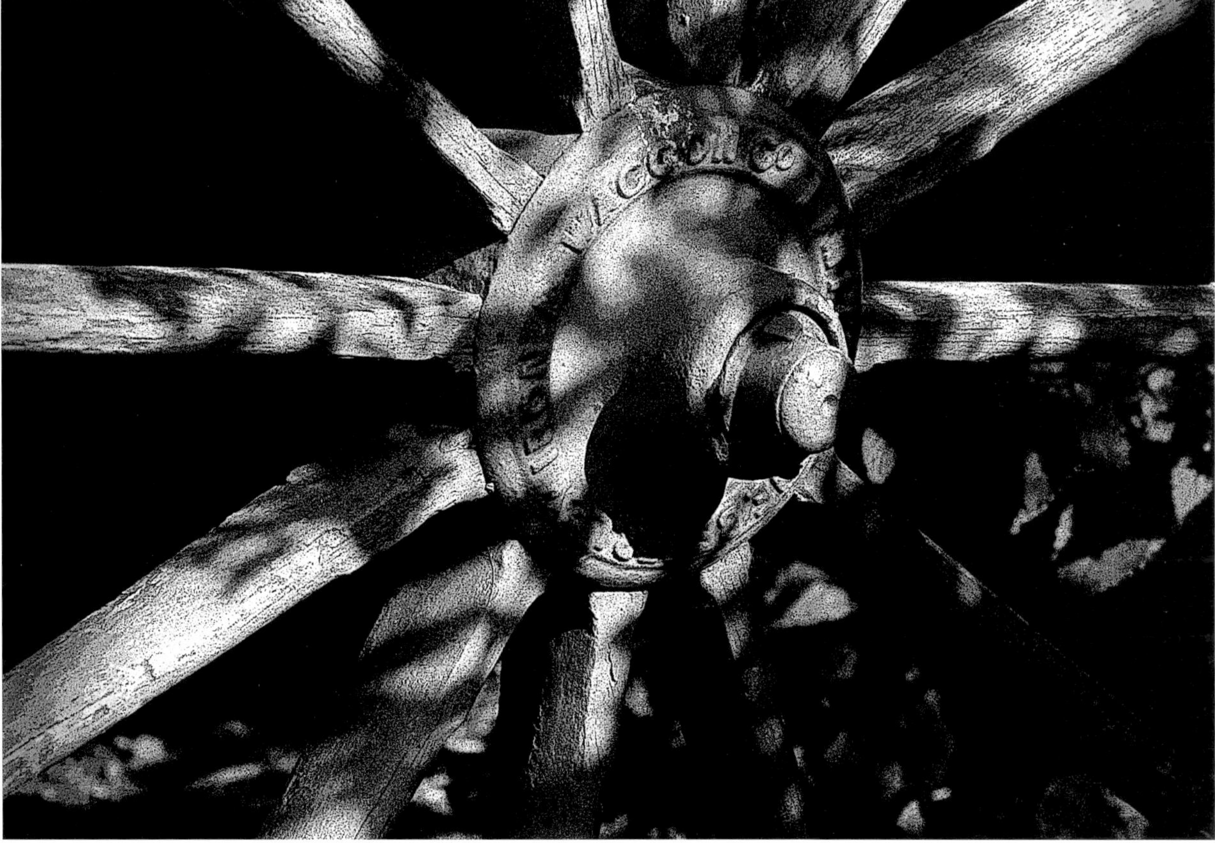

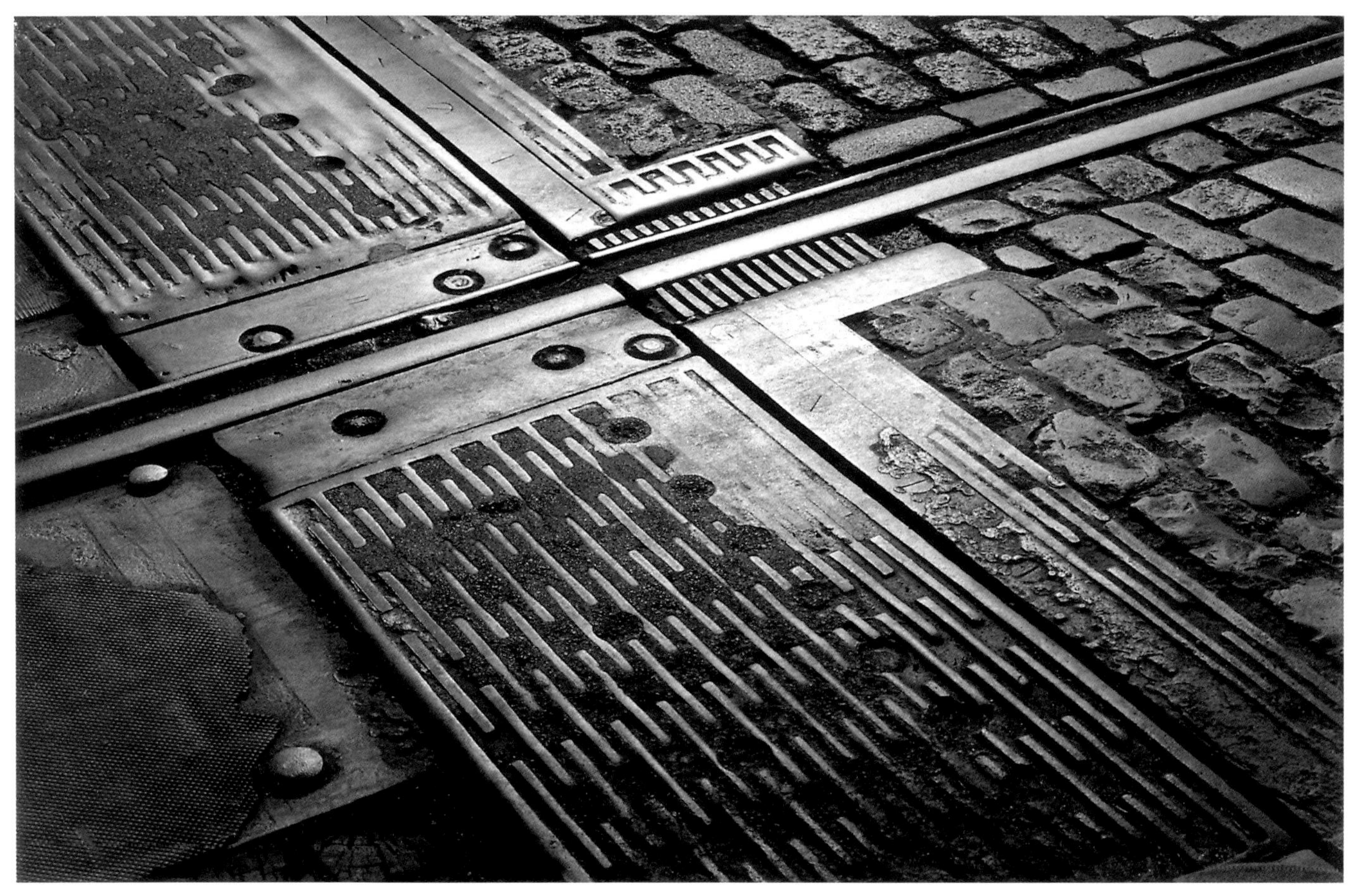

135
Criss Cross
Malcolm Hawkins

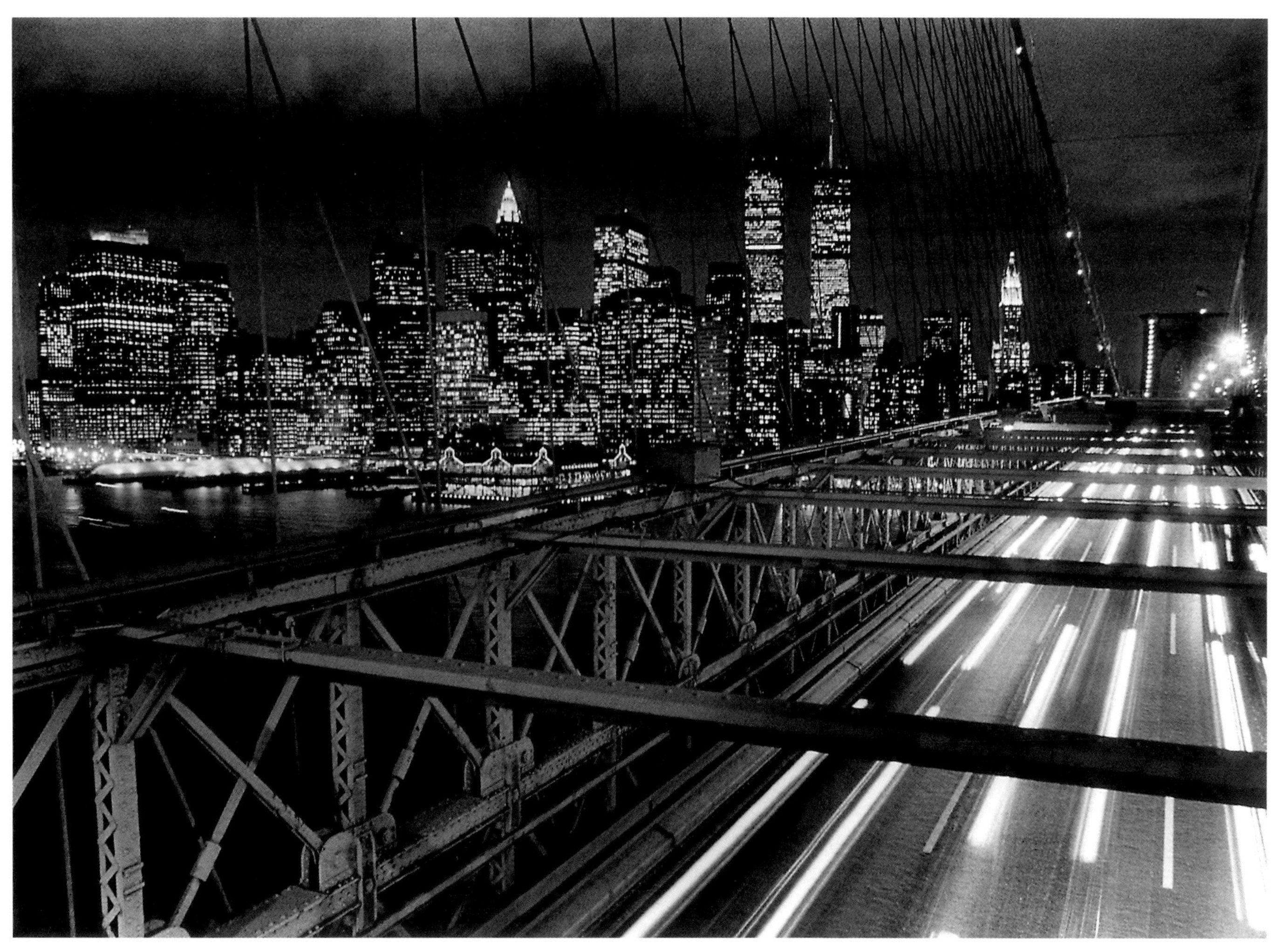

136
Rush hour, New York City
Andy Wilson

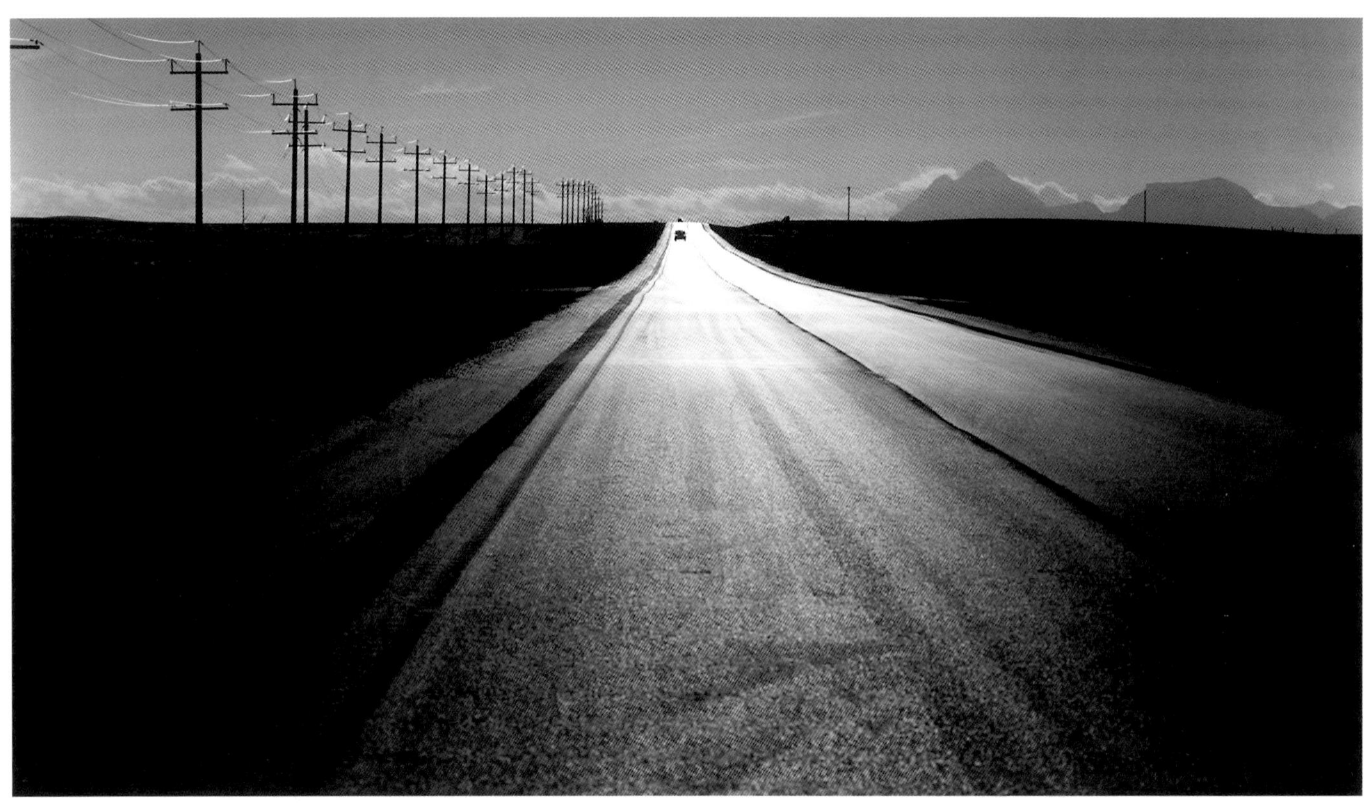

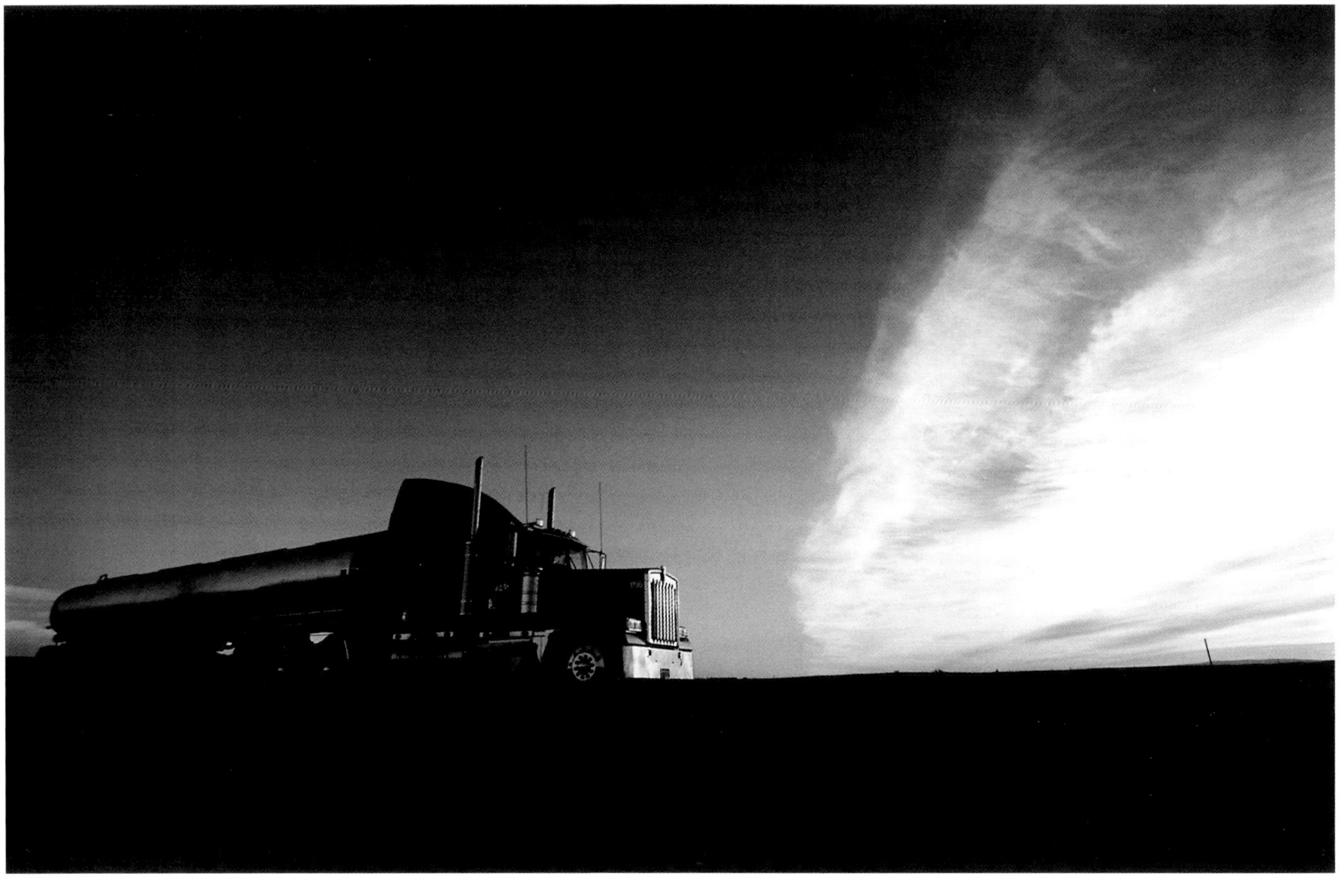

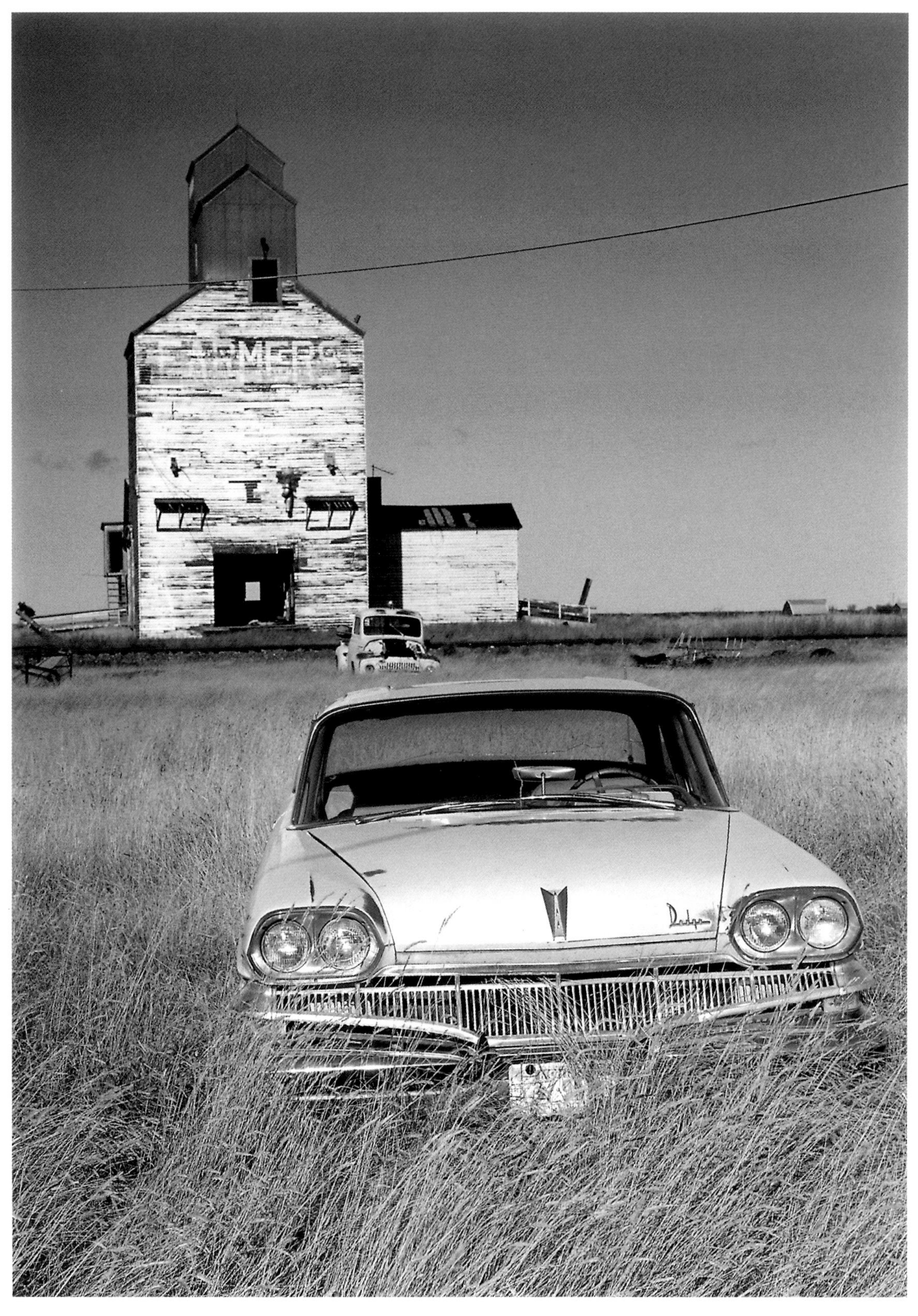

(left) 137 **Sunlit road, Canada**, *Leigh Preston*
(above top) 138 **Kenworth lorry, Green River**, *Leigh Preston*
(bottom) 139 **Old Dodge, Canadian border**, *Leigh Preston*

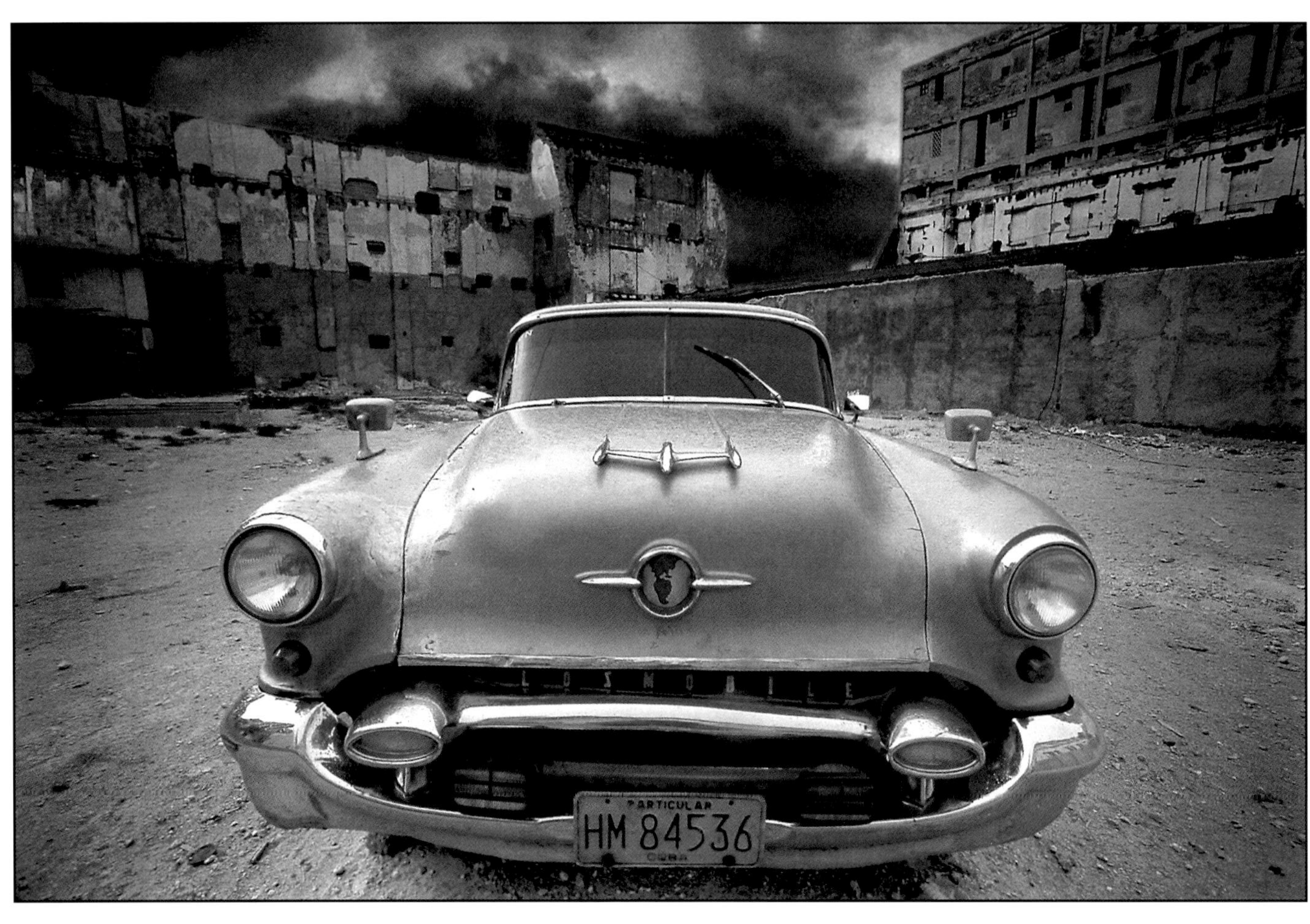

(above) 140 **Dominator**, *Kevin Adlard*
(right) 141 **Cuban classic**, *Kevin Adlard*

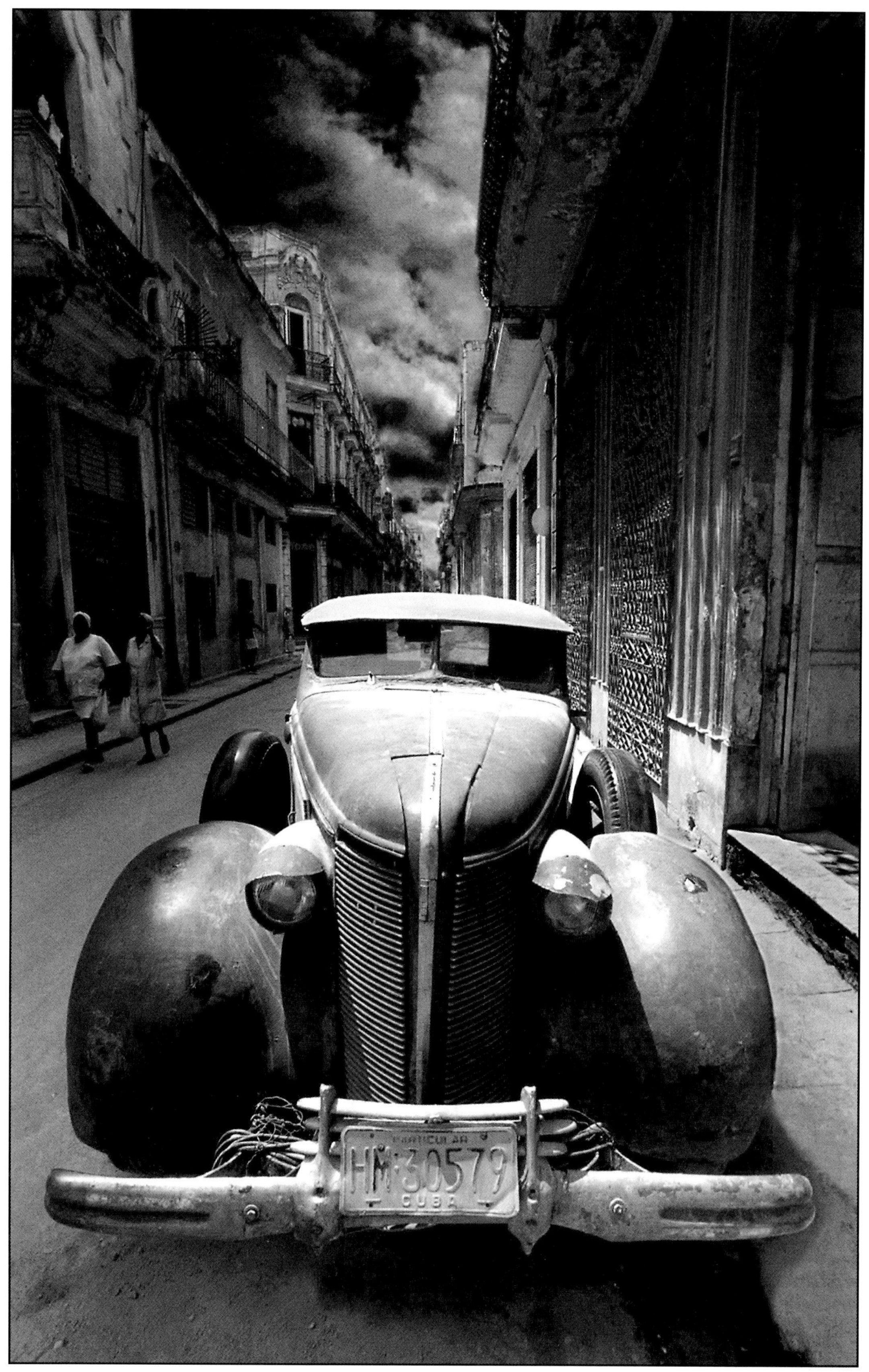
HM 30579
CUBA

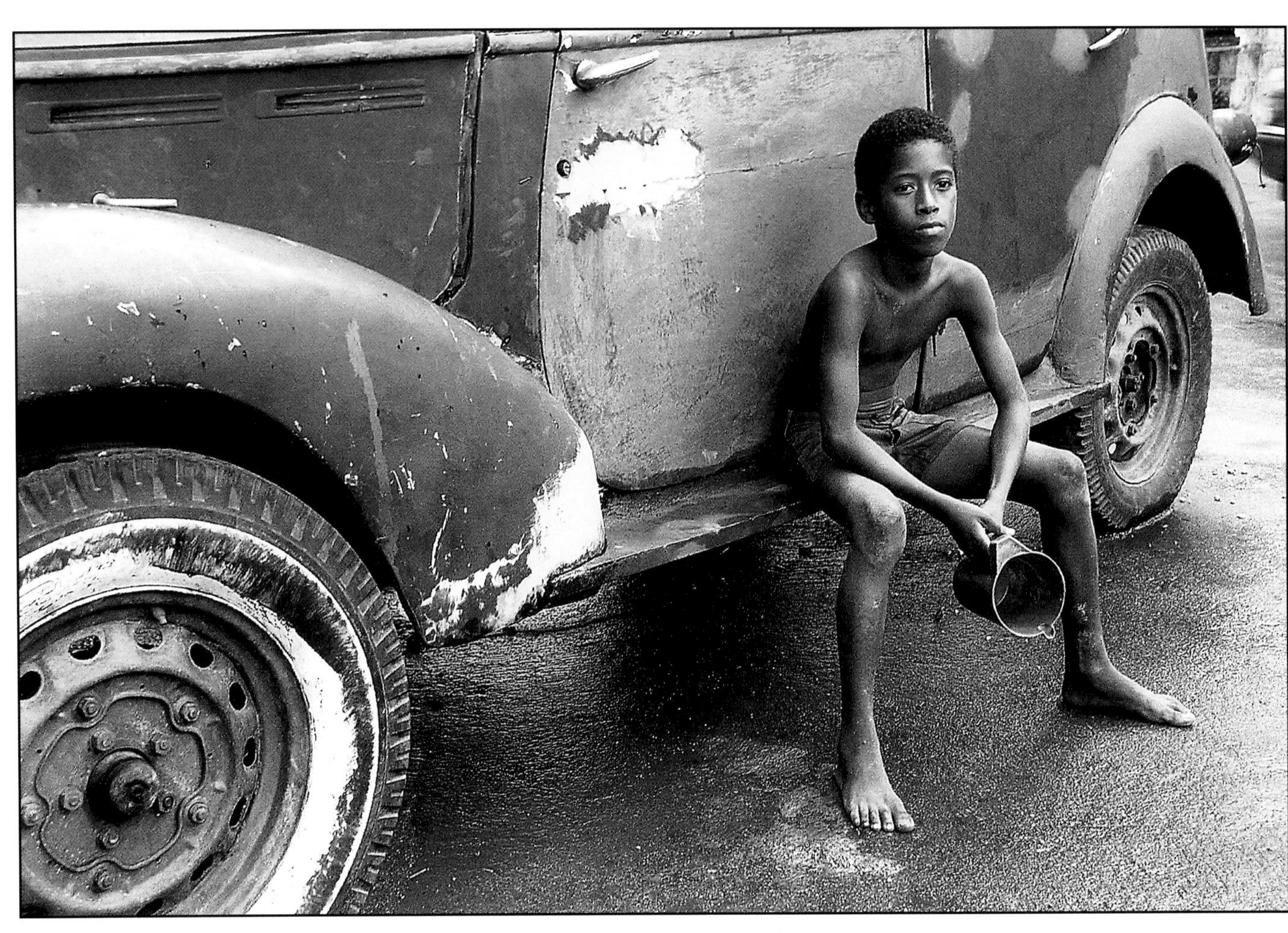

(above) 142 **Street kid, Havana**, *Kevin Adlard*
(top right) 143 **Cyclist**, *Roger Slade*
(bottom right) 144 **Cab driver (self portrait)**, *Ken Payne*

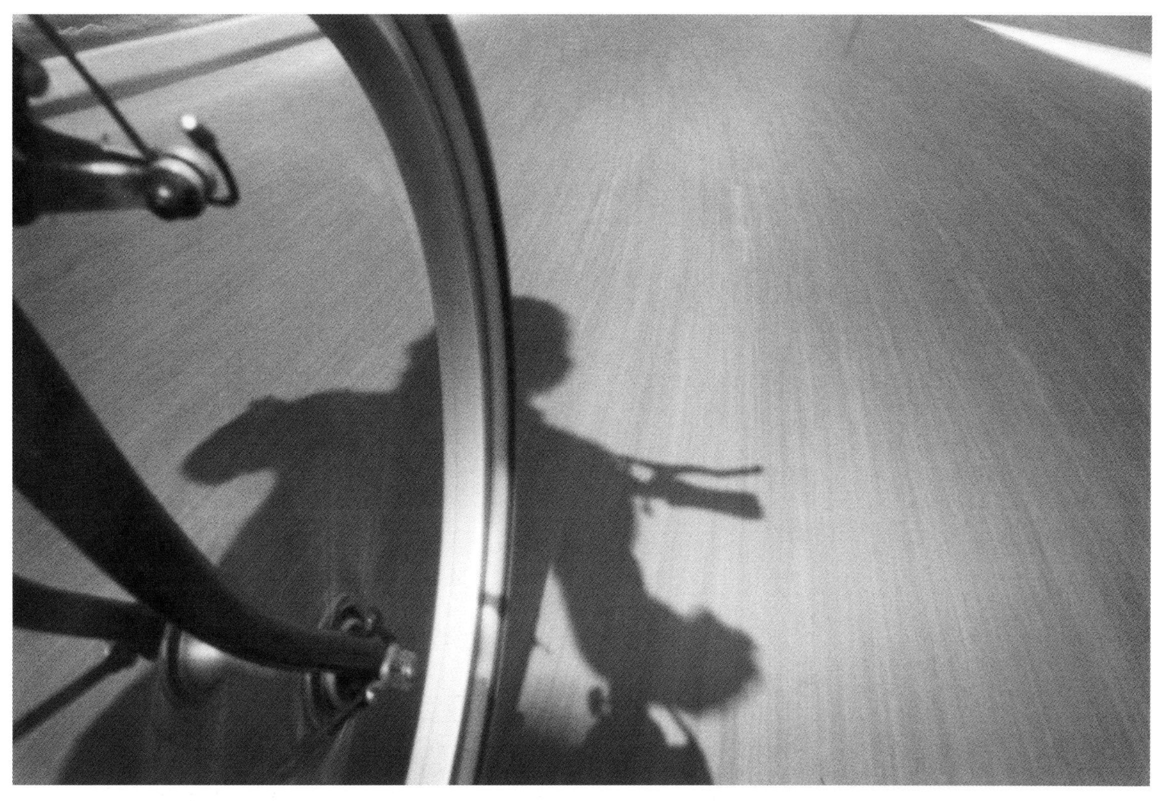

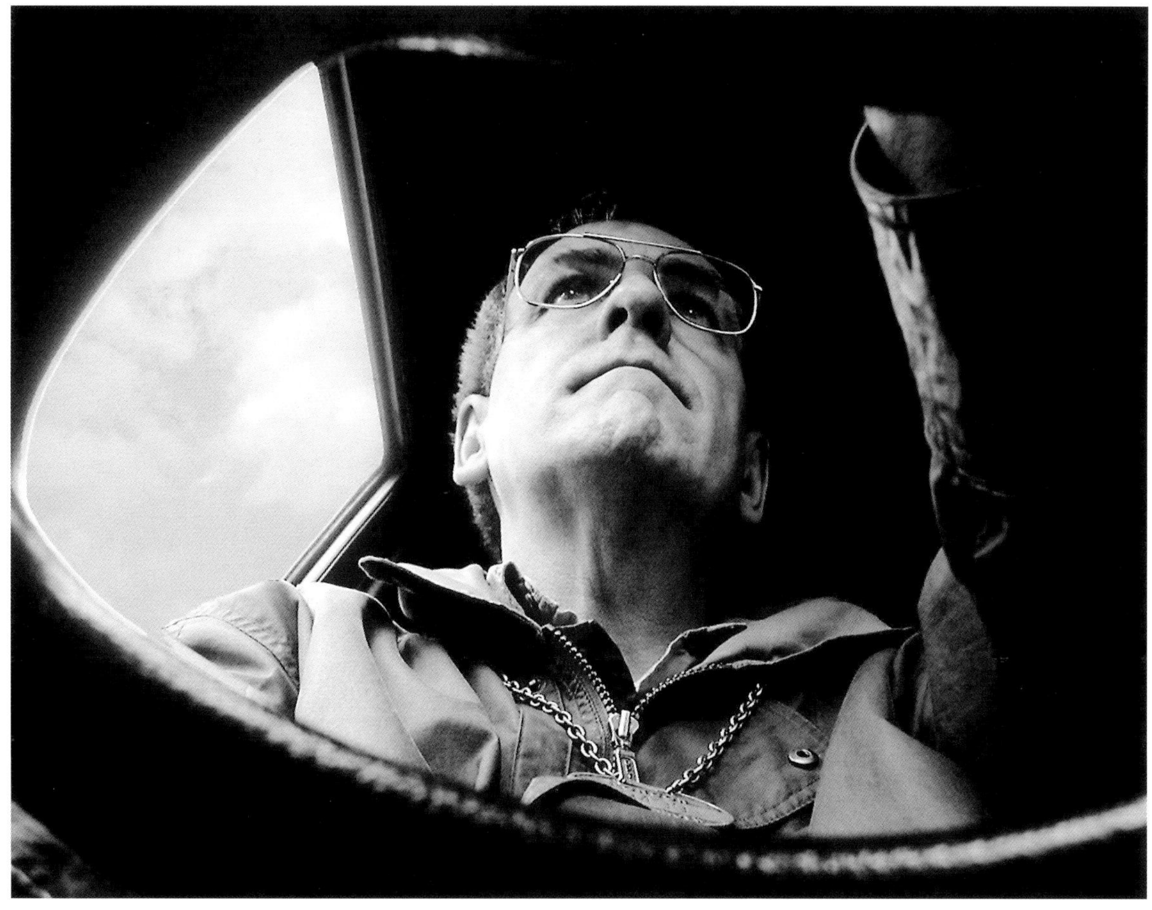

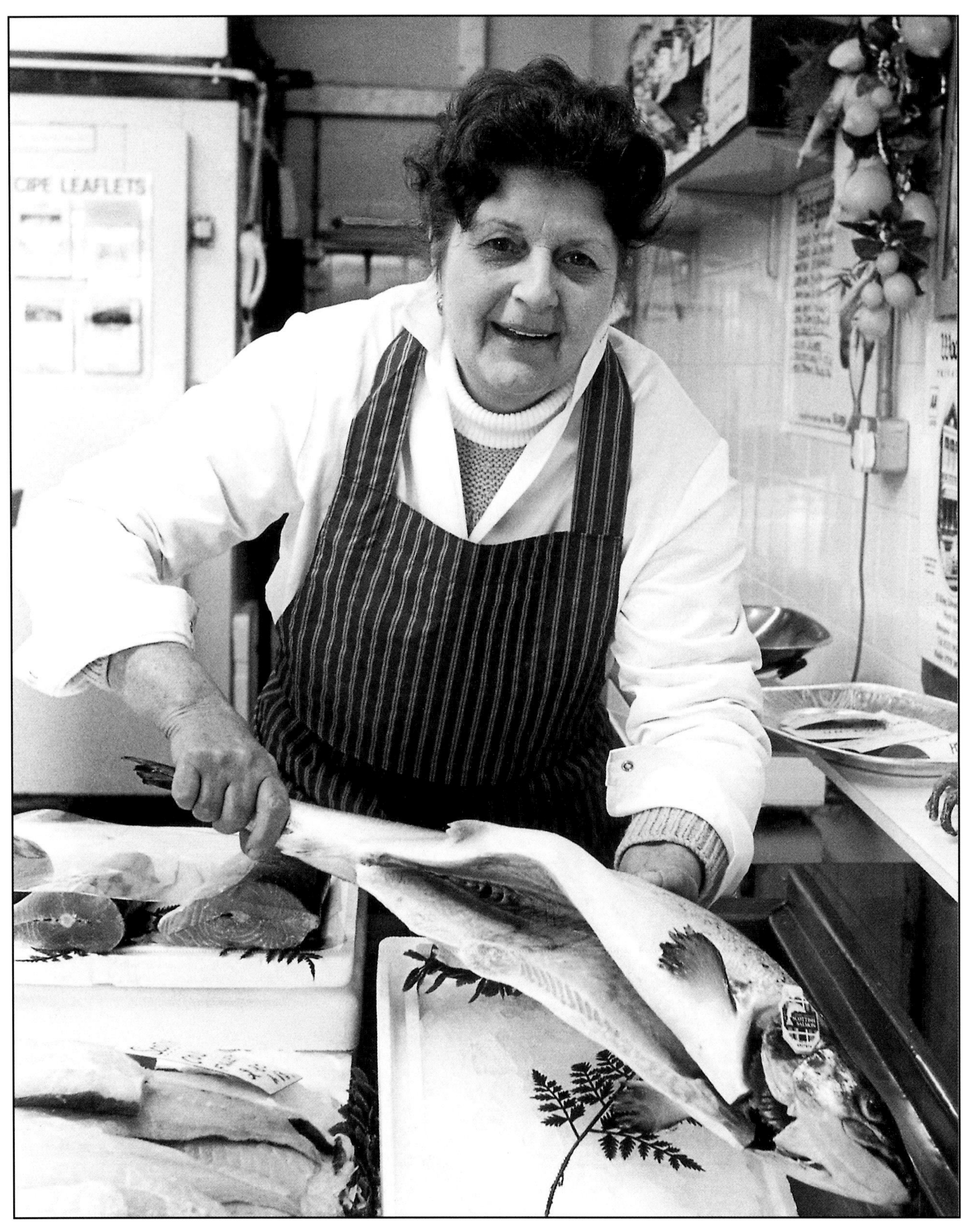

145
Dolly Atherton, fishmonger
John Fairclough

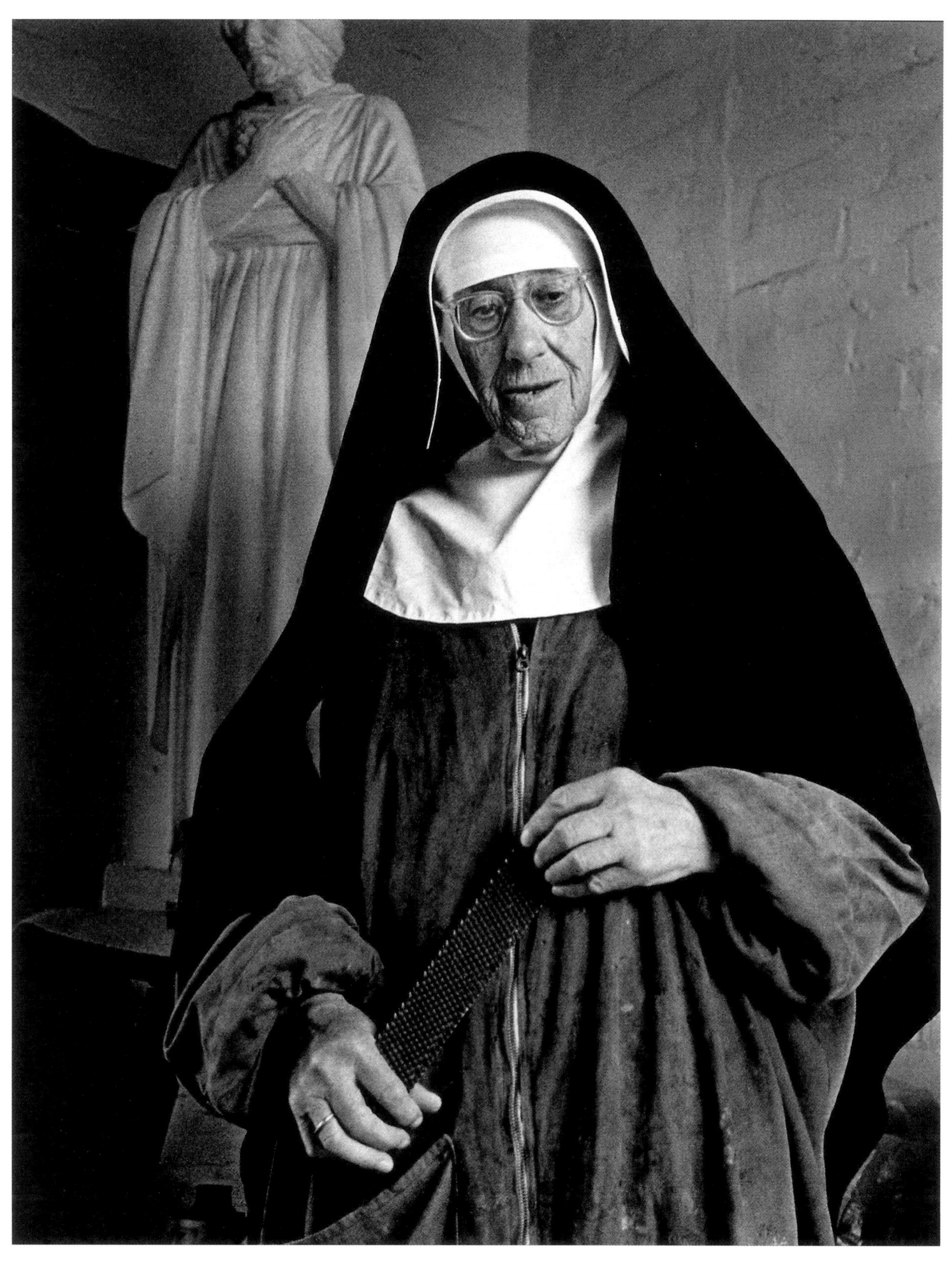

146
Nun in repair shop
Trevor Fry

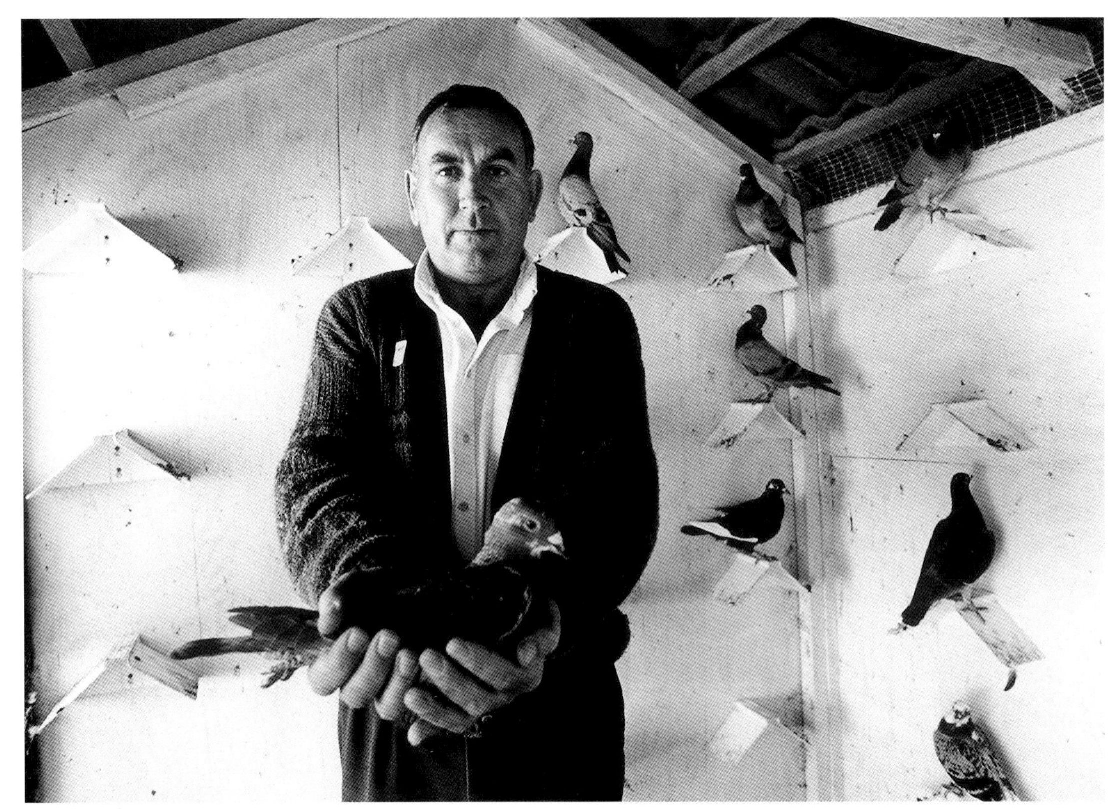

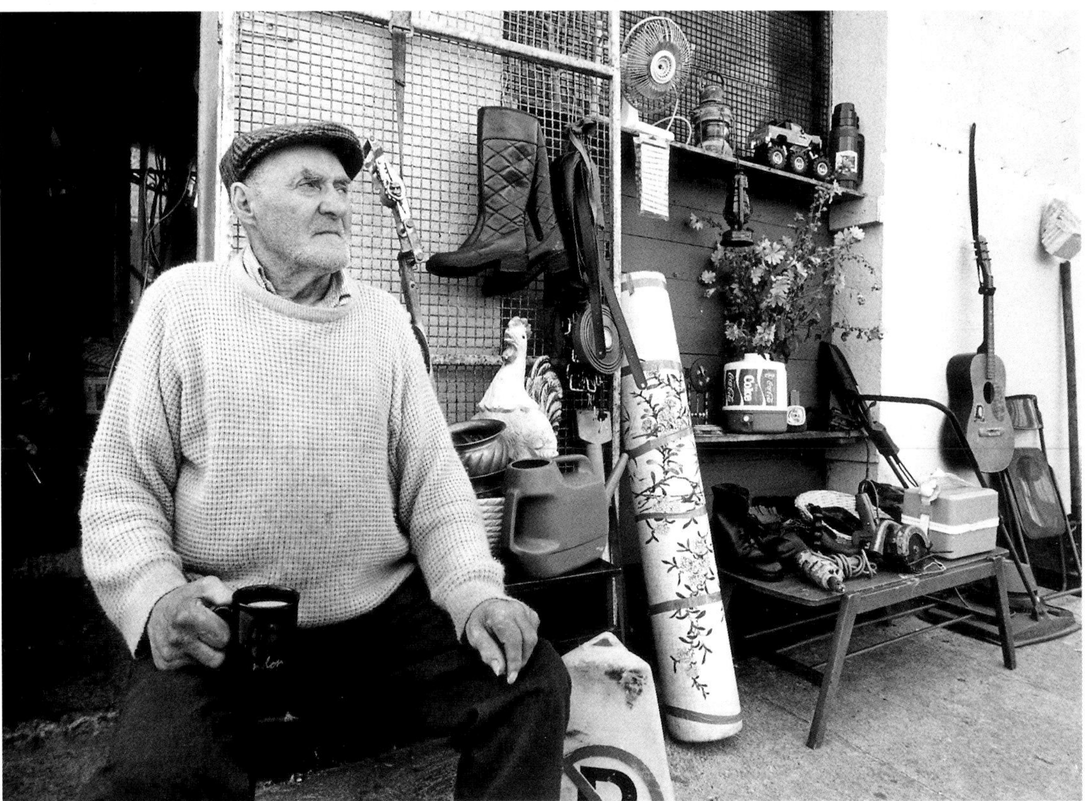

(top) 147 **Pigeon fancier**, *Michael Feeney*
(bottom) 148 **Tea break**, *Michael Feeney*

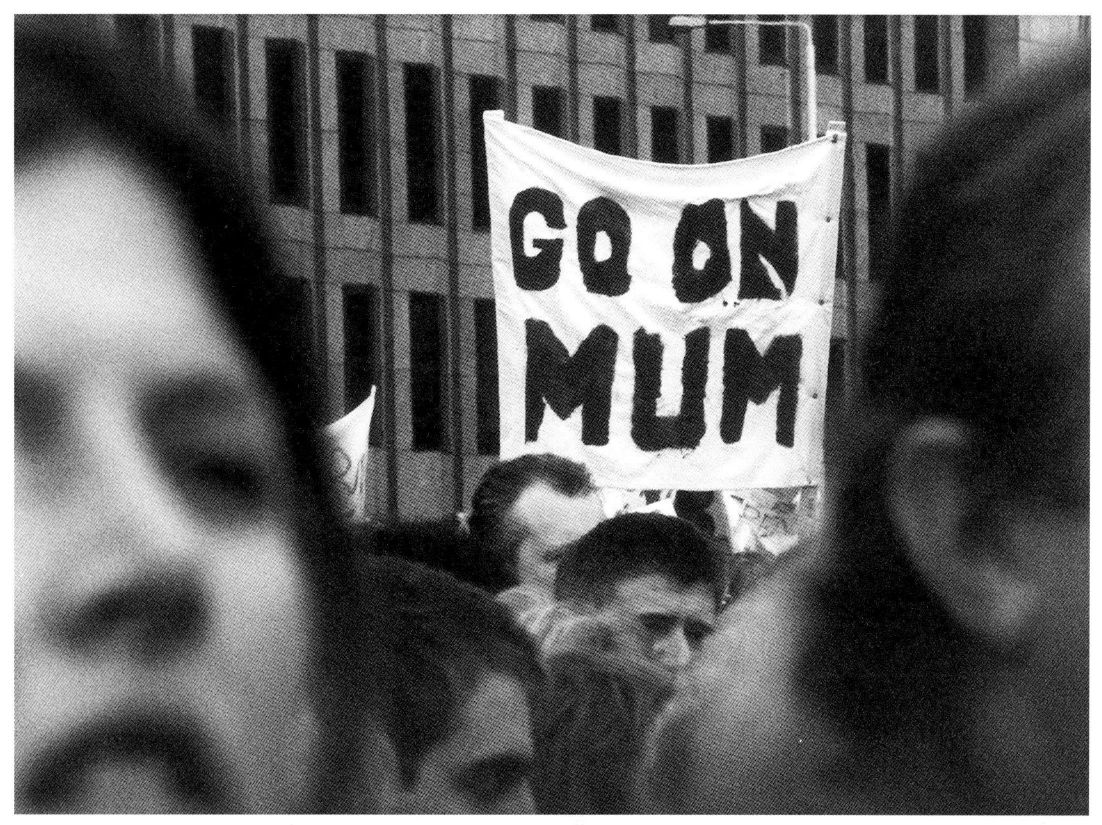

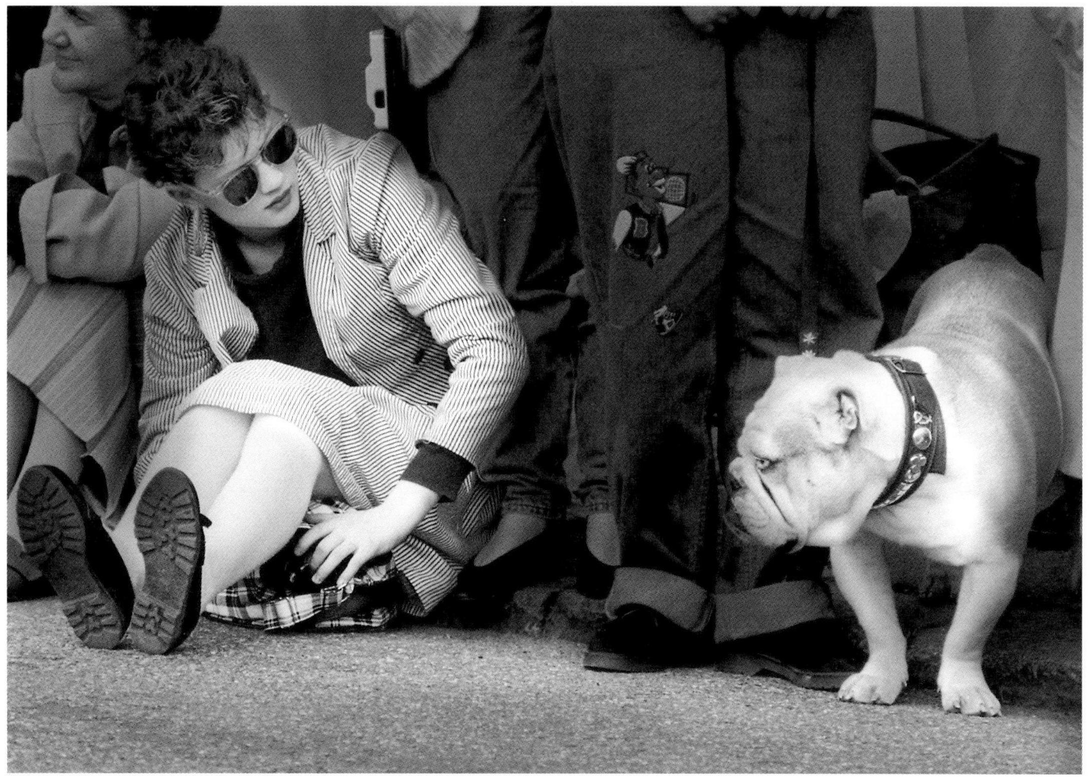

(top) 149 **Spirit of the London Marathon '99**, *Robert Arthur*
(bottom) 150 **Waiting for the parade**, *Paul Lambeth*

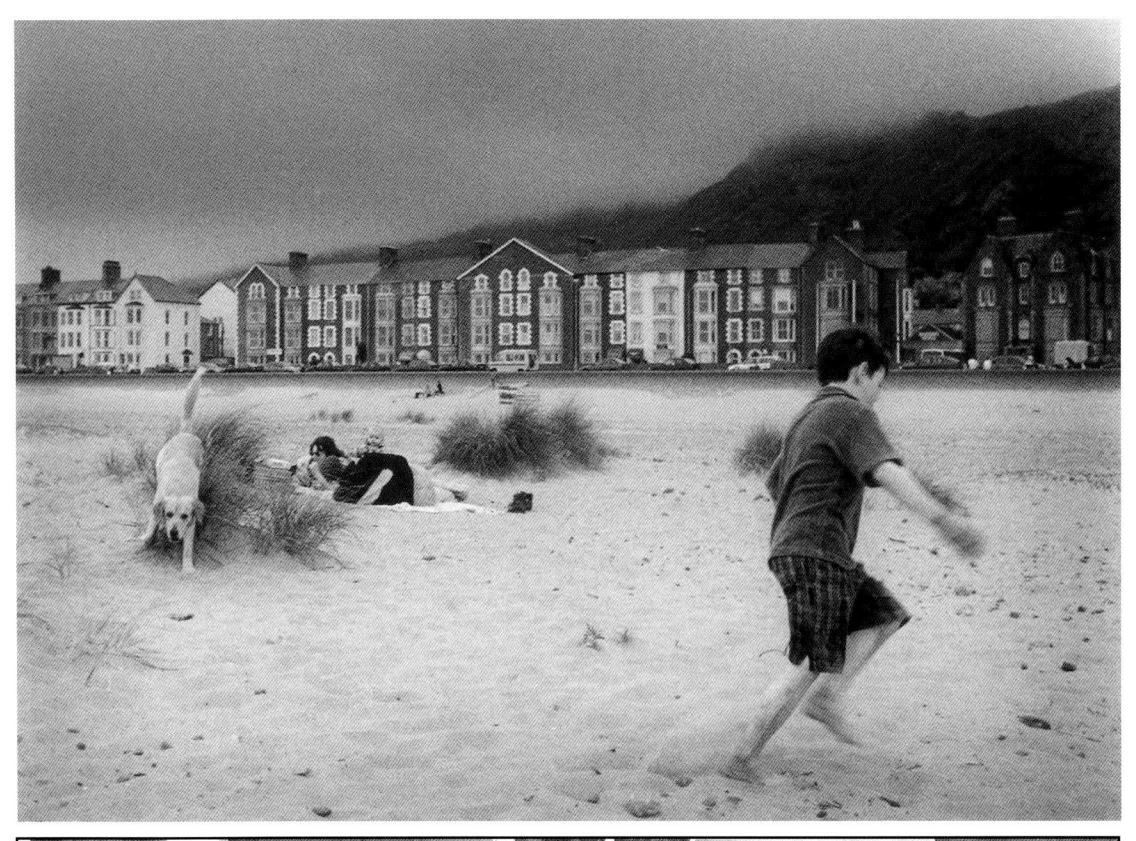

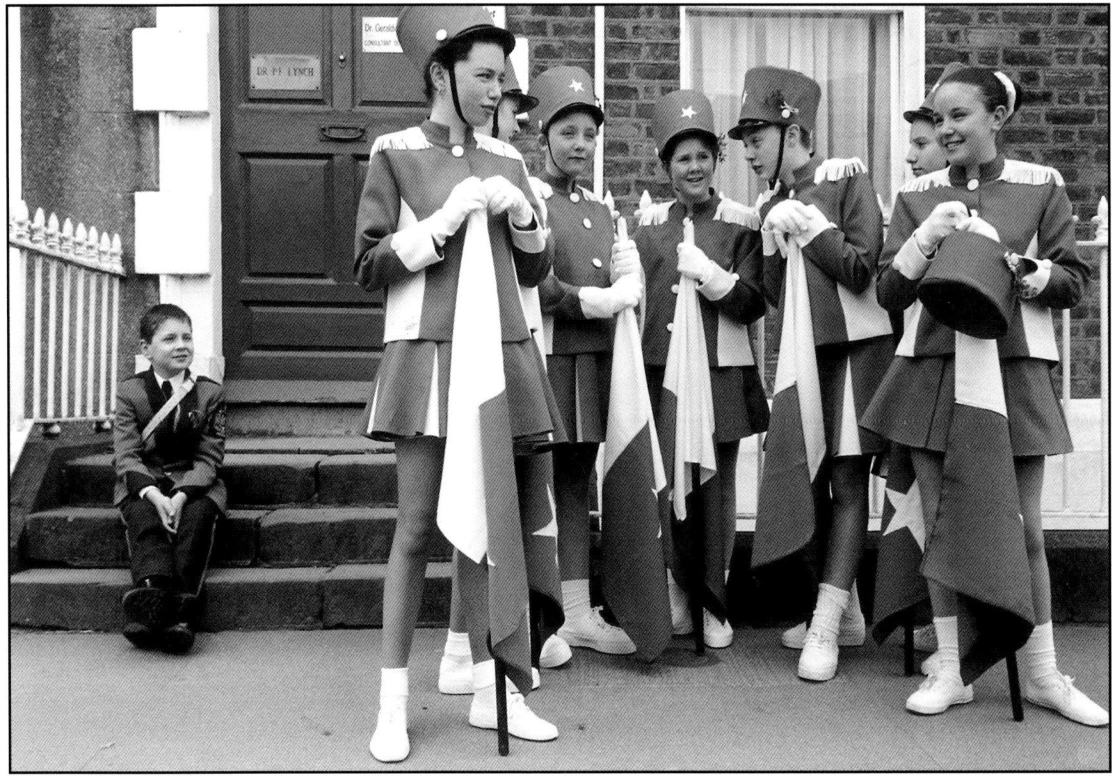

(top) 151 **Quintessentially English**, *Paul Silk*
(bottom) 152 **St Patrick's Day, Drogheda**, *Patrick Reilly*

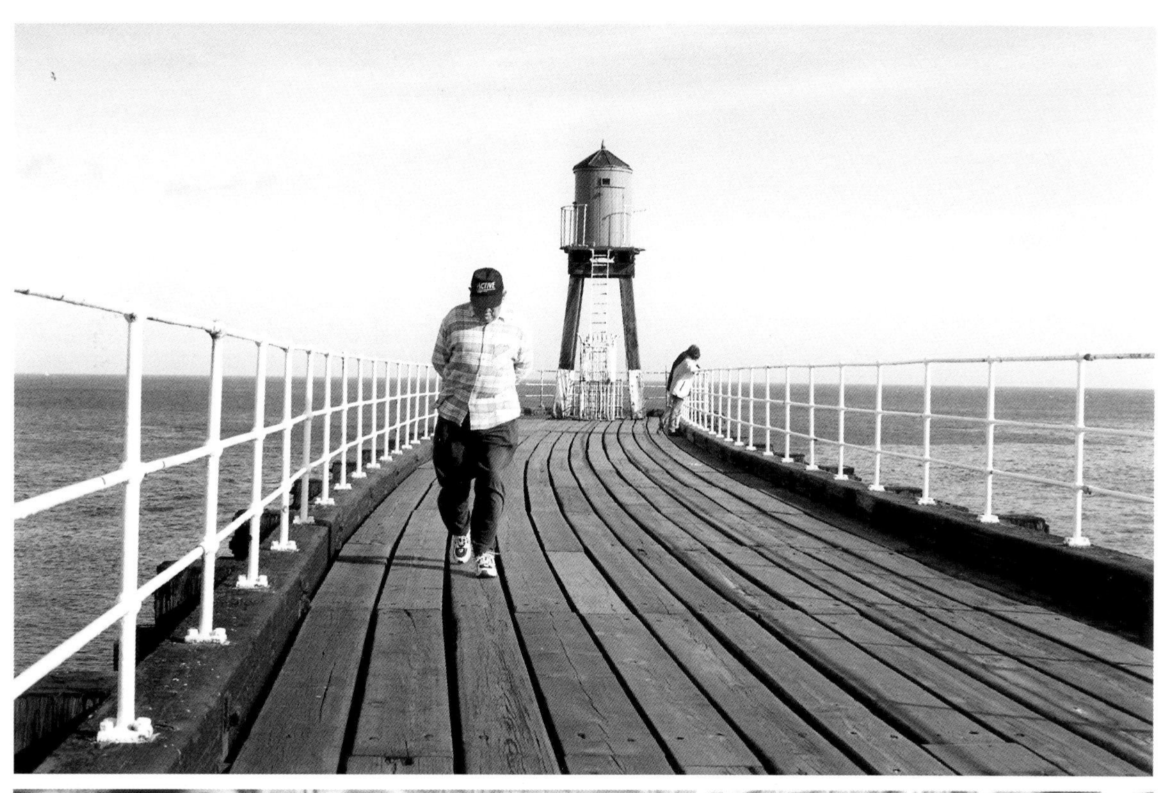

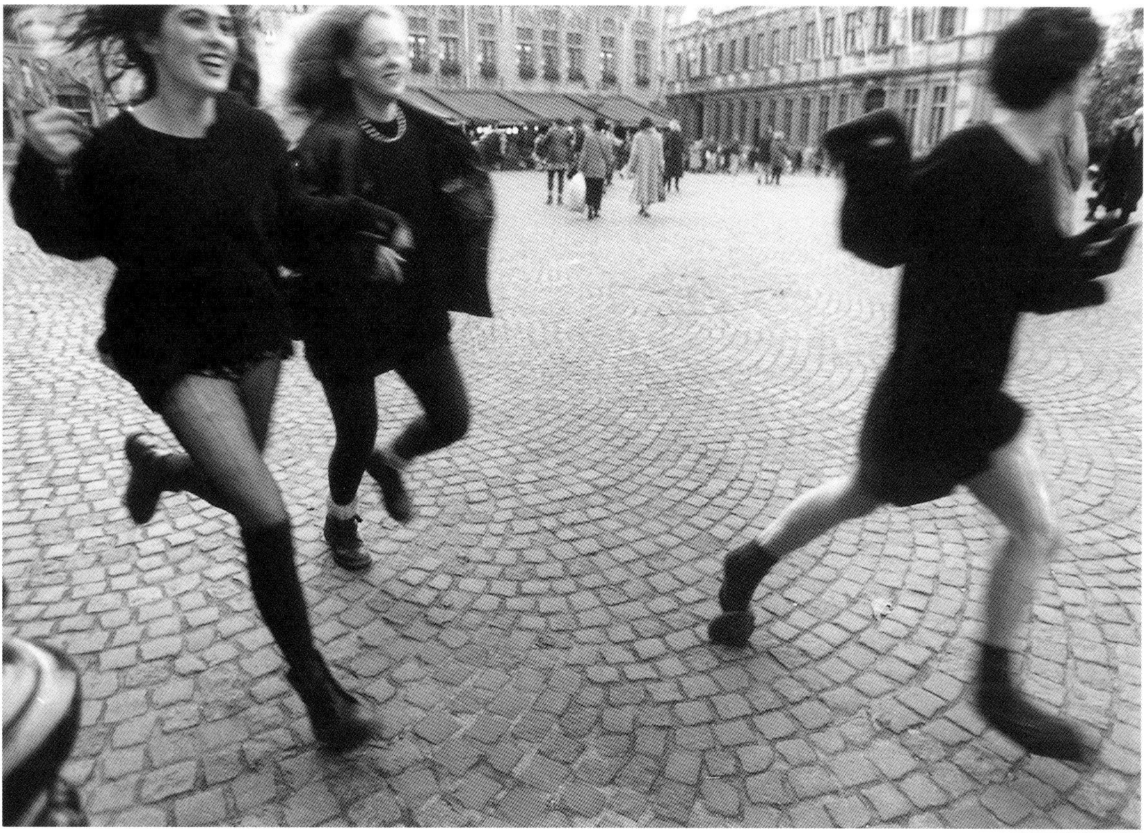

(top) 153 **On the boardwalk**, *Stephen Smith*
(bottom) 154 **Saturday night fever**, *Jim Mansfield*

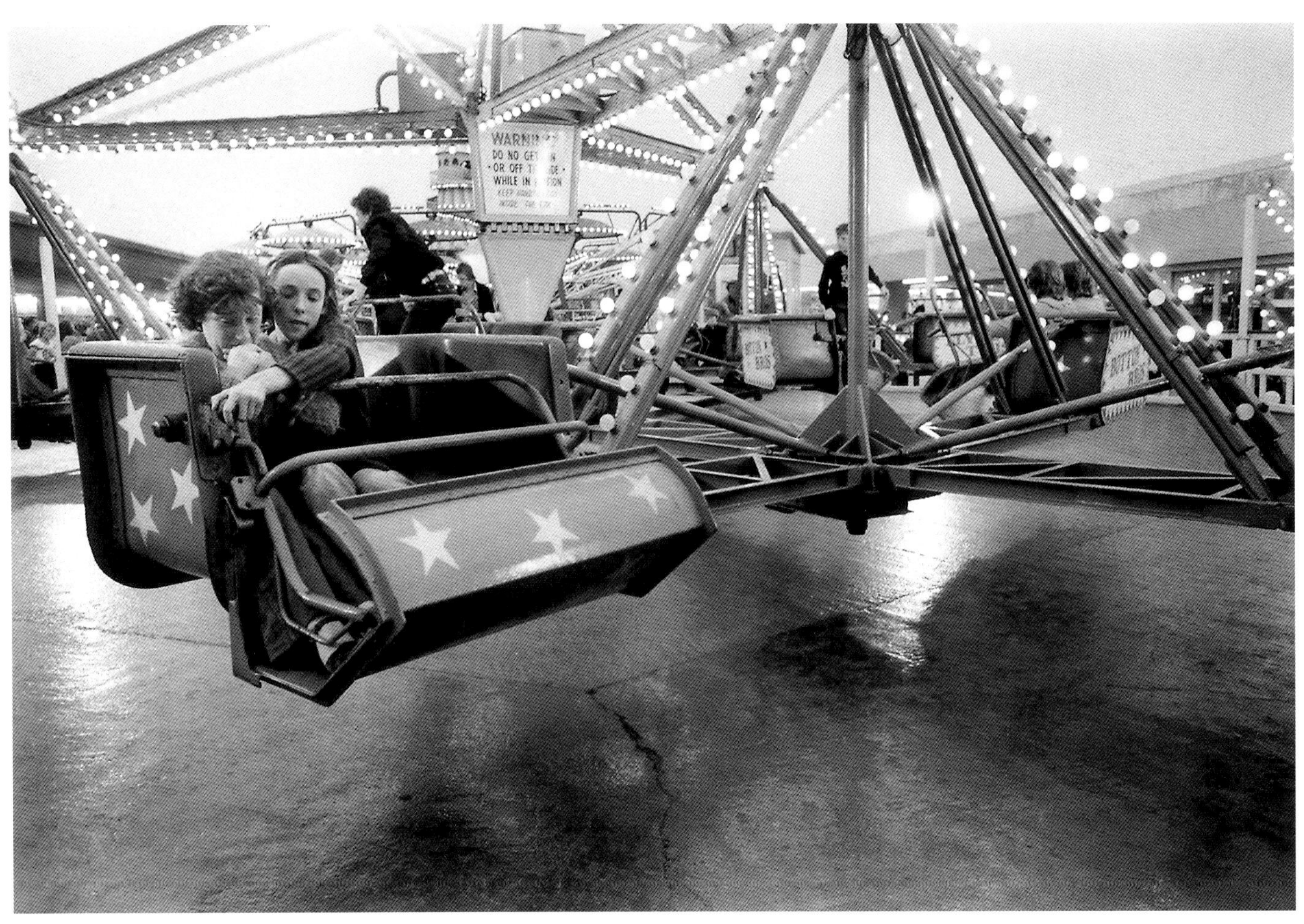

155
Terror ride
Keith Judge

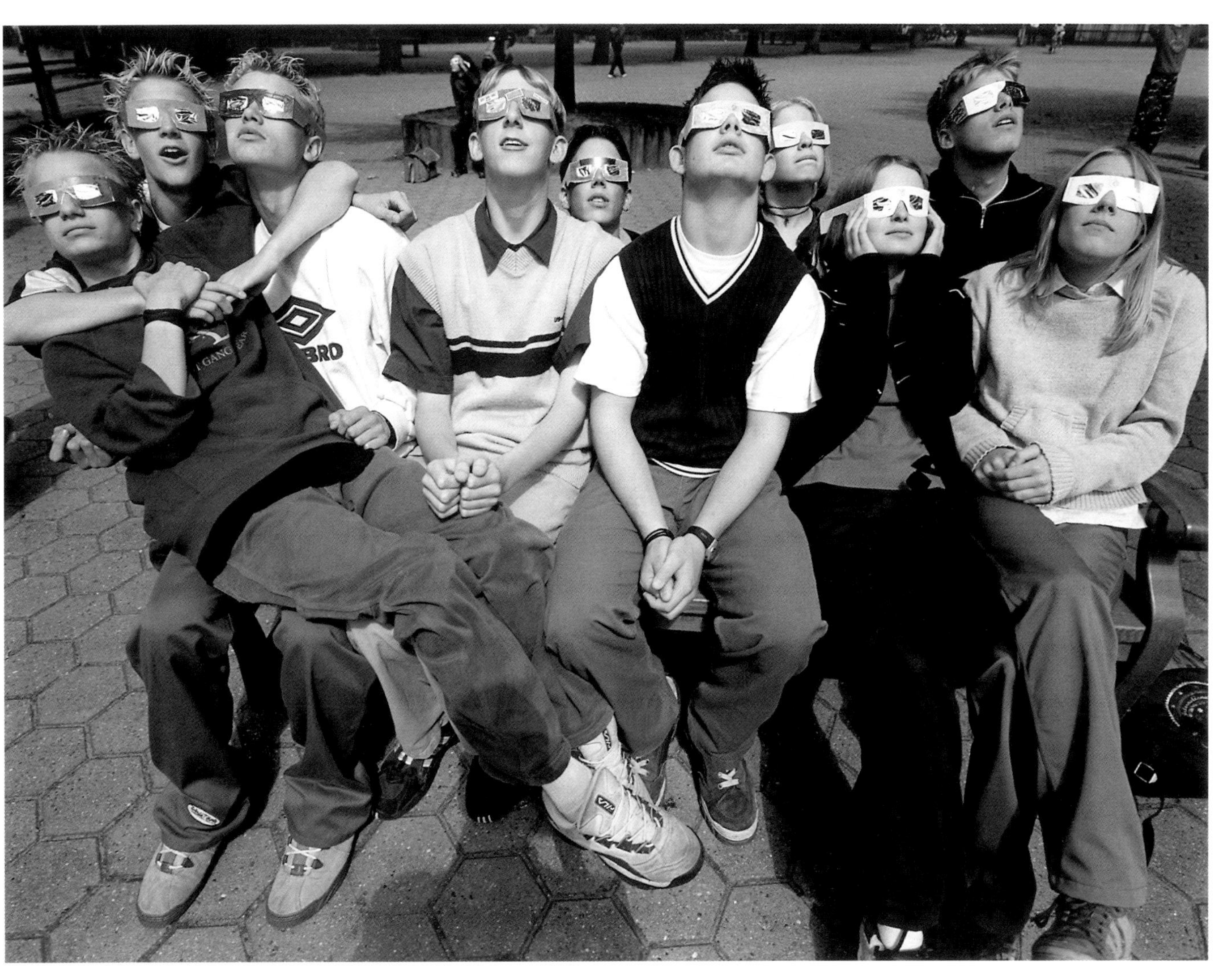

156
Visions (Eclipse day 1999)
Klaus Peters

Contributor profiles

Kevin Adlard *(Lincolnshire)*
Kevin is a well known international exhibitor who has recently gained the Fellowship of the RPS. His prints are mainly made by use of digital imaging. *(140, 141, 142)*

Jim Ainslie *(Canada)*
Jim has been working for the past 30 years or so with 35mm and a 4x5 inch view camera to capture aspects of the landscape. He enjoys exploration in the darkroom to "twist reality slightly", hoping that the resulting "visual enigmas" will provoke the viewer to take a second look. *(31)*

Gaston Alziary *(Berkshire)*
A monochrome worker since the early 1950s, Gaston started producing digital images in 1998. In 1999 (at 71), he entered prints in international salons for the first time and won a gold medal. He is a member of Newbury CC and an SPF judge. *(55)*

Ray Anderson *(South Glamorgan)*
Ray began photography 13 years ago as a therapy for stress at work. He joined a local club and quickly achieved his ARPS, with his main interest in monochrome landscape and architecture. His ambition is to get some of his work published so as to share his interest with a wider audience. *(131)*

Robert Arthur *(Surrey)*
Robert's keen interest in monochrome photography started in his teens. His work has been published in several magazines and this year he gained an acceptance from the London Salon. He achieved the ARPS in 1996 and is chairman of Capel CC. *(149)*

James Austin *(Cambridgeshire)*
James specialises in professional photography of architecture and works of art. Most of his output is now in colour, but his early photography was largely in black and white, and it remains his favourite medium for personal photographs. *(126)*

Ken Baldwin *(North Yorkshire)*
Until retirement, Ken was a professional photographer for almost 40 years. He specialised in promotional photography, mainly in architecture. For a period of five years, much of his work was concerned with the restoration of York Minster. *(9)*

Rex Bamber *(Kent)*
Rex joined the RAF as a photographer in 1941. He subsequently made photography his profession, working in many areas from photo-journalism and advertising to high fashion. Now retired, Rex is enjoying club photography at Croydon CC and also judges on the club circuit. *(41, 116)*

Charles Baynon *(Shropshire)*
A professional photographer for 16 years, Charles has recently opened an art gallery, where he sells his own photography as well as work by other artists in a variety of media. His main subject interests are landscape, still life and the nude. *(94, 95, 98)*

Jim Bennett *(Northern Ireland)*
Since retiring as a university lecturer, much of Jim's time and energy has been devoted to travel and photography. As well as commercial photo-journalism and travel photography, Jim enjoys working with the 'alternative' processes. *(54)*

Ronnie Bennett *(Hampshire)*
Ronnie began her career as a portrait photographer nearly five years ago on completing a C&G day-release photography course. She was the Fujifilm 1998 Portrait Photographer of the Year for the UK, has won two Kodak European Gold Awards for Portraiture and is also the 1999 Kodak Children's Portrait Photographer of the Year for the UK. *(49)*

Richard Bland *(Somerset)*
Richard lives in Somerset and teaches in Dorset. He has always enjoyed hill walking and much of his photography depicts open landscapes and isolated buildings, especially in the Hebrides. Nearer to home, the Somerset Levels provide a similarly quiet environment for photography. *(79)*

Anne Marieke Booij *(Holland)*
Anne Marieke was brought up in a family of very enthusiastic amateur photographers and was given her first camera on her ninth birthday. In 1991, after a holiday in Greece, she decided her photographs were not good enough and started taking courses in photography and darkroom techniques. She has been printing in monochrome since 1993. *(117)*

Paul Booth *(Isle of Skye)*
Paul has been taking photographs since 1996 when his father gave him his first camera for a school farm trip. He now works as a chef in his own hotel in the Trotternish Peninsula of the Isle of Skye, where he is also able to display and sell his photographs during the open season. *(108, 120)*

Carolyn Bross *(USA)*
Her husband's Valentine's Day gift of camera in 1985 started Carolyn's romance with photography and the path to a new career. Her monochrome images are often selectively hand-coloured to reflect her emotional response to the subject and these have been widely exhibited and published. *(47, 78)*

Alan Brown *(Staffordshire)*
A member of the Moorland Monochrome Group and Cannock PS, this is Alan's fourth consecutive appearance in Best of Friends. He holds distinctions of the PAGB and the BPE as well as having recently gained a Licenciateship of the RPS. Alan has achieved numerous acceptances and awards in national and international salons. *(61, 64)*

Clifford Brown *(Somerset)*
Clifford has been active in club photography since 1953. Although having produced colour prints, transparencies and – in the last few years – digital images, his abiding passion has always been in monochrome work, particularly infrared landscape photography. *(59)*

David Butcher *(Derbyshire)*
Starting photography in the early 1980s, David gained his RPS Associateship in 1987 and concentrates his work on monochrome landscapes and cityscapes. He is a member of Chapel-en-le-Firth CC and regularly gives lectures to other clubs. David has been selling framed prints for around 15 years and has also had prints published in books and magazines. *(23, 24, 25)*

Michael Cant *(Essex)*
Inspired by the Christmas gift of *Best of Friends 3*, Michael returned to photography in 1996 after several years away. His future plans include building a portfolio of monochrome pictures taken around Essex churches. *(38)*

Michael Chambers *(Surrey)*
Despite a long involvement with traditional photography, Mike has in recent years been seduced by the ease with which electronic manipulation and reproduction has enabled him to replicate darkroom skills – especially in colour. His inkjet prints have won him awards in national and international salons. *(106)*

Guy Cheeseman *(London)*
Guy has been an enthusiastic photographer for over 30 years. Guy says that, "Switching to transparency has given a quality boost to my colour work in recent years, but monochrome remains the more satisfying because of the control of the process". *(56)*

Peter Clark *(Staffordshire)*
A member of Eyecon and Cannock PS, his passion for monochrome continues unabated with a total emphasis on landscape. A regular exhibitor in international salons for the past 15 years, Peter is a Fellow of the RPS, holds the EFIAP Silver distinction and is a 4-star mono print exhibitor of the Photographic Society of America. *(21, 57, 71)*

Marj Clayton *(London)*
Marj's interest in photography started at age 12, when her father taught her the basics of monochrome. She studied photography at college in her native Canada, and has subsequently concentrated on photographing rural communities in Bolivia and Ghana – work which has been widely exhibited and published. *(51, 52)*

David Cobley *(West Yorkshire)*
(109, 114)

Gerry Coe *(Northern Ireland)*
Gerry is a professional portrait photographer working exclusively in monochrome. In his personal images, he works mainly to themes, but takes any subject that excites him. Gerry was awarded the Agfa UK and Ireland Portrait Photographer of the Year in 1998 and in 1999 obtained his Fellowship of the British Institute of Professional Photographers. *(2, 45)*

Colin Conway *(West Sussex)*
A member of The Camera Club in London, Colin finds that photography is an increasingly important part of his life, but too often neglected because of other pressures. He finds monochrome work an exciting challenge. *(58)*

Trevor Crone *(London)*
Trevor has had more images published in the *Best of Friends* series than any other photographer. His work has been exhibited and published widely. His personal perspective of Kent was published by Creative Monochrome as *The Intimate Garden*. *(30, 100, 101)*

Paul Damen *(Norfolk)*
Paul runs his own general photography business catering for both commercial and personal clients. He also has wide experience in tutoring photography, both full-time vocational and leisure courses for amateurs. He currently lectures part-time at Paston Sixth Form College in Norfolk. Paul is a member of Circle 11 of UPP and a member of the Licentiate Panel of the RPS. *(37, 86)*

Jerry Daniel *(Derbyshire)*
Jerry is a member of Chesterfield PS and Gamma Photoforum. He says he has used his photography to "be alone and escape the stresses of being a teacher". *(115)*

John Day *(Lancashire)*
John has been involved in photography for over thirty years now, setting up his first darkroom in 1968. His main subject interest is in landscapes, where he concentrates mainly on the abstract features contained within the landscape. *(17, 129)*

Simon Denison *(Shropshire)*
Simon divides his times between editing a popular archaeology magazine and making monochrome photographs for exhibition and sale. A portfolio of his landscape work was featured earlier this year in *Photo Art International*. *(104)*

Nick Després *(Guernsey)*
Nick has concentrated on colour slides for the past decade, but has recently rekindled his interest in monochrome. He is a Fellow of the RPS and, not leaving Guernsey much in recent years, has concentrated on the landscape of his native island. He is currently the reigning Ilford/Amateur Photographer Black and White Photographer of the Year. *(102, 113)*

Gary Dixon *(Cleveland)*
A keen photographer for over 20 years, Gary is the Secretary of Hartlepool PS. With a varied subject interest, his main passions lie in landscapes and candid people shots. Gary tends to work exclusively with Ilford HP5 film and usually prints on Ilford Multigrade papers. *(34)*

Signe Drevsjø *(Norway)*
Signe Drevsjø, who favours monochrome photography, has

been a serious photographer for more than 30 years. Signe has taken part in international exhibitions since 1969, gaining many worldwide prizes and the distinction of EFIAP. *(53)*

Glyn Edmunds *(Hampshire)*
An active photographer for over 10 years, Glyn has accumulated a string of distinctions, including the ARPS, EPIAP and DPAGB. He is a frequent exhibitor in national and international salons and has been a feature writer for *Mono* magazine for over a year. *(96)*

Roy Elwood *(Tyne & Wear)*
Roy works almost exclusively in monochrome. He is a Fellow of the RPS and holds the distinction of AFIAP. He is a regular feature writer for *Mono* Magazine and has had work included in every edition of *Best of Friends*. He likes exhibiting and is a popular lecturer. *(90)*

John Fairclough *(Lancashire)*
Introduced to photography when "nowt but a nipper", John first exhibited his images in 1955. He is an active member of Wigan PS. He works mainly in monochrome, where the thrill of seeing the latent image develop has never left him. His main subject interests are landscape and people. *(145)*

Terry Farnell *(Ireland)*
Terry spent six years living on Sherkin Island, off the coast of West Cork, producing an archive of island life at the end of the twentieth century, which has been published as a book. He has had several exhibitions in Ireland. *(82)*

Michael Feeney *(Ireland)*
Michael has been a member of Drogheda PC for 14 years and is happy working in both monochrome and colour media. Having main interests in sport and travel, Michael travels abroad extensively and is an avid canoeist. *(147, 148)*

Roy Frankland *(Tyne & Wear)*
Roy has had an interest in photography for only a couple of years and has been doing his own printing for around 8 months. His photography has been aided immensely by membership of Washington New Town CC. Roy has already had two pictures published in *AP*. *(8)*

Trevor Fry *(Essex)*
Trevor has enjoyed photography since the early 1950s, when he joined Epsom CC. He is currently a member of Cambridge and Saffron Walden clubs and has been a member of the London Salon of Photography for many years. He is a Fellow of the RPS and his work has featured in many exhibitions throughout the country. Although he works in colour, he retains a real love for monochrome, particularly for his favourite subject, people. *(146)*

Stephan Funke *(Thailand)*
Stephen is a member of the PSA and RPS, gaining his LRPS in 1998 and ARPS in 1999. He loves to work with theatre people and dance groups, and tries to do his own monochrome darkroom work in the tropical environment of Thailand. *(10)*

Wolfgang Gilges *(Germany)*
Wolfgang started to make photographic images around 10 years ago, with monochrome being the medium in which he finds he can express himself. His favourite subject is people, but he says he is still looking for his own photographic style. *(46)*

Edward Gordon *(Surrey)*
Edward took up photography about four years ago and has already achieved a national salon acceptance and the Licentiateship and Associateship of the RPS. He likes to photograph people and wants to spend more time in his native Ireland "before all the travelling people have disappeared or moved to London". *(89)*

Peter Handford *(Berkshire)*
Having developed his first print in 1950, Peter has "never lost the excitement of watching the image come up in the developer". His LRPS portfolio was published in the RPS Journal and he gained his ARPS in 1979. He is a member of Reading CC and the former Hyperion Group. *(40)*

Andy Hanson *(Cambridgeshire)*
Interested in photography since the late 1950s, Andy has been a member of six clubs. He gained the LRPS in 1981 and Associateship in 1983. He was awarded the APAGB in 1997 and is a regular lecturer on the club circuit. *(62)*

Kathleen Harcom *(Hampshire)*
Kathleen has been interested in black and white photography for almost 10 years and particularly enjoys pictures of the natural world. She often uses infrared film and lith printing to evoke a soft and ethereal atmosphere in her images. More recently she has started to explore still-life and portraiture. Kathleen is a Fellow of the RPS and a member of the Arena Group and Chimera Group. *(105, 121, 122)*

Clive Harrison *(Berkshire)*
Clive, who died this year, was a member of the London Salon of Photography and a founder member of the Arena Group. A regular exhibitor and competition winner, his photos have been printed in many British and European magazines. Clive's book of child photography, *Age of Innocence*, was published by Creative Monochrome. *(7)*

Malcolm Hawkins *(Wirral)*
Malcolm has been a black and white worker from his early teens with his father's encouragement. He studied at night school and is now a keen member of Hoylake PS. Monochrome photography is Malcolm's main interest, particularly landscape, travel and pictorialism, although he has "dabbled" recently in slide photography. Darkroom work remains Malcolm's passion in life. *(112, 135)*

Shelia Haycox *(Devon)*
Sheila is an enthusiastic amateur photographer, interested in all aspects of the medium, including mono, slide work and digital imaging. A member of Exmouth Photo Group and the West Country Creative Friends Travelling Portfolio, she says that "retirement is certainly not dull". *(85)*

Geoff Hodgson *(Worcestershire)*
An Associate of the RPS, member of UPP and the Vale of Evesham CC, Geoff has been an enthusiastic photographer for many years with, until recently, an over-riding interest in making monochrome prints in the darkroom. Conversion to digital imaging now allows, in the lightroom, creation of monochrome and colour prints, which have been widely exhibited within the local group known as "Infinity Plus". *(133, 134)*

Arnold Hubbard *(Tyne & Wear)*
Arnold has been a member of Sunderland PA for over 25 years. His work has been seen in many national and international exhibitions. A Fellow of the RPS and holder of the EPIAP distinction, Arnold is a popular lecturer and regular judge on the club circuit. *(32)*

Caroline Hyman *(Oxfordshire)*
Working principally in monochrome, Caroline specialises in hand-coloured still life of which she has held many solo exhibitions. At present she is working on a book of portraits and landscapes of the area in which she lives. She is a Fellow of the RPS, member of Arena and represented by Focus Gallery in London. *(80)*

Colin Ivison *(Warwickshire)*
Colin has decided to return to monochrome photography, having concentrated on colour for several years, as he feel it is a more creative medium. Colin attempts to take pictures that are interesting by using subject matter, lighting and atmosphere. *(118)*

Keith Judge *(Norfolk)*
Although growing up under the influence of 'social comment' photography, Keith says his work is now more concerned with "subtle, yet inescapable, symmetry" in figures and locations. *(155)*

Robert Kent *(Staffordshire)*
Enthusiastic about photography since his mid-teens, Robert spent 12 years as a professional photographer before joining a professional processing laboratory 21 years ago, where he remains in a senior position. A passionate devotee of monochrome, he is a founder member of the Moorland Monochrome Group. *(73)*

Mike Kielecher *(Lancashire)*
Mike has been seriously interested in photography since the early 1970s when he first joined a camera club. He works in both monochrome and colour and although he is interested in all aspects of photography, his successes are mainly in portraiture and figure work. Mike is a member of two local clubs: Bury PS and Oldham CC. *(92)*

Paul Lambeth *(Hertfordshire)*
A member of Welwyn Garden City PC, Paul has been making monochrome prints for around 20 years. He prefers to work in natural conditions rather than a studio. "I believe that good monochrome images are made as much in the darkroom as in the camera." *(150)*

Barbie Lindsay *(Suffolk)*
Barbie describes herself as a photographic artist, using her camera simply as a tool to produce her final images. She likes to work in all media, whether digital or darkroom: "They each have their own specialities which suit particular types of pictures." She enjoys judging as well as exhibiting nationally and is an active member of Ipswich & District PS. *(119)*

Jim Mansfield *(Hampshire)*
Jim has been interested in monochrome photography since the 1950s, joining Southampton CC in 1953. In 1983, Jim joined the RPS as a life member and became an ARPS in the same year. *(154)*

Bob Marsden *(Oxfordshire)*
Bob has always seemed to have had a camera "glued" to his right hand since childhood. "I find photographing children such fun that I've now got a little sideline to my full-time work in General Practice doing informal portraits of the children of friends and family. I'm continuing with night school to extend my skills." *(4)*

Bob Marshall *(Buckinghamshire)*
Bob is a member of Amersham PS where he has found inspiration from the work of his fellow members. He has enjoyed photography from childhood, when his father introduced him to monochrome and the darkroom. *(35)*

Pat Maycroft *(Co Durham)*
An Associate member of the RPS and part-time photography lecturer at Darlington College of Technology, Pat's first photograph was taken with a Box Brownie. Pat gained an honours degree in Photography at Cleveland College of Art and Design in 1998 and enjoys photographing a range of subjects. *(22)*

Maggie McCall *(Devon)*
Maggie has been interested in photography for over 20 years and having gained her LRPS is currently compiling a panel for the Associateship. Her favourite subjects are landscape and portraiture, but having recently given birth, baby portraiture is her current enthusiasm. *(1)*

Terrick Meakin *(Somerset)*
Having been taking photographs for many years, Terrick's first love is, "and always will be", monochrome. He is a member of Bath PS, Kingswood PS and the RPS. Three years ago, Terrick formed a group called 'Crown Monochrome' and about 30 members meet monthly to "indulge in an evening of traditional monochrome photography". *(132)*

Ian Mellor *(Buckinghamshire)*
A member of the New City PS in Milton Keynes, Ian enjoys many different aspects of photography, although his main success has been with figure and architectural subjects. He was awarded the ARPS and DPAGB in 1998 and has applied for the AFIAP, after five years of exhibiting photographs in international exhibitions. *(93)*

Caroline Mockett *(Essex)*
Caroline has been an avid photographer for over 10 years, joining her local club, Ingatestone in 1992. She was awarded the ARPS in 1999, and has just started as a PAGB judge. Favourite subjects include modern architecture, close-ups, abstracts and landscapes. She has had acceptances in several international salons for her slides. *(60)*

Johannes Müller *(Germany)*
Having studied geography, geology and botany, Johannes works freelance in landscape planning, landscape ecology, book publishing and university teaching. He has special interests in the geography of Asia, especially China and the Far East, railway history, rural architecture, landscape ecology and the development of the cultural landscape. (69)

Anne Newell *(Cornwall)*
Anne's main interest for some years has been in monochrome landscape photography. Recently, however, she has been "getting in closer" and really enjoys finding patterns, rhythms and texture in rocks, walls and trees. She gained her LRPS in 1993 and her ARPS in 2000. *(14, 18, 19, 36)*

James Ngai *(Mid-Glamorgan)*
James has been serious about photography since starting his own printing about seven years ago. Working mainly in medium format in both colour and monochrome, James started submitting prints to exhibitions and salons three years ago. He is a Licentiate of the RPS. *(5)*

Shay Nicol *(Cheshire)*
Shay began her photographic career in 1987 as a junior photographer/printer with a commercial photographic firm. She subsequently gained experience in press photography and is currently a photographer for Brittany Ferries. *(127)*

Stuart Noble *(West Yorkshire)*
Stuart has been a member of Halifax PS since the early 1950s and has held most of the official positions in the club, including president. He has never specialised in any type of photography, but has recently been "playing with" digital imaging. Stuart is the current treasurer of the Yorkshire Monochrome Group. *(83)*

O Tudur Owen *(Gwynedd)*
Since retirement five years ago, Tudur says his darkroom work has improved considerably, spurred on by acceptances in the previous four issues of *Best of Friends*. He is a member of Club Camera Blaenau Ffestiniog (where most meetings are held in Welsh). Most of his photographs are taken in the Welsh mountains within a mile of his home. *(26, 27, 91, 124)*

Ken Payne *(Hertfordshire)*
Ken started photography in 1959 and has worked for Kodak in Harrow making film emulsion and for Camera Press in London as a monochrome printer. For the past 18 months, Ken has been manipulating images on the computer. To date, Ken has had two pictures published in magazines. *(144)*

Len Perkis *(Norway)*
Len's main subject interests are landscape, nature and travel. His images have been widely published, including use as CM cards, and a major shipping line has used many of his landscapes to decorate its ships. *(123)*

Klaus Peters *(Germany)*
Klaus has been making photographs since 1967 and his work has been widely exhibited and published, including two books and four calendars. He holds the Artist distinction of FIAP. *(50, 156)*

Shirlie Phillips *(Australia)*
A keen photographer for the past eight years, Shirlie enjoys all subjects, and is now expanding her images to mixed media. Shirlie enters national and international competitions and her work was included in the book, *Four Peasants Digging. (88)*

Leigh Preston *(Gloucestershire)*
Leigh is a well known lecturer and judge on the club circuit and is a member of the RPS Licentiateship distinctions panel. A regular exhibitor in national and international salons, Leigh is the author of *Shadows of Change*, published by CM. *(137, 138, 139)*

Mike Preston *(Surrey)*
Encouragement from an enthusiastic schoolmaster was instrumental in making photography a life-long hobby for Mike. He specialises mainly in wildlife images and landscapes, generally working in monochrome. *(29)*

Jim Pymer *(Gloucestershire)*
Jim's photography is "purely for pleasure", with a particular interest in finding contemporary images in the landscape. Having been "bitten by the monochrome bug" only four years ago, Jim continues to develop his camera and printing techniques in order to improve his understanding of this art form as a means of self-expression. *(75)*

Peter Rand *(Surrey)*
Having been given his first 'decent' camera at 12, Peter soon discovered the magic of the darkroom. Monochrome has always been at the core of his work, which mainly covers landscape (his main focus), sport and portraiture. *(28)*

Christopher Read *(Buckinghamshire)*
Christopher has concentrated on monochrome photography for the past six years, gaining inspiration and guidance from fellow members of Amersham PS. He enjoys the control that monochrome allows. *(48)*

Patrick Reilly *(Ireland)*
Patrick has been taking photographs since the 1970s. Whilst enjoying many aspects of the medium, he still finds monochrome the most satisfying: "While I think about my work, I don't feel the need to explain it in detail: if other people like it, I see that as a bonus". *(152)*

Tom Richardson *(Lancashire)*
Tom has taken a serious interest in photography over the past

12 years, with the landscape as his preferred subject. His work has been accepted for numerous national exhibitions. He is an Associate of the RPS and the holder of a BPE distinction. *(74)*

Alastair Rucklidge *(Cambridgeshire)*
Alastair's interest in photography began five years ago when he joined Cambridge CC. He has worked in infrared for the past two years and mainly works in monochrome. Alastair has also recently begun to experiment in the digital medium. *(107)*

Martin Rushworth *(Cambridgeshire)*
Martin has been taking photographs for over 50 years, but more seriously since becoming a founder member of Bottisham & Burwell PC. He produces mainly slides and mono prints and has recently taken to the "masochistic" process of lith printing thanks to Dr Tim Rudman. *(16)*

Hazel Sanderson *(West Yorkshire)*
Using her keen appreciation of lighting, texture, tone and composition, Hazel has the exceptional ability to make a memorable image from a mundane subject. She is also the author of CM's book, *Dales of Yorkshire. (125)*

Keith Saunders *(Manchester)*
A former member of Warrington PS, Keith joined the UPP in 1998 and is now also a member of the Circle Eight Monochrome group. Keith recently gained his CPAGB with slides, but prefers the diversity of monochrome. *(72)*

Paul Schofield *(Staffordshire)*
Paul has been interested in photography since he was 14, when he went to night school classes with his dad. He took A-level photography "for something to do in the evenings"and gained an A grade. He is currently "playing" with various infrared films in black and white and colour. *(128)*

Jim Shipp *(Northumberland)*
After a number of years producing nature slides, Jim now prefers to work in monochrome, but still enjoys and appreciates all forms of photography. *(15, 76)*

Chris Shore *(Kent)*
For Chris, the joy of photography is to be in an isolated spot in good weather, finding an old derelict building and trying to turn it into a well composed image. He finds that his favourite haunts in the Romney Marsh offer these elements in abundance. *(103)*

Paul Silk *(West Midlands)*
Paul started photography eight years ago. For the last five years, Paul has been working exclusively in monochrome with some occasional hand colouring. He is a member of Great Barr PS and has had some success at national and international exhibitions, including PAGB medals. *(151)*

Roger Slade *(Essex)*
Roger has been interested in photography for many years, initially through borrowing his father's camera as a child. He is keen to keep developing a "seeing eye", to find new ways of looking at the world, largely through producing monochrome images of people and the landscape. *(143)*

Arthur Smith *(Tyne & Wear)*
Having joined Tynemouth PS eleven years ago, Arthur enjoys all aspects of photography, especially working in the darkroom and "waiting for one's latest, hopefully successful, creation to emerge from the final tray". He was thrilled to have a print selected for last year's *Best of Friends*, which has spurred him on to, hopefully, more success. *(99)*

Stephen Smith *(Derbyshire)*
During his 15 years working within an International Award winning Corporate Business Television department, Stephen has always had a passion for monochrome photography as a complementary interest in which he "can escape the world of the moving image and freeze-frame the achievements of nature". *(39, 153)*

Trevor Smithers *(Wiltshire)*
Trevor has been interested in photography on and off for over 30 years, concentrating mainly on monochrome. He is an Associate of the RPS and has started to enter national and international exhibitions with some success. Trevor now works mainly in medium format and although he used to have a wet darkroom set up, he is now exploring digital methods to replicate and print monochrome images. *(84)*

Mark Snowdon *(North Yorkshire)*
Mark developed his interest in photography in 1986 whilst living in South Africa. He works almost entirely in monochrome using medium format cameras. An active member of Northallerton CC, his preferred subjects are landscape and, more recently, portraiture. He gained his ARPS in 1991. *(3, 11)*

Neil Souch *(Devon)*
An Associate of the RPS, Neil works mainly in monochrome and his photography features the varied landscape of the west country. He counts himself fortunate to live in an area which has an abundance of subject matter to offer to the landscape photographer. Neil's current ambition is to gain his FRPS with a panel of locally inspired monochrome prints. *(110)*

Nick Stout *(France)*
Residing in Paris, Nick is an American amateur photographer and professional newspaper editor who, having come late to the hobby, has been photographing for about eight years. Passionate about street photography ("I'm a people-watcher first and foremost"), he has already had images accepted for some group exhibitions. Nick also finds himself drawn to objects and forms – "the shadows and shapes that convey the mood of the moment". *(63)*

Clifford Street *(Tyne & Wear)*
Clifford has been interested in photography from an early age and having brought his first serious camera about 16 years ago to record family events, joined Washington Camera Club in 1996. His photography is varied in subject matter and is done purely for pleasure. Concentrating on monochrome, Clifford has also competed in club competitions. *(130)*

Nigel Surtees *(Tyne & Wear)*
Introduced to photography 3 years ago by a friend who loaned him an SLR camera to take pictures of his child, Nick finds monochrome enjoyable because he has "complete control over the final image". He regularly enters club competitions as a member of the Washington Camera Club. *(12, 13)*

Luke Tan *(Singapore)*
(6)

Juha Taponen *(Finland)*
The west coast of Finland is Juha's favourite region for finding photogenic opportunities. Juha was involved in colour photography of nature for many years before turning to monochrome for rural and urban landscapes. He believes that photographs should tell a story. *(87)*

Caroline Taylor *(Gloucestershire)*
Caroline has been seriously interested in black and white photography for about twelve years, working both in medium format and 35mm. She gained her Licentiateship of the RPS in March 1999. Having a long-standing interest in fine art, she is inspired by the definition of photography as "painting with light". *(42)*

Steve Terry *(Isle of Skye)*
Steve is an Associate of the Royal Photographic Society and runs a photographic holiday centre and gallery on the Isle of Skye. He works in monochrome and colour and enjoys trying to capture the landscape in all it moods. *(70)*

David Thurlow *(West Yorkshire)*
David has been interested in photography for more than thirty years and his main love has always been monochrome. His subject interests are wide ranging – the sheer pleasure of taking photographs is what motivates him. He has his own tried and tested film/developer combinations, yet he loves experimenting with new ones, especially variations on the two-bath method which he mixes himself. *(65, 66)*

Kirk Toft *(West Yorkshire)*
Fascinated by bromoils since he first noticed etching-like illustrations in archival copies of *AP*, Kirk's "love affair" led him into two years of failed experimentation with the process. Six years on brought success and publication of work along with articles related to the process. Kirk is now also working in the obscure Oleobrom process. *(67, 68)*

Clive Vincent *(Cornwall)*
Although starting with colour, Clive is now a confirmed monochrome worker with roughly 15 years' experience of the medium. He tends to specialise in landscapes, primarily of his native Cornwall and his other great love, Dartmoor. A member of Penwith Photo Group, Clive has exhibited his work widely. *(111)*

Susanne Waldock *(Brunei)*
Hooked on monochrome after having started photography in colour ten years ago, this is the first time Susanne has had her monochrome work shown to anyone other than her supportive husband who still "languishes in transparency and digital colour". *(43, 44, 81)*

Alan Walmsley *(Dyfed)*
Finding monochrome a fine medium for interpretation, Alan is fascinated by line, pattern, shape, light and the land. His pictures "do not try to be representations of reality; they are not 'pictures of places', rather they are a way of seeing into things or 'pictures of feelings'". Most of Alan's work has been in monochrome after his father showed him how to develop and print in 1976. *(20)*

Emma Weal *(Devon)*
At a very young age, Emma was introduced to photography by her father. She has now gained her Associateship of the RPS. She works mainly in monochrome, specialising in nature, landscape and environmental portraiture. Her work has been widely exhibited, including two solo exhibitions. *(77)*

Colin Westgate *(East Sussex)*
Colin has been making photographs for over 40 years, most of that time as a member of Eastbourne PS. He is a member of the London Salon, the Arena Group, and UPP, and holds the MFIAP and FRPS distinctions. He now organises and runs workshops for both monochrome and colour photography. *(33)*

Andy Wilson *(Nottinghamshire)*
Andy is a member of Gamma Photoforum, the Print Project and Friend of, and exhibitor in, the London Salon of Photography. He is a founder member of the Triangle group of fine art monochrome printer/photographers and has had his images published in several photographic magazines. *(97, 136)*

GLOSSARY OF ABBREVIATIONS

BPE *British Photographic Exhibitor – 'Crown' awards based on submissions and acceptances in recognised national salons*

CC *Camera Club*

C&G *City & Guilds (vocational training and examination board)*

FIAP *(translated as) International Federation of Photographic Art: awards distinctions, including Artist, Excellence and Master, based mainly on acceptances in accredited salons*

PAGB *Photographic Alliance of Great Britain: central organising body for vast number of camera clubs in GB*

PS *Photographic Society*

PSA *The Photographic Society of America*

RPS *The Royal Photographic Society: awards distinctions at Licentiate (LRPS), Associate (ARPS) and Fellowship (FRPS) levels, mainly by assessed portfolio submissions*

UPP *United Photographic Postfolios – organising body for portfolios of members' work which are circulated by post for appreciation and comment.*